Randall J. Brewer

IT'S TIME TO GROW UP

THE QUEST FOR SPIRITUAL MATURITY

RANDALL J. BREWER

"Set your mind on things above, not on things on the earth. For you died, and your life is hidden with Christ in God" (Col. 3:2,3).

PUBLISHED by PARABLES
Earthly Stories with a Heavenly Meaning

Randall J. Brewer

Its Time To Grow Up: The Quest For Spiritual Maturity
Randall J. Brewer

Published By Parables
March, 2019

All Rights Reserved. No part of this book may be reproduced or utilized in any form or by any means, electronic or mechanical, including photocopying, recording, or by any information storage and retrieval system, without permission in writing from the author.

    ISBN 978-1-945698-46-0
    Printed in the United States of America

Readers should be aware that Internet Web sites offered as citations and/or sources for further information may have been changed or disappeared between the time this was written and the time it is read.

IT'S TIME TO GROW UP

THE QUEST FOR SPIRITUAL MATURITY

RANDALL J. BREWER

"Set your mind on things above, not on things on the earth. For you died, and your life is hidden with Christ in God"

Randall J. Brewer

-INTRODUCTION-

Saying you're a Christian does not have the same impact today as it did in times past. Everybody says they're a Christian even when there is no proof in their words and actions that support this claim. The sad reality is that there are too many spiritual hypocrites in the world and people are getting tired of hearing how religious you are. If you can't show them the love of Christ, it's best that you say nothing at all. As a born again believer, you have been called to be an ambassador for Jesus and this is why you need to be a doer of the Word and not a hearer only.

The bottom line is that it's time for the body of Christ to grow up. This truth should be burned into the hearts of every born again believer. Far too long has the ways of the world crept into the local church. It's gotten so bad that's it's almost impossible to tell the difference between a child of God and a child of the devil. Pastors have affairs with their church members while others perform marriage ceremonies for couples of the same sex. The leader of one church organization just told its one billion followers there is no hell. He said when sinners die they just disappear. In other words, why concern yourself with godly living?

Paul said in 1 Cor. 3:1-3 (NLT), "Dear brothers and sisters, when I was with you I couldn't talk to you as I would to spiritual people. I had to talk as though you belonged to this world or as though you were infants in the Christian life. I had to feed you with milk, not with solid food, because you weren't ready for anything stronger. And you still aren't ready, for you are still controlled by your sinful nature. You are jealous of one another and quarrel with each other. Doesn't that prove you are controlled by your sinful nature? Aren't you living like people of the world?"

Heb. 5:11-14 (MSG) says, "I have a lot more to say about this, but it is hard to get it across to you since you've picked up this bad habit of not listening. By this time you ought to be teachers yourselves, yet here I find you need someone to sit down with you and go over the basics on God again, starting from square one - baby's milk, when you should have been on solid food long ago! Milk is for beginners, inexperienced in God's ways; solid food is for the mature, who have some practice in telling right from wrong."

So unexpected were these words that the writer's intended readers never saw it coming. More than likely, you also will have the same response as those first century believers, shock and dismay. Hopefully, God now has your attention. He is saying to the church, "Enough is enough." He is calling believers all over the world to be strangers and pilgrims on the earth. He is calling His children to grow up and be different from the world, to become the type of people they were called to become. Daily the body of Christ needs to strive to be heavenly-minded and not earthly-minded.

A mature believer doesn't get caught up in the things of this world and they know spiritual growth doesn't come automatically. The goal of every believer is to be transformed into the image of Christ (Rom. 8:29). This will not happen unless you make a demand on yourself to make it happen. Diligently you must strive to "work out your own salvation with fear and trembling" (Phil. 2:12). Constantly you must study the holy scriptures to show yourself approved, to become a worker who does not need to be ashamed, rightly dividing the word of truth (2 Tim. 2:15).

What should you do? "Come out from among them and be separate, says the Lord. Do not touch what is unclean, and I will receive you. I will be a Father to you, and you shall be My sons and daughters, says the Lord Almighty" (2 Cor. 6:17,18). Before Jesus ascended on high, He gave this final command, "Go therefore and make disciples of all nations" (Matt. 28:29). In order to make disciples, you must first become a disciple. This will happen when you "grow in the grace and knowledge of our Lord and Savior, Jesus Christ" (2 Peter 3:18). Indeed, it is time for a change in the house of God. It's time to grow up.

Randall J. Brewer

-1-

"BORN TO GROW"

God is searching for people who want to grow up spiritually. He is looking for hearts that are receptive, hearts where He can plant His Word and watch it take root and grow. 2 Chron. 16:9 says, "For the eyes of the Lord run to and fro throughout the whole earth, to show Himself strong on behalf of those whose heart is loyal to Him." God doesn't force Himself or His Word on anybody. He wants you to have an unwavering desire to grow up spiritually, a desire so strong that nothing will stop you from becoming the person He wants you to be. You, and you alone, is who determines how fast and how far you will grow. Spiritual growth is not automatic like physical growth. It takes time, effort, perseverance, and a lot of determination and hard work. This is what Phil. 2:12 means when it says to "work out your own salvation with fear and trembling." The Message Bible says, "Redouble your efforts. Be energetic in your life of salvation, reverent and sensitive before God." The good news is that if you will hunger and thirst after righteousness, you will be filled (Matt. 5:6).

Spiritual hunger is the mark of a mature Christian. It means you're not satisfied with where you're at and you want more and more of God, as much of Him as you can get. When Paul says to work out your own salvation, he is saying to "carry it to the goal and complete it." It's like going into a gold mine and carrying out all the gold that is there. Sad to say, not everybody completes the work of spiritual growth. Sunday after Sunday millions of people go to church in an effort to fulfill their religious obligations. Their conscience is satisfied but inwardly their spirits are dry as a bone. They're going through the motions but are not growing spiritually. Why? Because they're dead inside and dead things don't grow. Some people just respond differently to the Word of God than others. Some stay committed and go on to bigger and better things, some don't. It's their choice for God does not make anybody do anything. How about you? Are you satisfied where you're at spiritually? Is there a hunger inside of you that is crying out to be filled?

Becoming Christ-like is what spiritual growth is all about. The goal of every believer should be to become "fully mature adults, fully developed within and without, fully alive like Christ" (Eph. 4:13 MSG). The degree to which you will grow is directly related to the degree of effort you put into it. It takes strict discipline and intentional effort for spiritual growth to happen. No more are you to be a spiritual baby who doesn't know what to do or what to believe. "God wants us to grow up, to know the whole truth and tell it in love - like Christ in everything" (vs. 14,15 MSG). Rest assured, God is with you every step of the way. As you put your life in His loving hands, He'll care for you and will impart to you the same infinite wisdom He has. Your response is to put your faith in Him and then do what He tells you to do. Vs. 16 (MSG) says, "We take our lead from Christ, who is the source of everything we do. He keeps us in step with each other. His very breath and blood flow through us, nourishing us so that we will grow up healthy in God, robust in love."

Just as a seed is planted to grow, you were born to grow physically, mentally, and spiritually. God's desire is for you to grow up and become who He made you to be. Things that don't grow die and this is why you must be forever believing that God will "work in us what is pleasing to Him" (Heb.

13:21). With spiritual eyes see yourself not where you are now but where God desires to take you. See yourself reaching your full potential. See yourself living a life with endless possibilities. Titus 2:11-14 (MSG) says, "God's readiness to give and forgive is now public. Salvation's available for everyone! We're being shown how to turn our backs on a godless, indulgent life, and how to take on a God-filled, God-honoring life. This new life is starting right now, and is whetting our appetites for the glorious day when our great God and Savior, Jesus Christ, appears. He offered Himself as a sacrifice to free us from a dark, rebellious life into this good, pure life, making us a people He can be proud of, energetic in goodness."

Getting saved is not the end of your spiritual journey, it's the beginning. It's the start of a life of continuous growing into the likeness of Christ. It is important that you understand there is no middle ground when it comes to spiritual growth. You're either growing or you're regressing and losing ground. You're either climbing the mountain or you're falling down the mountain. People need to stop making excuses for their failure to grow and face the harsh reality of where they're at spiritually. The truth is, an excuse is a fancy name for a lie and these people need to stop making excuses for why they don't read their Bible or go to church on Sunday. An excuse is never a reason for anything because people will always find a way to do those things that are important to them. The bottom line is that you should always be wanting more of God in your life. Don't settle for where you're now at but be like Paul who said in Phil. 3:14, "I press toward the goal for the prize of the upward call of God in Christ Jesus."

Let it be known that the biggest enemy of spiritual growth is to be satisfied with where you're currently at. Paul said in Phil. 3:12 (NLT), "I don't mean to say that I have already achieved these things or that I have already reached perfection. But I press on to possess that perfection for which Christ Jesus first possessed me." Paul is saying that he's not satisfied where he's at and he wants to keep growing and progressing. Today, right now, are you satisfied with your spiritual life? Have you reached the pinnacle of where you should be in your walk with the Lord? Or are there some things you still need to learn and do? Are there some areas in your life that need some spiritual growth? Paul prayed in Col. 1:9,10 "that you may be filled with the knowledge of His will in all wisdom and spiritual understanding; that you may have a walk worthy of the Lord, fully pleasing Him, being fruitful in every good work and increasing in the knowledge of God." The Message Bible says, "We pray that you'll live well for the Master, making Him proud of you as you work hard in His orchard."

God has plans for your life and He is thinking about you right now. Jer. 29:11 says, "For I know the thoughts that I think toward you, says the Lord, thoughts of peace and not of evil, to give you a future and a hope." The Hebrew word for "thoughts" is where the word "machine" comes from. A machine is created for a purpose and to accomplish a task. Everything that is created has a purpose. You are a prized creation of God and He sees what you were created to be. Know that God has a purpose and a final outcome for your life. It's between the revelation of that purpose and the fulfillment of it that life happens. It's where spiritual growth takes place. Jesus said to the Father in John 17:4, "I have finished the work which You have given Me to do." Live your life in such a way that when you stand before the Father you'll be able to say the same thing. God has a final outcome for your life but it's going to require spiritual growth on your part. You'll have to go deep into the things of God, deeper than you've ever gone before. It is then that He'll pull out of you everything that He placed inside of you.

You are in good company when it comes to spiritual growth. Luke 2:40 says, "And the Child grew and became strong in spirit, filled with wisdom; and the grace of God was upon Him." If Jesus had to grow in spirit, how much more do you have to grow? Vs. 52 says, "And Jesus increased in wisdom and stature, and in favor with God and men." Jesus had to grow. He grew in spirit and in wisdom showing that spiritual growth is an essential part of your Christian life. You must grow into the person God has called you to be. You need to grow in grace, in faith, in ability, and in wisdom. Some people think God loving them and His grace is sufficient for them so whatever will be, will be. They don't realize that the purpose of His grace is to empower you to go where He desires you to go, not keep you where you now are. It's spiritual growth that prepares you for your destiny. God anointed David to be king when he was a small lad but he didn't become king right away. No, he had to grow into being a king. He also had to kill a lion and a bear before he could kill Goliath.

Are you growing spiritually or have you become stagnant in your growth? Heb. 5:12,13 says, "For though by this time you ought to be teachers, you need someone to teach you again the first principles of the oracles of God; and you have come to need milk and not solid food. For everyone who partakes only of milk is unskilled in the word of righteousness, for he is a babe." Milk is a symbol of dependence. Babies are unable to pick up a fork and knife to feed themselves and are dependent on their mothers to feed them. Are you dependent on your spiritual leaders for your spiritual food or have you reached a point where you can feed yourself? Milk is a picture of the basic, elementary truths of the Christian faith. It is a good thing for a new believer to learn these things but there comes a time in the natural progression of spiritual growth that you begin to seek out the deeper truths of the Word of God. At some point you have to go deeper than reading a short devotional every day or a single verse in some promise box.

Jesus said in John 16:12, "I still have many things to say to you, but you cannot bear them now." Jesus wanted to speak some deep truths into the lives of the disciples but they were still drinking milk even after walking with Jesus for three years. Milk is predigested food that comes from the pastor to you. This is good for a season for even 1 Peter 2:2 says "as newborn babes desire the pure milk of the Word, that you may grow thereby." As you grow there will come a time when you'll have to study the Word of God for yourself. As you do this God will give you the same deep revelations that He gives your pastor and Bible teachers. Before long you'll take these advanced truths and fresh revelations that God gives you and become a distributor into the lives of other people. God wants His children to grow up and become mature believers, growing into the people He has called them to be. Jesus had to grow into the person God called Him to be. David did also and so do you. Ask yourself, are you eating meat or drinking milk? Can you discern truth from error?

Heb. 5:14 says, "But solid food belongs to those who are of full age, that is, those who by reason of use have their senses exercised to discern both good and evil." The Message Bible says, "Milk is for beginners, inexperienced in God's ways; solid food is for the mature, who have some practice in telling right from wrong." Can you detect false teaching when it's being taught? Do you have your spiritual senses trained to distinguish truth from foolishness and heresies? There are many false teachings being taught even in the church so you must learn for yourself what the Bible says. The best way to identify a false teaching is to know the truth of God's Word. A bank teller is not trained to know what a counterfeit bill feels like. They focus on what a real bill feels like and are then able to easily spot a counterfeit bill when it passes by them. When you study the truth of God's Word you'll be able to easily spot a false teaching. This is why you need to get into the Word of God and let the Word of God get into you.

Heb. 6:1 (NASB) says, "Let us press on to maturity." For that to happen, Paul says you must be "rooted and built up in Him and established in the faith, as you have been taught, abounding in it with thanksgiving" (Col. 2:7). The Message

Bible says, "You're deeply rooted in Him. You're well constructed upon Him. You know your way around the faith. Now do what you've been taught. School's out; quit studying the subject and start living it! And let your living spill over into thanksgiving." In order to be rooted in Jesus, you've got to go deeper than having a mere head knowledge of who He is. You've got to personally know Him better today than you did yesterday. Eph. 4:13 (AMP) says, "We might arrive at really mature manhood, the completeness of personality which is nothing less than the standard height of Christ's own perfection, the measure of the stature of the fullness of the Christ and the completeness found in Him." Vs. 24 (MSG) says you are to have "a God-fashioned life, a life renewed from the inside and working itself into your conduct as God accurately reproduces His character in you."

In order for spiritual growth to happen, you must be deeply rooted in the fertile soil of spiritual ground. The Parable of the Sower is a story Jesus told about spiritual growth. The blessing of this parable is that Jesus right away gives the meaning of what was said. Luke 8:5 says, "A sower went out to sow his seed. And as he sowed, some fell by the wayside; and it was trampled down, and the birds of the air devoured it." Vs. 11,12 says the seed was the Word of God and these birds are symbolic of the devil. Be aware for the devil always comes after you've heard the Word. 2 Cor. 4:4 (NLT) says, "Satan, who is the god of this world, has blinded the minds of those who don't believe. They are unable to see the glorious light of the Good News. They don't understand this message about the glory of Christ, who is the exact likeness of God." Some people just don't understand the message being preached. They hear the Word but their heart gets hard when they reject what they heard. The devil blinds them, binds them, and grinds them. This is precisely what he did to Samson.

Samson was an anointed man of God and his name is found in the Heb. 11 "Hall of Fame" of faith heroes in the Bible (vs. 32). He was a judge for twenty years but he played with sin and paid a heavy price for it. Judges 16:21 says, "Then the Philistines took him and put out his eyes, and brought him down to Gaza. They bound him with bronze fetters, and he became a grinder in the prison." Jesus is talking about those people who have a closed mind and because of their dullness of hearing the seed that was sown showed no sign of life at all. Their hearts and minds are void of spiritual perception. Just as the surface of a highway is hard, so is the hearts of those who don't give an attentive ear to the Word being taught to them. They sit in church thinking about what they're going to eat afterward or who's going to win the ballgame that afternoon. The spiritual eyes of these people need to be opened so they'll see their personal need of Jesus Christ. Their hearts are hard and they just can't grasp the importance and the meaning of what's being said to them.

Jesus continues in vs. 6, "Some fell on rock; and as soon as it sprang up, it withered away because it lacked moisture." He then said in vs. 13, "But the ones on the rock are those who, when they hear, receive the word with joy; and these have no root, who believe for a while and in time of temptation fall away." Some people are impulsive by nature and grasp at whatever is in front of them. On the outside it looks as if they're on the right path but when tribulation and persecution come they stumble and fall away. Their hearts are shallow and the Word can't take root in their lives. At first they were full of passion and excitement but you can't build your faith on an emotional experience. Emotions come and go but the Word of God doesn't change and it lasts forever. You are called to walk by faith and not your feelings because fickle emotions will never stand the test of time. People say they tried religion but it didn't work for them. They're blaming the gospel for their failure instead of putting the blame on themselves where it rightfully belongs.

G. K. Chesterton once said, "Christianity has not been tried and found wanting. It's been found difficult and not tried."

Another time he said, "The traveler sees what he sees, the tourist sees what he has come to see." Some people all they see are the trials of life not realizing that seeds not deeply planted will wither away in the blazing sun. These people respond quickly to the gospel message but their excitement soon fades away because they don't want to pay the price that spiritual growth and maturity demand. Christianity is not based on the emotion of the moment but if your decision to follow Christ is authentic it will stand the test of time. A person who walks away during hard times and does not come back into the fold was never a believer in the first place. 1 John 2:19 (MSG) talks about these non-committed people, "They left us, but they were never really with us. If they had been, they would have stuck it out with us, loyal to the end. In leaving, they showed their true colors, showed they never did belong."

You can grow but first you must want to grow. Success or failure is all based on the choices you make each and every day. You make your choices and your choices make you. The Word of God works and will produce good results in those who make the right choices and are dedicated in their quest for spiritual growth and maturity. Jesus next said in vs. 7, "And some fell among thorns, and the thorns sprang up with it and choked it." This was explained in vs. 14, "And the ones that fell among thorns are those who, when they have heard, go out and are choked with cares, riches, and pleasures of life, and bring no fruit to maturity." The Message Bible says "these are the ones who hear, but then the seed is crowded out and nothing comes of it as they go about their lives worrying about tomorrow, making money, and having fun." Seeds that are planted are always in a constant battle with weeds and thorns that continually try to stunt their growth. Jesus is saying that the Word is choked out of people's lives by the cares, riches, and pleasures of life.

Weeds grow randomly and they can grow anywhere. Notice that Jesus didn't say it was sin that chokes out the Word but rather the cares of this world. Yes, there are things in life that you must give careful attention to. Some things you can't ignore and it's a good thing that you apply time and effort resolving these issues. What Jesus is saying is don't let a good thing turn into a bad thing. There are people who have good intentions but there's a lot going on in their lives right now. They're very busy but they'll be sure to make a commitment to God when things settle down a little. Of course, it never happens and before you know it their life is over and they have nothing to show for it. Job 14:5 says, "You have appointed his limits, so that he cannot pass." The Message Bible says, "You set the boundary and no one can cross it." Don't get so caught up with the cares and pleasures of this life that you don't have time to do what's necessary for spiritual growth to come. If you're too busy for God, you're too busy.

Weeds and thorns are anything that crowds Jesus out of your life. You have a good heart, you mean well, but your priorities are out of balance. You care too much about the wrong things. Do not allow the things of this earth to become more important to you than the treasures of the kingdom of God. Paul called Demas a fellow laborer in Philemon 23 but tells a different story in 2 Tim. 4:9,10, "Be diligent to come to me quickly; for Demas has forsaken me, having loved this present world, and has departed for Thessalonica." This is why 1 John 2:15 says, "Do not love the world or the things in the world. If anyone loves the world, the love of the Father is not in him." The Message Bible says in vs.15-17, "Don't love the world's ways. Don't love the world's goods. Love of the world squeezes out love for the Father. Practically everything that goes on in the world - wanting your own way, wanting everything for yourself, wanting to appear important - has nothing to do with the Father. It just isolates you from Him. The world and all its wanting, wanting, wanting is on the way out - but whoever does what God wants is set for eternity."

Jesus ends His parable in vs. 8, "But others fell on good ground, sprang up, and yielded a crop a hundredfold." He explained this in vs. 15, "But the ones that fell on the good ground are those who, having heard the Word with a noble and good heart, keep it and bear fruit with patience." It's not always what you hear that counts, rather it's how you hear that makes a difference in your life. Jesus says you need to hear the Word with a noble and good heart. There are people who hear what's being said but it doesn't register down inside of them. They hear but are really not hearing. You need to give the gospel message your full attention with the godly intention of grasping its full meaning. This is so important because what and how you hear has the potential to impact your entire life. You will listen attentively if you believe your life depends on it. A good hearer receives the Word and keeps it. He takes it in and it becomes a part of him. He holds on to it and puts it to use in his life. He will then bring forth fruit with patience and endurance.

Spiritual transformation does not happen overnight. It's a gradual process. Conversion happens immediately but transformation takes a lifetime. Matt. 13:23 says the hearer understands the Word. He hears it, he follows it from beginning to end and never stops thinking about it until he grasps its full meaning. You need to chew on the Word and meditate on it instead of swallowing it whole. Some people read ten chapters a day and still do not know what it said. Slow down and ponder everything it's telling you. Those who hear the Word and understand it are made more responsible than those who don't. Soon you'll be a doer of the Word and not a hearer only (James 1:22). God expects you to act on what you heard for this is how spiritual growth comes and develops. The result of growing strong spiritually is that you'll produce fruit for the kingdom of God. No longer will you go to church just to receive something. Now you'll be going to make a positive contribution into the lives of others. This is what spiritual growth is all about. It's why you were born to grow.

Randall J. Brewer

-2-

"GIVING GOD GLORY"

There is nothing more important than to have your words and actions line up with your position in Christ. You've passed from death to life, from darkness to light, now it's time to act like it. You are a child of the living God so live up to who you are. Christ is in you so you must live up to that standard. In other words, become in practice what you are in position. Peter wrote two epistles and he begins and ends them with a mandate that you grow up and mature spiritually. He does this because there is nothing more tragic than a stunted believer who has not reached spiritual maturity. 1 Peter 2:2 says "as newborn babes, desire the pure milk of the Word, that you may grow thereby." He then says in 2 Peter 3:18, "But grow in the grace and knowledge of our Lord and Savior Jesus Christ. To Him be the glory both now and forever. Amen." Notice that Peter equates growing spiritually with giving God glory. Comprehend what Peter is saying. The master key to spiritual growth is understanding what it means to glorify God.

The greatest theme in the history of the universe is that God is to be glorified. When Jesus was born the angels declared, "Glory to God in the highest, and on earth, good will toward men!" (Luke 2:14). The concept of glorifying God is the reason the world exists. "The heavens declare the glory of

God" (Ps. 91:1) and so do the beasts of the field (Is. 43:20). You also were made to glorify God. It's why you exist. In 1647 the Westminster Shorter Catechism proclaimed that "the chief end of man is to glorify God and to enjoy Him forever." This lines up with what Paul said in 1 Cor. 10:31, "Therefore, whether you eat or drink, or whatever you do, do all to the glory of God." No matter what you do, even the most basic necessities of life like eating and drinking, do all to the glory of God. Jesus came to glorify the Father no matter what price He had to pay (John 12:27,28). You also need to aim your life at His glory and His purposes. When you realize that you are alive to give God glory, you will put yourself in the process of gaining spiritual growth and maturity.

Throughout history, the ultimate condemnation of man is that he didn't glorify God. Rom. 1:21,22 says, "Although they knew God, they did not glorify Him as God, nor were thankful, but became futile in their thoughts, and their foolish hearts were darkened. Professing to be wise, they became fools." It is a serious thing not to give God glory. Jer. 13:16 (NLT) says, "Give glory to the Lord your God before it is too late. Acknowledge Him before He brings darkness upon you, causing you to stumble and fall on the darkening mountains. For then, when you look for light, you will find only terrible darkness and gloom." The prophet is saying to give God glory or else! When people don't give God glory, they put themselves in a place of judgment. In Dan. 4:30 King Nebuchadnezzar claimed God's glory for himself and be became like a beast of the field for seven years, eating grass like oxen (vs. 32,33). In Acts 12:21,22 Herod blasphemed God and "immediately an angel of the Lord struck him, because he did not give glory to God. And he was eaten by worms and died" (vs. 23).

Those who fail to give God glory are cut off from the blessings of God. In their future is a Christless eternity where they'll be condemned forevermore. Rom. 1:28-32 (NLT) says,

"Since they thought it foolishness to acknowledge God, He abandoned them to their foolish thinking and let them do things that should never be done. Their lives become full of every kind of wickedness, sin, greed, hate, envy, murder, quarreling, deception, malicious behavior, and gossip. They are backstabbers, haters of God, insolent, proud, and boastful. They invent new ways of sinning, and they disobey their parents. They refuse to understand, break their promises, are heartless, and have no mercy. They know God's justice requires that those who do these things deserve to die, yet they do them anyway. Worse yet, they encourage others to do them, too." This doomed existence happens when people fail to glorify God, when their words and actions don't line up with His. Jesus said in John 8:44, "You are of your father the devil, and the desires of your father you want to do."

As a true believer in Christ, it should bother you when God is dishonored. David said in Ps. 69:9 (NLT), "Passion for your house has consumed me, and the insults of those who insult you have fallen on me." The Message Bible says, "I love You more than I can say. Because I'm madly in love with You, they blame me for everything they dislike about You." This same verse was quoted in John 2:17 after Jesus cleansed the temple by driving out the moneychangers who were there dishonoring God. This was something Jesus could not tolerate so He took a whip and drove them out. Concerning the church at Ephesus, Rev. 2:2 says "you cannot bear those who are evil." The people at Ephesus felt the pain of God being dishonored and not being given the glory He richly deserves. The greatest call of a believer is to glorify God, and this happens when you let His glory shine through you. 2 Cor. 4:6 (NLT) says, "For God, who said, 'Let there be light in the darkness,' has made this light shine in our hearts so we could know the glory of God that is seen in the face of Jesus Christ."

Adam and Eve lived in the presence of God. The glory of God engulfed them as they walked with Him in the cool of the day. When they sinned they were removed from the garden because fallen man cannot experience the glory of God nor can they give Him glory. From that moment on, God has endeavored to get man to see His glory. Adam saw it and now God wants you to see it as well. It was for this reason that He sent Jesus to walk the earth. Rom. 11:36 says, "For of Him and through Him and to Him are all things, to whom be glory forever. Amen." The Message Bible says, "Everything comes from Him; Everything happens through Him; Everything ends up in Him. Always glory! Always praise! Yes. Yes. Yes." The focus of your life is to glorify God and this happens when you confess Jesus as Lord (Phil. 2:9-11). You cannot give glory to God unless you give glory to His Son. Jesus said in John 5:23, "He who does not honor the Son does not honor the Father who sent Him." When Jesus is the Lord of your life, you will obey Him always and do the things He tells you to do.

Living a Christ-centered life is how you bring glory to God the Father. Col. 1:27 (GNT) says, "God's plan is to make known His secret to His people, this rich and glorious secret which He has for all peoples. And the secret is that Christ is in you, which means that you will share in the glory of God." In order for the world to see God's glory in you, you must grow spiritually. As you do that, you will be changed from one level of glory to a higher level of glory, You'll go from glory to glory (2 Cor. 3:18). The apostle Paul had to go through a growing process where God had to transform him so he could be used for the glory of God. You also have to go through this same process. In Acts 22:3 Paul tells how he was educated from his early days in the laws of the Jews and he grew up and became a strict Pharisee. He was very passionate and his religious zeal was displayed in his intense persecution of the church (Acts 29:9-11). In his own words Paul testified that "in raging fury against them I persecuted them even to foreign cities" (vs. 11 ESV). Then something stopped Paul dead in his tracks.

One day as Paul was traveling on the road to Damascus to persecute more Christians, he met the Lord Jesus Christ (Acts 9:3-5) and suddenly his misguided zeal came to a screeching halt. It was on this day that Paul's life was drastically changed. Like him, many people have been religious their entire life and yet have not been transformed into the image of Christ. They don't realize that spiritual growth is not a matter of knowledge only. It's what you do with that knowledge that determines the measure of your growth and maturity. In fact, 1 Cor. 8:1,2 says, "Knowledge puffs up, but love edifies. And if anyone thinks that he knows anything, he knows nothing yet as he ought to know." Also, spiritual growth has nothing to do with the works you do in and for the kingdom of God. Nobody was busier doing religious activities than the Pharisees but nobody was further from the truth than they were. Matt. 7:21-23 tells how being busy for God doesn't even qualify you for salvation let alone spiritual growth. What people need is a Damascus road experience, a face-to-face encounter with Jesus.

Paul went on to become a great apostle and wrote half the books in the New Testament. He started many churches and was used by God to ignite the miraculous growth of the first century church. Just like God did with Paul, He also wants to give you a new life, a new beginning. He wants to take you from darkness to light, from pride to humility, from glory to glory. God has a plan and a purpose for you just like He had for the apostle Paul. Eph. 2:10 says, "For we are His workmanship, created in Christ Jesus for good works, which God prepared beforehand that we should walk in them." The Message Bible says, "He creates each of us by Christ Jesus to join Him in the work He does, the good work He has gotten ready for us to do, work we had better be doing." God's plan is for you to have an ever-growing relationship with Him and a life that is supernaturally transformed so you'll become like Him. "As He is, so are we in this world" (1 John 4:17). God wants all of you, not just a part of you. He wants you to be set apart, wholly devoted to Him in every area of your life.

There is a role you have to play in order for this to happen. For sure, spiritual growth requires a lot of involvement on your part. You've got to actively abide in Christ and pursue a deeper relationship with Him. You need to yield to Him always and purposely set your minds on things above and not beneath (Col. 3:2). You have to choose to do these things. You have to choose to walk in the Spirit without giving in to the desires of the flesh (Gal. 5:16). It's by abiding in Christ that you'll have peace that passes all understanding (Phil. 4:7), joy unspeakable (1 Peter 1:8), and love that never fails (1 Cor. 13:8). You'll be unshaken even in the midst of difficult situations. You'll have an inner confidence that you can do all things through Christ who strengthens you (Phil. 4:13). People wrongfully believe that if they'll only get saved they'll automatically have love, joy, peace, and happiness all the days of their lives. No, it's the process of spiritual growth that brings all these blessings into your life. They come from an ever deepening relationship with Christ. They come from abiding in Him.

The power behind spiritual growth is the Holy Spirit. It is He who energizes your growth. 2 Cor. 3:18 (CEV) says, "So our faces are not covered. They show the bright glory of the Lord, as the Lord's Spirit makes us more and more like our glorious Lord." As you behold the glory of the Lord, as you gaze into His glory, the Holy Spirit begins the process of spiritual growth. David focused on the glory of God and his heart was made glad. Ps. 16:8,9 says, "I have set the Lord always before me; Because He is at my right hand I shall not be moved. Therefore my heart is glad, and my glory rejoices." Abiding in Christ is the channel through which this supernatural power flows. It's this power that allows you to thrive in your Christian life. It's this power that turns you from a nobody into a somebody but it takes involvement on your part. If you'll join God in the work He's doing, if you'll do your part, you can have the assurance "that He who has begun a good work in you will complete it until the day of Jesus Christ" (Phil. 1:6).

There is a commitment you can make that will give you the assurance that God's work of transformation will take place in your life. Paul tells you what that commitment is in Phil. 3. He begins in vs. 5,6 by telling how religious he was before he met Christ on the road to Damascus. His life was changed at that moment and he then writes in vs. 7 (NLT), "I once thought those things were valuable, but now I consider them worthless because of what Christ has done." He then shares the mindset you must have that brings true spiritual growth and maturity. "Yes, everything else is worthless when compared with the infinite value of knowing Christ Jesus my Lord. For His sake I have discarded everything else, counting it all as garbage, so that I could gain Christ and become one with Him" (vs. 8,9 NLT). Jesus Christ is everything and compared to Him everything else in the world is garbage. Committing yourself to having this mindset is the beginning of a radical transformation in your life. This is where the journey of spiritual growth begins.

Jesus said in John 15:4, "Abide in Me, and I in you." The God's Word translation says, "Live in Me, and I will live in you." If you want your life to be transformed, you must be in a continual living union with Jesus. The Amplified Bible says you have to be "vitally united" to Christ. The word "vitally" means 'essentially, critically, crucially, centrally.' You abide in Christ when you make your union with Him the central focus of your life. This is the mindset you must have in order for spiritual growth to happen. You must embrace the fact that nothing equals the infinite value of knowing Jesus and being found in Him. It's by abiding in Christ that God is able to pour the supernatural power of the Holy Spirit into your life. You must be willing to be in this for the long haul. The only way for you to thrive in life is to abide in Christ and this don't happen overnight. It's something that is cultivated and developed over time much like a branch slowly growing on a vine. Yes, it's hard work but well worth the effort.

To abide in Christ means to be immersed in His presence. No matter what you're going through, Jesus said "in Me you may have peace" (John 16:33). He's talking about abiding in Him. Believers who are stressed out all the time are not abiding in Christ. This is why the Christian divorce rate is the same as that of nonbelievers. The husband and the wife are not abiding in Christ and thus they don't have the power to overcome their marital trials. Sad to say, it has become the accepted norm that Christians in today's world act just like the unsaved. Why is this so? Because they don't abide in Christ and they haven't grown up spiritually. Jesus then said, "In the world you will have tribulation; but be of good cheer, I have overcome the world" (vs. 33). That alone should motivate you to bask in His presence every hour of every day. If you're not doing that, then it is doubtful that you'll be able to handle the trials of life that are sure to come. To unbelievers Jesus says, "Follow Me." To the born again Christian He says, "Abide in Me." By saying that, He is preparing you to live in a world of tribulation.

Most Christians never learn the concept of abiding in Christ. They try to walk the path of righteousness in their own strength not realizing that this is a futile and worthless effort on their part. Don't you do that. From this moment on you must learn to be immersed in your relationship with Jesus, to commune with Him, to walk with Him, to experience Him on a daily basis. No longer do you consider it a burden or an obligation to read your Bible but a joy and a privilege. A growing hunger for God is in your heart. You're not just satisfied with knowing about Him, now you want to know Him intimately in a personal way. As you grow spiritually, you'll have less and less desire for what the world has to offer. The closer you are to Him, the more He'll fill your life where in the past you tried to fill that void with the things of the world. No longer will you go in debt because of the wrongful use of credit cards. No longer will you throw away your weekly paycheck at the gambling casino. You are abiding in Christ and no longer is there a craving for worldly things.

The more you abide in Christ, the more your life will change for the better. You can now love people that you couldn't love in the past. You can accept people for who they are and not for who you want them to be. You've gone beyond loving those whose performance and conduct match your personal standard. It's now easier to forgive those who offend you. Jesus said on the cross, "Father, forgive them for they know not what they do." Do the people who hurt you know what they're doing? Probably not. They don't understand that when they harm you, they are in actuality harming themselves. They don't understand that there are long-term consequences that come from sinning against a child of God. Loving those who do you wrong is a sign of spiritual growth. The time it takes you to forgive a person gets shorter and shorter. No longer do you hold grudges and no more do you let the sun set while you're angry at somebody for doing you wrong. You're abiding in Christ and you love everybody with no strings attached.

More than that, your feelings of love for God are also increasing. There are inner feelings of intimacy for Him that were not there before. Along with that comes a deep desire to express that love. Praise and worship pour out of you like a never-ending river of love and compassion. You now have an increasing desire to obey Him and do what He tells you to do. His will becomes your will. No longer do you obey Him because you're afraid not to nor because of the consequences you believe disobedience brings. No, you obey Him for who He is. You obey Him because of your deep love for Him and His deep love for you. Your faith is also increasing. As you use your faith against the trials and challenges of life, it gets stretched little by little and slowly but surely begins to grow. The more of life's hardships you face and overcome, the greater your faith will be. And the more you're able to overcome, the more things God can trust you with. By standing in faith you're showing God you won't quit when the pressure is on. You won't walk away but will stand strong and fight the good fight of faith.

Phil. 3:10 is the verse that will launch you into a transformed life. The Amplified Bible says, "And this, so that I may know Him experientially, becoming more thoroughly acquainted with Him, understanding the remarkable wonders of His person more completely and in that same way experience the power of His resurrection which overflows and is active in believers, and that I may share the fellowship of His sufferings, by being continually conformed inwardly into His likeness even to His death, dying as He did." Paul is giving you the foundation on which spiritual growth is built on. That foundation is a progressive and passionate commitment to know Christ intimately. As you know Him more and more you will begin to be transformed into His image. That's the blessing that comes when you abide in Christ. After telling you to abide in Him, Jesus said in John 15:11, "These things I have spoken to you that My joy may be in you and that your joy may be full." Jesus is not talking about your circumstances here, He's talking about fixing your heart "for out of it spring the issues of life" (Prov. 4:23).

Paul then says in vs. 11, "If, by any means, I may attain to the resurrection from the dead." He is not talking here about what happens after you die. The Amplified Bible gives more understanding to what Paul is saying, "That if possible I may attain to the spiritual and moral resurrection that lifts me out from among the dead even while in the body." This verse is talking about being raised from the deadness of this life and living a life of spiritual growth and maturity. Eph. 2:1 says, "And you He made alive, who were dead in trespasses and sins." Rom. 6:11 says, "Likewise you also, reckon yourselves to be dead indeed to sin, but alive to God in Christ Jesus our Lord." To be alive with the divine life of God is the goal for which every believer should be striving for. That's the goal of spiritual growth. Vs. 12 says, "I press on" to lay hold of the new resurrected life. Get up every morning committed and determined to live the divine life Jesus has called you to live. Press on to possess the perfection and maturity with which Jesus first possessed you.

No longer live life nonchalantly. Press on to know Christ better. Put to death that old life and walk in the new resurrected life. It's the pressing in that's your part. It's what you must do morning, noon, and night. It's a choice you must make every single day of your life. Vs. 14,15 says, "I press toward the goal for the prize of the upward call of God in Christ Jesus. Therefore let us, as many as are mature, have this mind; and if in anything you think otherwise, God will reveal even this to you." The Message Bible says, "I'm off and running, and I'm not turning back." Paul says you need to focus on one thing. You need to forget the past and look forward to what lies ahead. You've been forgiven so don't let the past pull you down and prevent you from looking to what God has planned for you. Paul is saying he will press on and not give up. That's his part and that is your part also. If you want true transformation in your life then this is the commitment you must make. Press on and never give up.

Randall J. Brewer

-3-

"ABIDING IN CHRIST"

Jesus said in John 10:10, "I have come that they may have life, and that they may have it more abundantly." What a lot of unbelievers don't understand is that all the promises of God are conditional. For example, Jesus said in Matt. 11:28, "Come to Me, all you who labor and are heavy laden, and I will give you rest." That's conditional. Before you can find rest for your souls, you must first come to Jesus just as you are. As you surrender your life to Him, He'll give you the rest you need. Another example is a verse believers quote often not realizing that the promise given is also conditional. Rom. 8:28 says, "And we know that all things work together for good to those who love God, to those who are called according to His purpose." This promise is only for those who truly love God and demonstrate that love by submitting to the call God has on their life. Clearly not all believers are doing that. Likewise, the abundant life Jesus came to give you is also conditional. You must abide in Him and grow up in order to have the blessings of abundant life manifested in your life. Abiding in Christ is the source of the abundant life Jesus came to give you.

The more you immerse yourself in your personal relationship with Jesus, the more you abide in Him, the more you'll experience life in abundance. Rest assured, you can do this.

Jesus said, "For My yoke is easy, and my burden is light" (Matt. 11:30). The word "easy" means 'well-fitting.' The life Jesus called you to live fits perfectly with your personality and God-given abilities. Don't resist your heavenly call but put on the life God made for you. On the road to Damascus the Lord said to Paul, "It is hard for you to kick against the goads" (Acts 9:5). A goad was a stick with a pointed piece of iron on its tip. The farmer would prick the animal to steer it in the right direction. Sometimes the animal would rebel by kicking at the goad and the sharp point would be driven further into its flesh. The more the animal rebelled, the more it suffered. The fact of the matter is, those who resist the call of God on their lives are only punishing themselves. Prov. 13:15 says, "The way of the unfaithful is hard." Solomon also wrote in Prov. 15:10, "Harsh correction is for him who forsakes the way."

Jesus is saying to take the life He's molded and shaped for you and put it on. Surrender your life to Him and stop demanding your own way. The farm animal no longer gets pricked when it does what the farmer wants it to do. The yoke around its neck fits perfectly and it's no struggle to do what it's been made to do. You don't have to work hard to abide in Christ, you just have to stop resisting the call and surrender your life to Jesus. Just like that big ox, if you rebel you'll get pricked but if you surrender you'll get peace. The choice is yours. The good news is that when you surrender to God and abide in Him, He'll step forward and go to work in your life. Phil. 2:13 (NLT) says, "For God is working in you, giving you the desire and the power to do what pleases Him." The Message Bible says, "Be energetic in your life of salvation, reverent and sensitive before God. That energy is God's energy, an energy deep within you, God Himself willing and working at what will give Him the most pleasure."

The success of your life is not based on you calling yourself a Christian or whether or not you go to church. Success comes only when you abide in Christ. It comes when you surrender to Him and grow in that intimate knowledge of who He is. Jesus is the author and finisher of your faith (Heb. 12:2) and He came to give you abundant life. He even tells you what to do in Matt. 11:29, "Take My yoke upon you, and learn from Me." He is telling you to abide in Him "for I am gentle and lowly in heart." He is saying that you can trust Him at all times "and you will find rest for your souls." Gone will be the inner conflict that so many believers struggle with because they're being pricked by reason of rebellion and disobedience. The Message Bible says, "Learn the unforced rhythms of grace. I won't lay anything heavy or ill-fitting on you. Keep company with Me and you'll learn to live freely and lightly." Success comes when you and Jesus walk together. Ps. 16:11 says, "You will show me the path of life; In Your presence is fullness of joy; At your right hand are pleasures forevermore."

Abiding in Christ should be the deepest longing in your heart. It's your intimate feelings for Him that drive you into His presence each and every day. This love is real and tangible and can be seen by those around you. It's a love you can't hold inside but like a bursting dam it overflows all around. This is so important because your entire Christian life depends on the quality of your love relationship with Jesus Christ. Many people say they love Jesus but do they really? Is it tangible? Can people see it? Is there proof that what they say is true? If not, maybe they don't love Christ as much as they say they do. They want Him to forgive their sins and they want to go to heaven but do they love Him enough to surrender their life to Him? Do they love Him enough to do the things He tells them to do? Do they love Him enough to abide in Him? If not, they better get back on the path God has called them to take. They need to heed the warning of Prov. 14:12 which says, "There is a way which seems right to a man, but its end is the way of death."

You can't abide in Christ if you're continually distracted by the cares and pleasures of this world. The devil knows this and is the reason he endeavors to put roadblocks on the path you're traveling on. God has a plan and purpose for your life and the devil is a thief trying to steal your destiny from you. He'll try to pull you in every direction so you won't know if you're coming or going. Don't let this happen to you. 2 Cor. 2:11 says "we are not ignorant of his devices," of his well planned out schemes and tactics. The best way to avoid being distracted in your walk with God is to forever put Him first place in your life. As you abide in Him and He abides in you, the devil will be unable to pull you off the narrow road you're on. So important is your love for God that Deut. 6:4,5 says, "Hear, O Israel: The Lord our God, the Lord is one! You shall love the Lord your God with all your heart, with all your soul, and with all your might." The word "hear" in Hebrew is a command that demands a response. The writer is commanding you to hear what he's saying and then respond to it.

Picture somebody grabbing you by the shirt collar and screaming out loud, "Listen to me!" This is what this verse is saying. "Listen to me! Love the Lord your God with all your heart, with all your soul, and with all your might." Jesus repeats this verse in Matt. 22:37 when He was asked what was the greatest commandment in the law. The greatest thing you can do is love God with everything you've got. Doing this will change the way you live your life. Deut. 6:6-9 goes on to show you what your life will look like if you're loving God like you're supposed to. Vs. 6 says, "And these words which I command you today shall be in your heart." There's that word "command" again. Loving God is not a suggestion, it's a command. The NLT says, "And you must commit yourselves wholeheartedly to these commands that I am giving you today." If loving God is the top priority of your life, vs. 7 says it is your responsibility to teach these words diligently to your children. Prov. 22:6 says, "Train up a child in the way he should go, and when he is old he will not depart from it."

The Bible even tells you when to talk to your children about Jesus. Deut. 6:7 says you "shall talk to them when you sit in your house, when you walk by the way, when you lie down, and when you rise up." That covers about everything, doesn't it? In other words, you should never stop talking to your family about Jesus. Abraham was one of the greatest men in all the Bible and Gen. 18:17-19 tells why this is so. The Lord said, "Shall I hide from Abraham what I am doing, since Abraham shall surely become a great and mighty nation, and all the nations of the earth shall be blessed in him? For I have known him, in order that he may command his children and his household after him, that they keep the way of the Lord, to do righteousness and justice, that the Lord may bring to Abraham what He has spoken to him." Think about that for a moment. Jesus was in the bloodline of Abraham and this is how all nations are blessed through him. The reason this was able to happen is because Abraham trained his children in the ways of righteousness. If you love God, open your mouth and tell somebody about it.

Deut. 6:8 tells you what to do next with the words telling you to love God with all your heart, soul, and might, "You shall bind them as a sign on your hand, and they shall be as frontlets between your eyes." You work with your hands and everything you do is motivated by your deep love for God. When your love for God is bound between your eyes, it will change what you think about and the decisions you make. When you abide in Christ, your thoughts and actions will all be for the glory of God. Vs.9 says, "You shall write them on the doorposts of your house and on your gates." It should be evident when visitors come to your house that Jesus is Lord of your life. There's a calm, peaceful atmosphere in your house that's not found outside in the world. The children are well disciplined and the dishes are clean and put away. Christian music is playing on the radio and everybody is treated with the love and respect they deserve. Unity and intimacy abound for they are all one in Christ Jesus, one in heart, mind, and will. Jesus is Lord and it is evident for all to see.

The importance of abiding in Christ is found in the parable of the two builders. Matt. 7:24-27 tells how a wise man built his house on a rock and a foolish man built his house on the sand. A great storm came and the house on the rock stood strong whereas the house on the sand collapsed and fell. The difference between these two men is that the wise man abided in Christ and did what the Word said to do, the foolish man did not. Both of these men experienced the same storm but one of them had overcoming peace while the other ignored the Word and great was the fall of his life. It is a sad day when Christians respond to their marriage problems the same way unbelievers do. Instead of abiding in Christ they get divorced and then move on to another doomed marriage. Also, there are just as many Christians out of work as there are non-Christians. Why is that? Because they're not abiding in Christ and experiencing the peace and victory that Jesus promises those who do. Yes, trials will come but those who abide in Christ don't respond to them like unbelievers do. They rest in God and believe He'll work a miracle on their behalf.

Those who abide in Christ are immersed in who He is and have learned to rest in His promises. They believe Jesus when He said, "These things I have spoken to you, that in Me you may have peace. In the world you will have tribulation; but be of good cheer, I have overcome the world" (John 16:33). Who can rest and be cheerful when they've been laid off from their job? Those who abide in Christ. They know God is on their side and a new and better job is in their near future. Those who murmur and complain, those who doubt and fear, are those who built their house on the sand and they can expect to be out of work for a long, long time. For you to live victoriously in life you've got to abide in Christ.

You've got to be immersed in Him and remain in Him. If you don't, you will never experience the joy and power of the abundant life. If you're not sold out in your commitment to Jesus, if you're not abiding in Him, then you will not have life and have it more abundantly. The blessings of God are conditional. If you're not abiding in Christ then don't shake your fist at God when bad things happen to you.

In order to experience the rest of God, you've got to put on the yoke He made for you. It's the secret to a rich, fulfilled life. No longer do you live for yourself but now you've put on the life God made for you. A well-fitting yoke is the secret to painless work for the ox and so it will be in your life. When you do what He has called you to do, it will be no burden to you and peace will be present in your life. When trials come, when the winds blow, you will find rest for your soul. You are abiding in Christ and He is abiding in you. When you wake up in the morning your house will still be standing. Phil. 4:6,7 (NLT) says, "Don't worry about anything; instead, pray about everything. Tell God what you need, and thank Him for all He has done. Then you will experience God's peace, which exceeds anything we can understand. His peace will guard your hearts and minds as you live in Christ Jesus." The Message Bible says, "Before you know it, a sense of God's wholeness, everything coming together for good, will come and settle you down. It's wonderful what happens when Christ displaces worry at the center of your life."

When you learn to abide in Christ, there is nothing the devil can do to harm you. You'll be able to walk in victory through any situation the evil one and this world throws your way. Jesus promised in John 15:7, "If you abide in Me, and My words abide in you, you will ask what you desire, and it shall be done for you." This is a great promise but don't forget the conditional word "if" at the beginning of this verse. Victory in life is all based on whether or not you're abiding in Christ and His words are abiding in you. Jesus is also saying that those who abide in Him need to have a prayer life that is second to none. It sounds easy but it really isn't. Most people have a hard time finding time to pray. This is a busy, fast-paced world and the devil will do anything to keep you from spending time alone with God. For the born again believer, prayer should be the same as breathing for it is the ultimate test that reveals the condition of one's inner man. There is nothing that reveals the condition of your spirit more than prayer. If you're abiding in Christ, you must find time to pray.

Jesus was always in constant contact with the Father. Morning after morning He would go off by Himself to pray and be alone with the Father. It was here that He received direction for His life, where He learned what to say and what to do. Jesus said in John 5:19, "Most assuredly, I say to you, the Son can do nothing of Himself, but what He sees the Father do; for whatever He does, the Son also does in like manner." He also said in John 8:28, "I do nothing of Myself; but as My Father taught Me, I speak these things." Again He said in John 12:49, "For I have not spoken on My own authority; but the Father who sent Me gave Me a command, what I should say and what I should speak." The last thing you want to do is face this world all by yourself. You're just not that tough. Nobody is. The world faces life with its own knowledge and ability and look at the condition it is in. Don't be like the world. Like Jesus, be in continual contact with the Father. If you're not getting the victory through prayer, then the devil is getting the victory through your lack of prayer.

One thing that scares people about prayer is they think they have to pray for an hour at a time. No, you don't have to do that, but you should never go an hour without praying. Remember, prayer should be as common as breathing. You don't think about breathing, it just comes naturally. This is how it should be with talking to God. You're abiding in Him and He's abiding in you. You think about Him all the time so it should be as natural as breathing to commune with Him. He's your friend and He wants to hear your deepest thoughts. Tell Him anything and everything that concerns you. Talk to Him while you're washing the dishes and when you're mowing the lawn. Talk to Him at work and at play. Talk to Him morning, noon, and night. Pray without ceasing (1 Thess. 5:16). Don't allow the devil to crowd out of your life your time to pray. Rearrange your life to ensure that you are in constant communion with God. Just like you need to breathe in order to live, much more do you need time with God to survive in this crazy, mixed-up world. It truly is a matter of life and death.

Jesus made it clear that if you are to abide in Him, then you must abide in the Word. He said in John 8:31,32, "If you abide in My word, you are My disciples indeed. And you shall know the truth, and the truth shall make you free." Why is it that so many Christians are not being set free by the Word of God? Because they're not abiding in it. The Message Bible says, "If you stick with this, living out what I tell you, you are My disciples for sure. Then you will experience for yourselves the truth, and the truth will free you." Abiding in the Word shows that you are His disciple. Being a disciple goes way beyond being a mere Christian. It puts you in the inner circle of Jesus' closest friends. It sets you apart from the world and those Christian believers who don't take the time to abide in Christ. A disciple is one who applies the teachings of the Word into their own life. They do the things Jesus did and say the things Jesus said. In order to know what to do and say, you must abide in the Word at all times. This will give you special knowledge of the truth and this is what sets you free.

For some people, studying the Bible can be a frustrating experience because they don't know what to do or where to start. It can seem to be a bit overwhelming and for this reason many people lay their Bible aside and don't read it at all. The truth is, reading your Bible should be fun and interesting, something you look forward to. You don't want to read your Bible just for the sake of reading it. No, you read it to get something out of it. You read it so you can apply its principles and Godly wisdom into your life. You read it to draw closer to Jesus. You read it to become His disciple. There are many ways in which you can read your Bible. One way is to pick a book in the Bible that you want to read and commit yourself to reading that book over a certain period of time. Read it in different translations so that you can get a deeper perspective of what that book is all about. Get a study Bible and get the background to the book before you read it. You need to be able to place this book into the bigger context of the Bible story.

You may also want to study a particular topic in the Bible. You may want to learn more about faith or love or divine healing. Get a concordance or a topical Bible and look up all the references on whatever subject you're studying. This will give you an idea of what the entire Bible says on this particular topic of study. Another exciting thing you may want to do is study a particular character in the Bible. Abraham is called the father of our faith so you may want to learn about him. David was a man after God's own heart so you may want to study and find out why this was so. Esther and Ruth were great women in the Bible and you may want to study their background and find out what it was that made them so special. You'll see how God was working in their lives. You'll learn about their strengths and weaknesses and the life lessons you can learn from their lives. You'll see how God responded to the things they did and this will give you a deeper insight into who God is and the things that are important to Him.

To abide in Christ is to know Him. In Greek the word "know" refers to the intermingling of two lives together. If you'll abide in His Word, you'll have an 'ever-increasing, intimate, personal, experiential knowledge' of who He is. It's that knowledge that will set you free from all the bondage of the enemy. The good news is that the knowledge of the truth never ends. There is always something more to learn, another truth to build upon. This is why you need to read your Bible every day. Prov. 4:20-22 says, "My son, give attention to my words; Incline your ear to my sayings. Do not let them depart from your eyes; Keep them in the midst of your heart; For they are life to those who find them, and health to all their flesh." So, are you a disciple or just a Christian? A disciple is one who follows his Master so closely that he becomes like Him. This is what abiding in the Word will do for you. It will transform you into His image and cause you to become just as He is. That should be the goal of every believer. Just open up your Bible and abide in it.

God said in Jer. 29:12,13, "Then you will call upon Me and go and pray to Me, and I will listen to you. And you will seek Me and find Me, when you search for Me with all your heart." God is on your side and He has a good plan and a good purpose for your life. He is a good God but He must be sought after to be found. This is why you must persevere as you abide in Him and in His Word. Hold on to Him and never let go. If you'll do that, Jesus promised that He'll do everything else. As you abide in Christ, you'll grow spiritually and this is what allows you to "run with endurance the race that is set before us, looking unto Jesus, the author and finisher of our faith" (Heb. 12:1,2). The devil only wins if you quit, if you stop abiding in Christ. But if you'll cling to Him morning, noon, and night, you'll be able to say what David said in Ps. 59:16,17, "But I will sing of Your power; Yes, I will sing aloud of Your mercy in the morning; For You have been my defense and refuge in the day of my trouble. To You, O my strength, I will sing praises; For God is my defense, the God of my mercy."

-4-

"ALONE WITH GOD"

Why are you here? You are here to have a relationship with the living God. Know that God loves you and He wants to have a close, personal relationship with you. It was for this reason that man was created in the first place. God wanted a family He could commune with, a family He could call His own. This is why the fall of man was so devastating. It broke God's heart because the sin that entered in now hindered Him from having a close relationship with His most prize possession. He sent Jesus to the earth to remove the barrier of sin and now the doors are wide open for fellowship between God and man to be restored. Jesus said in John 17:25,26 (NLT), "O righteous Father, the world doesn't know You, but I do; and these disciples know You sent Me. I have revealed You to them, and I will continue to do so. Then your love for Me will be in them, and I will be in them." Getting saved is all about having a relationship with God. Living your life and growing spiritually is all about relationship as well.

God wants you to walk with Him the way Enoch did in Gen. 5:24, "And Enoch walked with God; and he was not, for God took him." Imagine that. Enoch walked with God so closely that one day God just took him home to heaven. Noah also walked with God. Gen. 6:9 says, "Noah was a just man, perfect in his generation. Noah walked with God." The

Young's Literal Translation says Noah walked with God "habitually." To grow spiritually, you must do the same thing. You must walk with God habitually. Walking with God indicates movement. You're going somewhere. Hopefully, you're going where He wants to take you. Many people may have had an encounter with God early in their lives but have gone no where since. There's no movement in their life and they've become stagnant in their relationship with God. Their lives are now dull and void. They may be saved but there is no fellowship with the One who saved them in the first place. Walking with God is not a one time experience. It's a journey where He takes you from glory to glory.

God is a God of progression. He never changes but He never stays in the same place. He's a God of movement and you must walk with Him to keep up with where He's going. It's that movement that will produce a positive change in your life. You'll grow spiritually and will be changed into His glorious image. Having a healthy and close relationship with God is all about spending time alone with Him. It's about fellowship and this is what determines how much you'll grow spiritually and how far you'll go in this life. Not only are you to know the Word of God, you've got to know the Author of the Word of God. Paul said "for I know whom I have believed" (2 Tim. 1:12). He didn't say what he believed but rather who he believed in. Faith and fellowship with God are inseparable. Knowing the scriptures without knowing who God is produces a form of godliness but will lack the power to do any good in your life. Jesus said in John 17:3, "And this is eternal life, that they may know You, the only true God, and Jesus Christ whom You have sent."

1 John 1:3,4 (NLT) says, "We proclaim to you what we ourselves have actually seen and heard so that you may have fellowship with us. And our fellowship is with the Father and with His Son, Jesus Christ. We are writing these things so that you may fully share our joy." The Amplified Bible says "this fellowship that we have, which is a distinguishing mark of a Christian, is with the Father and with His Son Jesus

Christ, the Messiah." Did you catch that? John said the distinguishing mark of a Christian is the fellowship they have with God. The strength of any relationship is fellowship and this is what sets believers apart from anybody else in the world. Ex. 33:11 says, "So the Lord spoke to Moses face to face, as a man speaks to his friend." That's fellowship. Moses said in vs.13 (AMP), "Show me now Your way, that I may know You, progressively become more deeply and intimately acquainted with You, perceiving and recognizing and understanding more strongly and clearly, and that I may find favor in Your sight."

God wants to get personal with you and you should want to be personal with Him. This is what fellowship is all about. It's the key to walking with God and walking with God is the key to change in your life. David said in Ps. 27:1, "The Lord is my light and my salvation. The Lord is the strength of my life." David made his relationship with God personal. He said to God in vs. 8, "When You said, 'Seek My face,' my heart said to You, 'Your face, Lord, I will seek.'" God needs to become real to you and this happens when you spend quality time alone with Him in fellowship. David said in vs. 4, "One thing I have desired of the Lord, that I will seek: That I may dwell in the house of the Lord all the days of my life." David was confident in his relationship with God. In the same verse David said he wanted "to behold and gaze upon the beauty, the sweet attractiveness and the delightful loveliness of the Lord and to meditate, consider, and inquire in His temple" (AMP). Is it any wonder David was called a man after God's own heart (Acts 13:22)?

Fellowship with God will lead you to a place of confidence. 1 John 5:14,15 says, "Now this is the confidence that we have in Him, that if we ask anything according to His will, He hears us. And if we know that He hears us, whatever we ask, we know that we have the petitions that we have asked of Him." Fellowship produces confidence, and confidence produces a powerful life. Moses was able to do the things he did because he had fellowship with God and this increased his confidence. David was able to kill Goliath because of the confidence that came as a result of his fellowship with God. Another word for "confidence" is "faith." Faith comes when you have close fellowship with God. Fellowship is what connected Jesus to the Father, and it will connect you to Him as well. Let the desire to fellowship with God be the strongest craving in your life. Ps. 42:1,2 says, "As the deer pants for the water brooks, so pants my soul for You, O God. My soul thirsts for God, for the living God."

God loves you so much that He desires to have fellowship with you. He wants you to walk with Him the same way Adam did before he sinned. So strong is His desire for fellowship that He said in 2 Cor. 6:16, "I will dwell in them and walk among them. I will be their God, and they shall be My people." When your desire for fellowship matches God's desire, you'll be able to say what the psalmist said in Ps. 84:10, "For a day in your courts is better than a thousand. I would rather be a doorkeeper in the house of my God than dwell in the tents of wickedness." The Message Bible says, "One day spent in Your house, this beautiful place of worship, beats thousands spent on Greek Island beaches. I'd rather scrub floors in the house of my God than be honored as a guest in the palace of sin." These words reveal the heart of a man who walked with God. Those who are called into fellowship with God don't get caught up in the things of the world. They are "strangers and pilgrims on the earth" (Heb. 11:13) and walking with God is all they think about.

1 Cor. 1:9 says, "God is faithful, by whom you were called into the fellowship of His Son, Jesus Christ our Lord." The Amplified Bible says you "were called into companionship and participation with His Son, Jesus Christ our Lord." God loves you and you've been called into fellowship with Him. It's your fellowship with Him that will establish your faith and cause it to grow. It's what causes you to grow up and mature spiritually. If you want your life to change, if you

want to be transformed into the image of Christ, then you must develop the habit of spending time alone with God. This goes way beyond the casual reading of scripture or skimming through some devotional where you forget what you've read ten minutes later. This desire to spend time alone with God needs to be genuine and you need to be fully committed to doing it on a daily basis. Transformation comes no other way. It's the God-designed method through which your life becomes radically changed. You go from glory to glory only by having a continual, personal, and ongoing relationship with the living God.

Yes, you need fellowship with other believers but it's that time spent alone with God that your relationship with Him grows and thrives. Most believers go to church but how many get alone with God in the privacy of their own homes? The truth be told, the majority of Christians fail to do this not realizing that this is the very place God has designed to meet with them and bring growth and change into their lives. There is no escaping the need to get alone with God and meet Him in a life changing way on a daily basis. People perform religious rituals every day of the week but that doesn't mean they're acquainted with the great God of the universe. They don't know Him because they don't fellowship with Him. They go to church and hear about God but they don't experience Him down in the core of their being. God designed you to have a close, personal relationship with Him. You need to be alone with God so you can be honest and transparent about how you feel and what you're going through. You can't do that in a crowd and this is why quality time alone with God is so important.

When Jesus died on the cross, the veil in front of the ark of the covenant was torn in two making it possible for you to have a one-on-one, face-to-face encounter with God. However, it is your responsibility to get alone with Him, to step into the "Holy of Holies" where the presence of God dwells. You purposefully meet the Lord in such a way so that His Word and His Spirit can transform you into the image of Jesus. David said in Ps. 62:1,2, "Truly my soul silently waits for God; From Him comes my salvation. He only is my rock and my salvation; He is my defense; I shall not be greatly moved." The Message Bible says, "God, the one and only - I'll wait as long as He says. Everything I need comes from Him, so why not? He's solid rock under my feet, breathing room for my soul, an impregnable castle: I'm set for life." David said his soul waits in silence. The truth be told, most people don't wait very well. You need to realize how different your life will be if you will learn to wait on God alone. Ps. 46:10 says, "Be still, and know that I am God."

Your quiet time with the Lord is what brings transformation power into your spiritual life. And it's this power that will carry you through any hardship or trial that comes your way. This is why you must stop what you're doing and be still so you can know He is God. Stop being consumed by the things of the world. This world is not your home and it's certainly not your friend. You're a pilgrim here, you're just passing through. Paul said in Phil. 3:20, "For our citizenship is in heaven, from which we also eagerly wait for the Savior, the Lord Jesus Christ." The Message Bible says, "But there's far more to life for us. We're citizens of high heaven!" If this world is not your home, then why allow it to control your time and thoughts? Why allow it to determine what choices you make in life? Why allow it to put you on a path you shouldn't be on? The hard truth is, you must daily make a choice to reject the world's way and follow Jesus Christ. You need to break away from the addiction of the smart phone and go off by yourself and be still in God's presence.

Unseen forces can control what people do with their lives based on the ungodly things that show up on that little screen they hold in their hand. Too many people are being led like an ox with a ring in its nose. They're being controlled by the world and don't even realize it. This is why you've got to put that phone down and no longer allow it to determine what you give your attention to. You need to get alone with God and interact with Him instead of feeding your flesh with that smart phone. As a believer, you are in the world but not of the world. It's time for you to experience a real relationship with God. You need to interact with Him in His Word and respond accordingly. The world takes no prisoners and it treats Christians and non-Christians the same way. It offers nothing but pain and destruction yet the majority of people let the world control what they say and do. You've got to purposefully stop this from happening and the first step is to get alone with God. This is a commitment you must make and keep every single day of your life.

You've fed your flesh long enough, now it's time to feed your spirit. It's time to hear what God has to say about your life instead of hearing what the world has to say. Set aside a time and a place where it's just you and God communing with one another. Say "no" to all the distractions that are sure to come and commit to getting alone with God. You can do this if you'll make up your mind to do it. Consider what Jesus did in Luke 5:15,16, "Great multitudes came together to hear, and to be healed by Him of their infirmities. So He Himself often withdrew into the wilderness and prayed." Jesus would withdraw Himself from the crowds of people because He knew time alone with the Father was necessary in order for Him to complete the work He was sent to do. Jesus often walked away from the demands of those who wanted to be ministered to so that He could be alone with the Father (Mark 6:31). Mark 6:46 says, "And when He had sent them away, He departed to the mountain to pray." How much more do you need to do the same thing?

Mark 1:35 says, "Now in the morning, having risen a long while before daylight, He went out and departed to a solitary place; and there He prayed." Jesus was overwhelmed with ministry but He still took time to get alone with God and pray. The exact opposite is true with most believers today.

They make excuses and say they're too busy to spend time alone with God. The truth is, Jesus was too busy not to pray. He knew He couldn't complete His work on earth if He didn't have constant and continual fellowship with the Father. It's this time alone with God where He'll transform your life and give you the direction you need to fulfill your destiny. He told Ezekiel, "Arise, go out into the plain, and there I shall talk with you" (Ezek. 3:22). 1 Sam. 3:9,10 tells how the young boy Samuel heard God speak when he "went and lay down in his place." He was quiet and alone and, sure enough, God spoke to him. Likewise, to effectively and powerfully hear from God, you must get in His presence quietly and alone.

Jesus said in Matt. 6:6, "But you, when you pray, go into your room, and when you have shut your door, pray to your Father who is in the secret place; and your Father who sees in secret will reward you openly." The Message Bible says, "Here's what I want you to do: Find a quiet, secluded place so you won't be tempted to role-play before God. Just be there as simply and honestly as you can manage. The focus will shift from you to God, and you will begin to sense His grace." Spiritual growth starts when you make a regular commitment to get alone with God. Your quiet time with Him creates the environment by which you may grow spiritually. Ps. 119:147,148 says, "I rise before the dawning of the morning, and cry for help; I hope in Your word. My eyes are awake through the night watches, that I may meditate on Your word." The psalmist took time to get alone with God, even to the point of doing so in the middle of the night. He was very busy but not too busy to spend time alone with God.

God's desire is to transform you more and more into the image of Christ but that can't happen if you're too busy to spend time alone with Him. 2 Cor. 3:18 says you "are being transformed into the same image from glory to glory, just as by the Spirit of the Lord." It's the Holy Spirit who changes you into the image of Christ but it is your responsibility to remain in an environment where the Holy Spirit can do His work. This happens when you spend quality time alone with

God. If you'll do that, the Message Bible says, "And so we are transfigured much like the Messiah, our lives gradually becoming brighter and more beautiful as God enters our lives and we become like Him." The key to finding time to be alone with God is to have a strong desire to do so. People make time for things that are important to them. If you desire to know God in a personal way, you're going to have to spend time alone with Him. It's the degree of that desire that determines the effort you make to change your calendar and make time to be alone with God.

When you put your foot down and commit to spending time alone with God on a daily basis, you start the process of being changed from glory to glory. Your hope and faith in God is strengthened as you sit quietly alone in His presence. Say to him what the boy Samuel said, "Speak, for Your servant hears" (1 Sam. 3:10). God will indeed speak to you but you first must give Him time to speak. The world will bombard you with things to distract you but you need to set your eyes on spiritual things. You must make that choice because if you don't you'll continue to be led by the world and its evil ways. How can God lead you and transform you if you never give Him a chance to do so? Look beyond the horizon of the day and set your heart on things eternal and not temporal. Phil. 4:8 (NLT) says, "And now, dear brothers and sisters, one final thing. Fix your thoughts on what is true, and honorable, and right, and pure, and lovely, and admirable. Think about things that are excellent and worthy of praise."

Col. 3:2,3 says, "Set your mind on things above, not on things on the earth. For you died, and your life is hidden with Christ in God." The things of this world are temporary and not worthy of your constant attention. God, however, is eternal and He is worthy of all your attention. He is the one you should keep your eye on. He is the one who should be consuming all your thoughts and time. Allow God to feed your spirit instead of allowing the world to feed your flesh. It takes a serious commitment to do this. You need to fight through the distractions of this world. You need to take heed to the words of Jesus spoken in Mark 6:31, "Come aside by yourselves to a deserted place and rest a while." In the midst of a hectic and crazy world, you've got to realize the importance of getting alone with God. David had a thirst for God and he wrote in Ps. 63:1, "O God, You are my God; Early will I seek You; My soul thirsts for You; My flesh longs for You in a dry and thirsty land where there is no water." David's thirst for God drove him to spend time alone with Him. You must do the same.

Randall J. Brewer

-5-

"IN HIS PRESENCE"

The Bible is full of stories of people who met God and had a close encounter with Him. In fact, God drawing near to you and you drawing near to Him is the theme of the entire Bible. So much does God want to have a personal relationship with you that He put into each person the desire to get to know Him better, Eccl. 3:11 says, "He has put eternity in their hearts." Some people tap into this desire, many don't. He wants you to be aware of His presence and this is why you need to turn away from all the distractions in the world and give Him your full, undivided attention. "Draw near to God and He will draw near to you" (James 4:8). Yes, people long for God but because of sin and selfishness this desire for Him has been warped and twisted. They don't seek to be in His presence as they should and this is why many times in the Bible it was God who drew near to man. In the Old Testament no man had more encounters with God than Moses, and it all began with God drawing near to him at the burning bush.

Moses knew about God but he didn't know Him personally. He had killed a man in Egypt and was forced to flee to the back side of the desert where for forty years he attended the flock of his father-in-law Jethro. What started out as a promising life was now reduced to an old man wandering aimlessly through the barren wilderness. Then one day God shows up. Ex. 3:2 says Moses saw a burning bush but was amazed that it was not consumed by the flames. When it comes to God, you must always expect the unexpected. This is God's way of getting your attention. He wants a relationship with you and He'll go to great lengths to draw you to Himself. If something happens in your life that you don't understand, consider the possibility that maybe God is trying to get your attention. He'll make the first move but you must make the second. Moses is curious so he says in vs. 3, "I will now turn aside and see this great sight, why the bush does not burn."

Don't ignore those things that seem to be out of the ordinary. Moses turned aside and went to the burning bush to investigate not realizing that God was drawing him in so that He might reveal Himself to him. "So when the Lord saw that he turned aside to look, God called to him from the midst of the bush and said, 'Moses, Moses!' And he said, 'Here I am'" (vs. 4). God wanted to get personal with Moses so He called him by his name. He'll also call you by your name. Is. 43:1 says, "I have called you by your name; You are Mine." God was going to use Moses to deliver His people from Egyptian bondage but first He wanted Moses to know Him in a personal way. He wanted Moses to have an intimate relationship with Him, an encounter so deep and so meaningful that he'll never be the same again. This all began at the burning bush. Moses was drawn in and he even asked God what His name was. God answered and said "I AM WHO I AM" (vs. 14). In life you only give your name to a person you want to have a relationship with. God knows your name and it's a true blessing when He tells you His name.

God is a good God but He is not a tame God. He is holy and this is why after calling Moses by name He says to him, "Do not draw near this place. Take your sandals off your feet, for the place you stand is holy ground" (vs. 5). Your true self is exposed in the presence of a holy God. Peter said to Jesus in

Luke 5:8, "Depart from me, for I am a sinful man." You know you're drawing near to God when your heart convicts you of sin. You are in the presence of a just and holy God just like Moses and vs. 6 says, "And Moses hid his face, for he was afraid to look upon God." Moses should have been consumed in the presence of a holy God but he wasn't. God is merciful and 2 Peter 3:4 says He "is longsuffering toward us, not willing that any should perish but that all should come to repentance." The same God who tells you to remove your sandals had His own sandals taken off at the cross. Jesus died for your sins and, because of that, in His presence you will never be the same again. You can now be a burning bush to others.

Elijah had an encounter with God at one of the lowest points in his life. He was in a cave hiding because Jezebel had vowed to kill him (1 Kings 19:2). He is in great fear, he wants to die, and he is overcome with self-pity. Is there a cave you're hiding in? Does the darkness and confusion of life make you want to runaway and hide? If so, there is hope. God met Elijah in his cave and He'll meet you in your cave. You can find relief knowing that you can be in His presence even during your darkest hour. Surprisingly, this low point in Elijah's life came shortly after one of the greatest miracles in all the Bible. He and the prophets of Baal were in a showdown to see whose God was the real God. Each had built an altar and put a slaughtered bull on top. The God who answered by fire would be the one true God (1 Kings 18:24). To prove his point, Elijah even had water poured over his sacrifice and the wood under it. Nothing happened on the altar of the false prophets but the fire of the Lord came and consumed the burnt offering and licked up all the water in the trench (vs. 38).

Elijah had won a great victory over the prophets of Baal on Mt. Carmel. He then brought all the false prophets to the Brook Kishon and executed them there (vs. 40). Jezebel heard about this and vowed that Elijah would be dead by this time tomorrow. It was then that Elijah rose up and ran for his life. He traveled forty days and forty nights and went to Horeb, the mountain of God (1 Kings 19:8). This threat from Jezebel was not what he expected. Something wonderful had just happened and now there are people seeking to take his life. This sudden change was more than he could handle. He had an idea of how things were supposed to be and the exact opposite happened. He feels like a complete failure and now he wants to end it all and die. He prayed and said, "It is enough! Now, Lord, take my life, for I am no better than my fathers!" (1 Kings 19:4). Have you ever felt this way? Have you grown tired of standing in faith that you don't think you can stand anymore? If so, then get ready. God is about to show up in your cave.

Elijah was not the only person in the Bible who wanted their life to end when their expectations were not met. Moses wanted to die (Num. 11:15) as did Job (Job 3:11) and Jeremiah (Jer. 20:17). Even Jonah said, "It is better for me to die than to live" (Jonah 4:8). These verses show that even the greatest prophets in the Bible had moments of despair. Yes, life gets tough but you can never forget that God has a divine plan for your life. Joseph was imprisoned in a strange land and in less than a day he was second-in-command in the most powerful nation on the earth. Joseph never gave up and neither should you. Rest assured, God will be there for you in your darkest hour. He'll meet you in the cave of despair. Elijah was in his cave and the Lord came to him and said, "What are you doing here, Elijah?" (1 Kings 19:9). He asks this question because He wants to engage Elijah in a conversation. He wants to communicate with him just like He wants to talk to you. God said in Is. 1:18, "Come now, and let us reason together." He knew Elijah needed to get some things off his chest and this is why the question was asked.

Elijah did not hesitate to tell God what was bothering him. He was very zealous for God but yet people are seeking to kill him. This isn't right, it isn't fair, it shouldn't be this way.

Certainly things should have turned out differently. Have you ever felt this way? Of course you have. The good news is that God gives you the freedom to tell Him what's on your heart. He then tells Elijah to go outside and stand on the mountain before the Lord. 1 Kings 19:11,12 says, "And behold, the Lord passed by, and a great and strong wind tore into the mountains and broke the rocks in pieces before the Lord, but the Lord was not in the wind; and after the wind an earthquake, but the Lord was not in the earthquake; and after the earthquake a fire, but the Lord was not in the fire; and after the fire a still small voice." If you want to hear from God, don't look for the spectacular but listen for a soft, gentle whisper. People listen more carefully and pay closer attention when spoken to in a whisper. God whispers because He's drawing you close to Him. You can't hear a whisper from a great distance away. This is why you need to be still and know He is God.

Before Elijah heard God's still, small voice, he first had to weather the storm that took place outside that cave. The wind blew, the ground shook, and then a fire came. Finally, after enduring all that, he heard the whisper of God. These natural calamities happened because God was trying to get his attention. Elijah was so wrapped up in self-pity that he couldn't hear God's gentle voice. What happened here was the exception and not the norm. Normally, if you'll listen, God will speak to you in the midst of your storm, not after it has passed you by. This He did with Job and this He'll do with you also. Job is the oldest book in the Bible and it deals with the oldest question known to man, "Why do good people suffer?" Job was a good man. He "was blameless and upright, and one who feared God and shunned evil" (Job 1:1). You don't get any better than that. He was blessed with a wonderful family and had great possessions of wealth and livestock. He was the greatest of all the people of the East (vs. 3). Still, he was about to suffer beyond human comprehension.

As Job was busy living his good life, up in heaven a conversation was taking place between God and the devil. Satan was standing among holy angels who presented themselves before the Lord and God called him out. He asked him, "From where do you come?" (vs. 7). Satan said he was going to and fro across the earth. He was looking for someone to devour (1 Peter 5:8) but he didn't tell God this. God knew what his intentions were so He asked him, "Have you considered My servant Job?" (vs. 8). He then told the devil what a great man Job was. The devil counters this by saying that Job only feared and served God because he'd been blessed with so many wonderful things. Take away those possessions and surely he will curse You to Your face (vs. 11). God knows the heart of Job so he gives the devil permission to take those things away from him, the only restriction being that the devil can't touch the body of Job. Within hours an enemy army came and stole his cattle and killed his servants, lightning burned up his sheep and consumed his other servants, and a great wind blew down his oldest son's house, killing all his sons and daughters who were inside (vs. 14-19).

Rarely, if ever, will anybody suffer the level of this calamity. One minute Job was riding on the high clouds of success, the next minute he had nothing. What did he do? "Then Job arose and tore his robe and shaved his head, and he fell to the ground and worshiped" (vs. 20). How amazing is that? How would you respond if a similar thing happened to you? Job did not turn his back on God but kept trusting and worshiping Him. He loved God for who He was and not for what he could get from Him. Even after everything Job went through, the devil wasn't finished with him. He went back to God and reminded Him that Job still had his health. Take that away from him "and he will surely curse You to Your face!" (Job 2:5). God replied, "Behold, he is in your hand, but spare his life" (vs. 6). Satan then went out from the presence of the Lord and struck Job with painful boils from the sole of his foot to the crown of his head (vs. 7). The Message Bible says, "Job had ulcers and scabs from head to foot. They itched and oozed so badly that he took a piece of broken pottery to scrape himself" (vs. 7,8).

The only person left in Job's life is his wife and she turns on him as well. She said, "Do you still hold to your integrity? Curse God and die!" (vs. 9). Job answered her, "You speak as one of the foolish women speaks. Shall we indeed accept good from God, and shall we not accept adversity?" In all this Job did not sin with his lips (vs. 10). He was down, but he was not out. Three of his friends came and sat with him and in time they said surely he had to have done something wrong for all this to happen to him. They jumped to their own conclusions and accused Job of doing evil (Job 4:7;8:20;11:14,15). Job's wife said, "Blame God," his friends said, "Blame yourself." This puts Job on an emotional rollercoaster. One moment he wishes he had never been born (Job 3:11) and the next he says, "For I know that my Redeemer lives, and He shall stand at last on the earth; And after my skin is destroyed, this I know, that in my flesh I shall see God" (Job 19:25,26).

Job debated with his three friends for thirty-seven chapters and then, in Job 38, God arrives on the scene. Job had heard enough of the foolishness his friends were saying to him and God definitely had heard enough. Job 38:1 says, "Then the Lord answered Job out of the whirlwind." The Message Bible says, "And now, finally, God answered Job from the eye of a violent storm." God spoke to Elijah in a still, small voice. He wasn't in the storm with Elijah but with Job He was. Job is in the midst of the greatest storm any person has ever gone through and God came to him in a great whirlwind. Job had wanted an audience with God so he could state his case and put God on trial (Job 23:3,4). God now speaks to Job but He doesn't give him the explanation he wants. Instead, He asks him a series of questions in an effort to put everything into perspective. The first question is asked in Job 38:2, "Who is this who darkens counsel by words without knowledge?" The

Message Bible says, "Why do you talk without knowing what you're talking about?"

In all, sixty-four questions are asked of Job. God asks him if he was there at the moment of creation (vs. 4). "Were you there when I made the sea (vs. 8) and the clouds (vs. 9) and put the stars in place (vs. 31-33)? Can you control the weather and tell lightning where to go (vs. 35)? Do you know the reproductive cycle of mountain goats (Job 39:1)? Have you given the horse strength (vs. 19)?" In other words, "Do you have the same perspective of how the universe works that I do?" Job stammers and doesn't know what to say so he puts his hand over his mouth (Job 40:4). God's not through talking and again Job 40:6 says "the Lord answered Job out of the whirlwind." He asks Job if he would like to run the universe for a day and to hand out punishment where it is needed. This went on for two chapters until finally Job's perspective was changed. He yields to God and to His perspective. The anguish is gone and so is all the pain. He is now at peace. God then told him to pray for his friends and when he did "the Lord blessed the latter days of Job more than his beginning" (vs. 12). One hundred and forty years later, "Job died, old and full of days" (vs. 17).

Isaiah was one of the major prophets in the Old Testament. He lived seven hundred years before the birth of Jesus and predicted the coming of the Messiah to save mankind from the ravages of sin. He was commissioned when he had one of the closest encounters with God that anyone has ever had. It was in His presence that Isaiah's life was forever changed. This encounter is a blueprint of what the Christian experience is all about. Is. 6:1 says this encounter happened in the year that King Uzziah died. At this time in history the nation is in a crisis. King Uzziah had served the tribe of Judah for fifty-two long years. He was a good king and did what was right in the sight of the Lord. The people prospered and looked up to their king with awe and respect. So successful was their nation and their lives that they began to drift away from God. King Uzziah became conceited and proud and thought he could do anything he wanted. He disobeyed God and went into the temple to burn incense to Him. Only priests could do this and suddenly leprosy appeared on his forehead (2 Chron. 26).

James 4:6 says that "God resists the proud." God was displeased with what King Uzziah did and he had leprosy for the rest of his life. He was no longer allowed in the temple or in his own palace. His son Jotham lived there and ruled in his place. Since Uzziah had leprosy, he could not be buried in a royal tomb. Instead, he was buried in a nearby cemetery that the kings owned. The king was adored by Isaiah but it wasn't until Uzziah died that the prophet had his encounter with God. Isaiah is about to learn that there is a King far greater than any mortal man. For five chapters Isaiah has been prophesying to the people in an effort to get them to see the error of their ways. He said in Is. 5:20, "Woe to those who call evil good, and good evil; Who put darkness for light, and light for darkness; Who put bitter for sweet, and sweet for bitter!" On and on he goes. Woe to you! Woe to you! Woe to you! The nation is in a crisis and the people don't know what's going to happen next. The future looks bleak and the people are looking for answers. It was at this time that Isaiah had his encounter with God.

Isaiah went to the temple to worship God and he writes in Is. 6:1, "In the year that King Uzziah died, I saw the Lord sitting on a throne, high and lifted up, and the train of His robe filled the temple." What a magnificent sight this must have been. The temple was ninety feet long, thirty feet wide, and forty-five feet high and the train of the Lord's robe filled this place. Above the throne were angelic beings called seraphim (vs. 2). Each one had six wings. With two they covered their face, with two they covered their feet, and with two they flew. Their faces were covered because they could not stare at the holiness of God. They cried out to one another, "Holy, holy, holy is the Lord of hosts; The whole world is full of His glory!" (vs. 3). Isaiah was in the presence of God and the place where he stood was engulfed by the glory of it all. "And the posts of the door were shaken by the voice of him who cried out and the house was filled with smoke" (vs. 4). Isaiah then said, "Woe is me, for I am undone! Because I am a man of unclean lips, and I dwell in the midst of a people of unclean lips; For my eyes have seen the King, the Lord of hosts" (vs. 5).

Isaiah told the people, "Woe to you!" but here he says, "Woe is me!" This is what happens when you are in the presence of a holy God, when you see a God who is high and lifted up. In His presence all self-esteem is shattered and all confidence in oneself is destroyed. Isaiah searched his inner man and said "Woe is me!" because he realized he was part of the problem. Don't allow yourself to get high-minded because God used you in some special way. Stay humble and give all the praise and honor to God. Isaiah confessed that he dwelt in the midst of a people with unclean lips. Be careful who you associate with. 1 Cor. 15:33 says, "Do not be deceived: 'Evil company corrupts good habits.'" The Message Bible says, "Bad company ruins good manners." In Isaiah's vision something unusual then happens. The word "seraphim" means 'burning ones' and vs. 6,7 says, "Then one of the seraphim flew to me, having in his hand a live coal which he had taken with the tongs from the altar. And he touched my mouth with it."

The seraphim came with a burning coal from the altar of God who is "Holy! Holy! Holy!" These words tell what type of God He is. Isaiah sees a holy God but then he sees himself. The presence of God is beautiful but it can also be terrifying. In His presence comes the reality of who you are. For sure, nothing is hidden in the presence of a holy God. Isaiah would later write, "But we are all like an unclean thing, and all our righteousnesses are like filthy rags" (Is. 64:6). Before finding comfort in the presence of God you must pass through the conflict of realizing that without Jesus in your life you are unclean. You must be forgiven of your sin and this is what happened to Isaiah. The angelic creature touched the mouth of Isaiah with the hot coal and said, "Behold, this has touched your lips; Your iniquity is taken away, and your sin purged" (vs. 7). Isaiah is now cleansed and his confidence has returned. He heard God ask, "Whom shall I send, and who will go for Us?" Without hesitation Isaiah responds, "Here am I! Send me" (vs. 8).

God wants you to have your own personal encounter with Him so you can know how good He is. And He wants these encounters to happen daily. There are many more people in the Bible who met God and each one's life was radically changed. Then again, how can anybody meet God and not be changed? There is a promise given to all people that if they will call on the Name of the Lord, they will experience an encounter with Him. They'll "taste and see that the Lord is good" (Ps. 34:8). Christianity is not about following a bunch of rules and strict regulations. It's not about religion, it's about relationship. God wants to be the most real person in your life. Look at everything He's already done to get you to focus your full and complete attention on Him. He's standing there in front of you with opened-wide arms. He's drawn near to you and now He's waiting for you to respond and draw near to Him. Remember, Jesus died so this moment can happen. Stop looking only at what is seen but look to Him who is unseen. What are you waiting for? Draw near to Him today! Do it now!

Randall J. Brewer

-6-

"FIRST THE BLADE"

It is in the presence of God that spiritual growth takes place. God wants you to grow, to increase, and to multiply. He wants you to "be strong in the Lord and in the power of His might" (Eph. 6:10). He wants the image of Jesus to be manifested in every area of your life. For that to happen, you've got to grow up spiritually. One of the first things you need to learn about spiritual growth is that a person does not develop and mature overnight. It's a long, continual process much like one's physical body that grows and matures. The difference is that you have some say-so when it comes to how fast you develop in the things of God whereas your body grows at its normal, slow pace. Insight into this growing process was given by Jesus when He told the parable of the growing seed in Mark 4:26-29. He said in vs. 28, "For the earth yields crops by itself: first the blade, then the head, after that the full grain in the head." Yes, spiritual growth is a process and your efforts determine how fast or how slow you will grow.

This growing process is also outlined in Is. 28:9,10, "Whom will he teach knowledge? And whom will he make to understand the message? Those just weaned from milk? Those just drawn from the breasts? For precept must be upon precept, precept upon precept, line upon line, line upon line, here a little, there a little." The prophet is saying there is no shortcut to spiritual growth. You grow precept upon precept, line upon line. This corresponds to what Jesus says happens when a person plants the Word of God by speaking it out of their mouth. The seed grows, first the blade, then the head, after that the full grain in the head. You need to learn at the start of your spiritual journey that nothing has a greater impact on spiritual growth than to study and meditate on the Word of God. The best time to do this is when you are alone with God. Read your Bible and then be still and know He is God. Listen to Him as He reveals to you the meaning of what you just read. As you ponder the things He tells you, as you listen to His voice, you'll learn how to apply the Word to your everyday life.

God said in Josh. 1:8, "This Book of the Law shall not depart from your mouth, but you shall meditate in it day and night, that you may observe to do according to all that is written in it. For then you will make your way prosperous, and then you will have good success." Don't just read your Bible but meditate on it day and night (Ps. 1:2). The Hebrew word for "meditate" involves a low murmuring, a talking to oneself. Speak out loud what you've read and ponder its meaning. Meditating on God's Word is dwelling on, reflecting, mulling over, and the pondering of holy Scripture that results in a life changing encounter with God. Paul spoke of this often in his writings. Phil. 2:5 says, "Let this mind be in you which was also in Christ Jesus." He said in Phil. 4:8 to meditate on godly things and Col. 3:2 says, "Set your mind on things above, not on things on the earth." He told Timothy, "Meditate on these things; give yourself entirely to them, that your progress may be evident to all. Take heed to yourself and to the doctrine. Continue in them, for in doing this you will save both yourself and those who hear you" (1 Tim. 4:15,16).

Meditation is the first step you take toward spiritual growth. It's the "blade" Jesus talked about in the parable of the growing seed. The purpose of meditation is to replace your thinking with God's thinking. God's thoughts are revealed in the Word of God and 2 Tim. 3:16,17 says, "All Scripture is given by inspiration of God, and is profitable for doctrine, for reproof, for correction, for instruction in righteousness, that the man of God may be complete, thoroughly equipped for every good work." You meditate on the Word of God so God can reveal to you how to apply it to your daily life. The Word won't do you much good if it's not taking you from glory to glory, if it's not consistently transforming you into the image of Christ. Don't allow the Word to go in one ear and out the other. Don't read so much of it that you forget what you've read by the time you're through. No, read line upon line, here a little, there a little. Read a few verses at a time and then stop and meditate on what you've read. You're alone with God, now ask Him to show you how to put into practice what you've read.

The purpose of meditation is to get you to realize that in the Bible, God is speaking to you personally. Everything written there is for you and your benefit. This is why you need to reflect on what you've read and give the Holy Spirit time to impress upon you how it applies to your daily Christian walk. You are alone with God, you are meditating on and pondering the Word, and you are engaging God in conversation. Slowly but surely spiritual growth is happening. This is why you need to meditate on the Word of God every day of your life. Heb. 4:12 (NLT) says, "For the Word of God is alive and powerful. It is sharper than the sharpest two-edged sword, cutting between soul and spirit, between joint and marrow. It exposes our innocent thoughts and desires." The Bible is a limitless ocean of wonders. It is full of wisdom and blessings that will take your life to a higher realm of glory. As you study the Bible and meditate on it, your life will change for the better. You are alone with God and He is transforming your life in a radical way.

The more you know God, the more you'll grow spiritually and the better your life will be. 2 Peter 1:2,3 (MSG) says, "Grace and peace to you many times over as you deepen in your experience with God and Jesus, our Master. Everything that goes into a life of pleasing God has been miraculously given to us by getting to know, personally and intimately, the One who invited us to God. The best invitation we ever received!" God, who He is and how He thinks, is found in the pages of your Bible and this is why you must meditate on it day and night. Ps. 119:15 (ESV) says, "I will meditate on Your precepts and fix my eyes on Your ways." Vs. 97 (ESV) says, "Oh how I love Your law! It is my meditation all the day." Also consider vs. 130 (ESV), "The unfolding of Your words gives light; it imparts understanding to the simple." To develop this same love and desire for God's Word is life changing. You need to crave the Word more than anything else in this world. It's the source of life, a light in a dark place. Ps. 119:105 says, "Your word is a lamp to my feet and a light to my path."

One of the greatest benefits of meditating on God's Word is that it renews your mind. The thoughts, ideas, and opinions of the human mind all come from the flesh and the world. They are contrary to the thoughts of God and this is why Paul wrote in Rom. 12:2, "And do not be conformed to this world, but be transformed by the renewing of your mind, that you may prove what is that good and acceptable, and perfect will of God." The Message Bible says, "Don't become so well-adjusted to your culture that you fit into it without even thinking. Instead, fix your attention on God. You'll be changed from the inside out." Your mind is renewed and God's thoughts become your thoughts when you daily meditate on the Word. This is a supernatural transformation that is taking place. "Old things have passed away; behold, all things have become new" (2 Cor. 5:17). Don't limit your life to where it's been or where it is now. Allow the Word of God to penetrate your heart and transform you into the image of Christ. You must see life differently than you have in the past. You must see it like God sees it.

Meditation is to be a daily discipline. Jesus said to pray to the Father, "Give us this day our daily bread" (Matt. 6:11). He was saying you can't live off the bread you ate yesterday. Transformation is progressive and people who don't get alone with God and meditate in His Word don't grow spiritually. They're living like they did before they got born again. Paul wrote about this in Eph. 4:17-24 (NLT), "Live no longer as the Gentiles do, for they are hopelessly confused. Their minds are full of darkness; they wander far from the life God gives because they have closed their minds and hardened their hearts against Him. They have no sense of shame. They live for lustful pleasure and eagerly practice every kind of impurity. But that isn't what you learned about Christ. Since you have heard about Jesus and have learned the truth that comes from Him, throw off your old sin nature and your former way of life, which is corrupted by lust and deception. Instead, let the Spirit renew your thoughts and attitudes. Put on your new nature, created to be like God - truly righteous and holy."

Paul is saying you can't grow spiritually and still live like you did in times past. The Message Bible says, "Everything - and I do mean everything - connected with that old way of life has to go. It's rotten through and through. Get rid of it! And then take on an entirely new way of life - a God-fashioned life, a life renewed from the inside and working itself into your conduct as God accurately reproduces His character in you." Now is the time for you to be transformed into the image of Christ. This happens when your mind is renewed by the daily revelations given to you as you meditate on the Word of God. A mind not renewed limits your ability to see things from God's perspective. It will cause you to follow the ways of the world instead of the ways of God. You don't want this to happen. Rom. 12:2 (NLT) says, "Don't copy the behavior and customs of the world, but let God transform you into a new person by changing the way you think." Understand that your thoughts and imaginations shape and form your future. Meditating on the Word removes those worldly thoughts and replaces them with the thoughts of God.

If you don't like where you're at in life, then change the things you think about. Get alone with God and begin to meditate on His holy Word. Don't be pressured to think the way those around you think. Joshua and Caleb stood out from the crowd when the children of Israel allowed fear to stop them from entering the Promised Land. Caleb said, "Let us go up at once and take possession, for we are well able to overcome it" (Num. 13:30). Before he said this he first "quieted the people before Moses." In other words, he didn't want to hear what they had to say. He didn't want to hear their worldly thoughts. You also need to be different. Grow up and think godly thoughts instead of worldly thoughts. Don't allow the world to fit you into its mold. Don't be influenced by what ungodly people think and say. Let God mold and shape you into the person He wants you to be. Is. 64:8 says, "But now, O Lord, You are our Father; We are the clay, and You are our potter; And all we are the work of Your hand." The Message Bible says, "All of us are what You made us."

In the beginning, man was created to think like God. God walked with Adam in the cool of the evening and together they shared their thoughts with one another. The day then came when Adam and Eve listened to the words and thoughts of the evil one and sin entered the earth. No longer did the thoughts of God prevail in the hearts of men. "Then the Lord saw that the wickedness of man was great in the earth, and that every intent of the thoughts of his heart was only evil continually" (Gen. 6:5). Thoughts are powerful. They form your decisions and your decisions dictate what your actions will be. Thoughts mold and shape you into the person you will become. You're where you're at today because of what you thought about yesterday. This is why it's so important to get alone with God and think about the things He wants you to think about. Allow the Word of God to renew your mind which will cause you to think godly thoughts. This in turn will produce godly words and godly actions. You'll grow up spiritually and will be molded into the person God wants you to be.

Be careful what you think about. Rom. 8:6 says, "For to be carnally minded is death, but to be spiritually minded is life and peace." Remember, you become what you think about. Prov. 23:7 says, "For as he thinks in his heart, so is he." You can change your life by changing the things you think about. It's true, your life will go in the direction of your most dominate thought. Vs. 26 (NLT) tells you what to do, "O my son, give me your heart. May your eyes take delight in following my ways." God is saying to give all your thoughts to Him. The Message Bible says, "Dear child, I want your full attention; please do what I show you." Meditating on the Word of God gives Him the opportunity to mold and shape your thoughts. This is what renewing your mind is all about. You gave Him your heart when you got saved but now you have to give Him your thoughts. Allow His thoughts to become your thoughts. Ps. 92:5,6 (GNT) says, "How great are Your actions, Lord! How deep are your thoughts! This is something a fool cannot know; someone who is stupid cannot understand."

You were created to grasp and hold onto the thoughts of God. Jesus died for your sins and this allows you to talk with Him the way Adam did in the Garden of Eden. You tell Him your thoughts and He'll tell you His. In time, your mind will be renewed and His thoughts will become your thoughts. You'll have something in common with God because you'll both be thinking about the same things. The result of all this is that you'll grow spiritually and God will take you from glory to glory. You'll have life and have it more abundantly. God told Abraham he would be the father of many nations. He then took him outside and told him to look up at the stars. God told him, "So shall your descendants be" (Gen. 15:5). What was God doing? He was giving Abraham something to think about. Reading your Bible is how God gives you something to think about. This is why you need to meditate on it day and night. Abraham's thoughts changed his life and your thoughts will change your life as well.

One of the greatest revelations you can learn in life is that your thoughts are seeds that get planted in your heart. Whatever you put there will grow. Your destiny is determined by what you think about. Your thoughts determine your future and whether or not you succeed in life. Gal. 6:7 says, "Do not be deceived, God is not mocked; for whatever a man sows, that he will also reap." Don't fool yourself by thinking your thoughts don't matter. Don't think you can meditate on bad things and still live a good life. The Message Bible says, "Don't be misled: No one makes a fool of God. What a person plants, he will harvest." God is saying you can't keep doing the same things in life and expect different results. If you want something you've never had before, you've got to do something you've never done before. You've got to plant seeds of success and victory down in your heart. You've got to take responsibility for your future and the first step is to get alone with God and mediate on the Word of God. "First the blade, then the head, after that the full grain in the head."

Your life is composed of whatever it's being influenced by. This is why Prov. 4:23 (NLT) says, "Guard your heart above all else, for it determines the course of your life." The Good News Translation says, "Be careful how you think; your life is shaped by your thoughts." Be diligent and monitor the things you think about. 2 Cor. 10:5 says, "Casting down imaginations and every high thing that exalts itself against the knowledge of God, and bringing into captivity every thought to the obedience of Christ." The Message Bible says, "Fitting every loose thought and emotion and impulse into the structure of life shaped by Christ." You need to protect your heart because it is the center of who you are. Every decision you make is based on what's in your heart "for out of it springs the issues of life" (NKJV). If you don't protect your heart, you'll never be able to change the direction your life is going. You change your future by changing the things you think about today. This is how you grow up and become the person God wants you to be. Your life will drastically change when you realize the things you think about really do matter. So much so that it's a matter of life and death.

The bottom line is that you need to change the way you think. Rom. 8:5 says, "For those who live according to the flesh set their minds on the things of the flesh, but those who live according to the Spirit, the things of the Spirit." Renewing your mind is vitally important for it's the ongoing process through which God takes you where He wants you to go. The good news for those who seriously desire to grow up spiritually is that the Bible tells you specifically what things you should be thinking about. Phil. 4:8 says, "Finally, brethren, whatever things are true, whatever things are noble, whatever things are just, whatever things are pure, whatever things are lovely, whatever things are of good report, if there is any virtue and if there is anything praiseworthy - mediate on these things." The Message Bible says to meditate on "the best, not the worst; the beautiful, not the ugly; things to praise, not things to curse." If you'll continue to ponder and think about these good things, you'll never have to worry about bad things coming in and taking root in your mind. This is what renewing your mind is all about.

As you mediate on godly things, Phil. 4:7 (NLT) says, "Then you will experience God's peace, which exceeds anything we can understand. His peace will guard your hearts and minds as you live in Christ Jesus." The Amplified Bible says this peace "shall garrison and mount guard over your hearts and minds in Christ Jesus." That is a military term. As you focus your mind and meditate on the right things, there will be a military force around your heart and mind. It's this spiritual force that gives you the power to cast down and throw away every negative thought and imagination. As you do this, your mind is renewed and you grow up spiritually. The word "renew" means 'to renovate; to reconstruct; to build down and build anew.' All things have passed away, behold, all things have become new. Take an inventory of your thought life and see if there are some things you need to cast down so that you can build anew. Replace those negative thoughts with things that are "true, noble, reputable, authentic, compelling, gracious" (Phil. 4:8 MSG). Your life will be much better if you'll think on the positive things in life and not the negative.

Your perspective, the way you see and understand what's going on around you, is key to your success in life. You need to understand that right thinking equals successful living. You can hear the Word of God but if your thinking and perspective isn't right, you'll limit what the power of that Word can bring into your life. The world will tell you it's the flu season but Ps. 91:10 says, "No evil shall befall you, nor shall any plague come near your dwelling." Who are you going to believe? What's your perspective on the matter? Your answer determines if you'll get sick or stay healthy. Hosea 4:6 says, "My people are destroyed for lack of knowledge." This verse can also be translated, "My people are destroyed for lack of a proper perspective." The army of Israel feared Goliath but David said, "The Lord, who delivered me from the paw of the lion and from the paw of the bear, He will deliver me from the hand of this Philistine" (1 Sam. 17:37). David had a different perspective and was able to slay the giant. On the other hand, Jeremiah was called to be a prophet to the nation but he told God, "I cannot speak, for I am a youth" (Jer. 1:6). He had the wrong perspective.

Your perspective of God and yourself is what determines how great your life will be. Will you trust God and chop that giant's head off or will you run away in fear? Will you enter the promised land with Joshua and Caleb or will you die off in the wilderness with all the others? It's your perspective that makes all the difference in the world. Gideon said, "Indeed my clan is the weakest in Manasseh, and I am the least in my father's house" (Judges 6:15). He said this only moments after the Angel of the Lord called him a "mighty man of valor" (vs. 12). Isaiah asks, "Who has believed our report? And to whom has the arm of the Lord been revealed?" (Is. 53:1). Whose report will you believe? If the world gives you a report that is contrary to the Word of God, Rom. 3:4 says, "Let God be true and every man a liar." Abraham did not consider his old body or the deadness of Sarah's womb. He believed the report of the Lord when He said, "So shall your descendants be" (Gen. 15:5). Abraham was "fully convinced that what He had promised He was also able to perform" (Rom. 4:21). He had the right perspective and in time became the father of many nations just like God said he would.

Rise up and control the things you think about. If you don't control your thought life, then for sure the devil will. Know also that God is keeping a sharp eye on the things you think about. David told his son Solomon, "Know the God of your father, and serve Him with a loyal heart and with a willing mind; for the Lord searches all hearts and understands all the intent of the thoughts" (1 Chron. 28:9). The Message Bible says, "Serve Him with a whole heart and eager mind, for God examines every heart and sees through every motive." Stop watching ungodly television and stop listening to ungodly radio shows. It's things like this that cause ungodly thoughts to get planted in your mind. The things that are said may not seem to be that bad but it's "the little foxes that spoil the vines" (Song of Solomon 2:15). Know with certainty that little foxes not dealt with will grow into big foxes. James 3:5 (NLT) says "a tiny spark can set a great forest on fire." Walk away from those family members and coworkers who gossip all the time. Go off by yourself and get alone with God. Meditate on the things He wants you to think about. If you'll do that, your life will never be the same.

Randall J. Brewer

-7-

"WORTH WAITING FOR"

When it comes to spiritual growth, there is nothing more important than spending time alone with God and meditating on His Word. God is pleased when you do this because it shows Him how much you love Him and desire to be transformed into the image of Christ. It reveals your passion to be in His presence and your willingness to wait on Him no matter how long it takes. Never be in a hurry when it comes to God and understand that the best things in life are worth waiting for. What better thing is there than knowing God in a personal way? There is no denying that it takes time to develop good relationships. It's true in the natural realm and even more true in the spiritual realm. Truly, He is worth waiting for. In fact, waiting on God is an essential part of spiritual growth. You must learn to wait on Him and give Him time to bring to pass the things He promised He would do. People want God to tell them what to do yet they struggle if He tells them to do nothing but sit still and wait on Him. They don't realize that waiting on God is one of the most powerful and beneficial things they can do.

People cringe at the idea of waiting for something to happen. They're always in a hurry and waiting is not a part of who they are. What Christians need to understand is that the Biblical definition of waiting is different than man's. In the Bible the word "wait" means 'to be in a position of readiness;

to stay in a place of expectation; to look for watchfully; to bind together with expectation that is looking forward to something.' It paints a picture of a person sitting on the edge of their seat expecting something wonderful to happen at any moment. Waiting on the Lord is fun and exciting. At least it's supposed to be. People struggle because they're waiting on the wrong thing. They're waiting for their circumstances to change instead of waiting on God. They're trying to put the cart before the horse. They're waiting on the natural and not the spiritual. These people need to wait on God who has the power to change the natural. Ps. 27:14 says, "Wait on the Lord; Be of good courage, and He shall strengthen your heart; Wait, I say, on the Lord!" The Amplified Bible says, "Yes, wait for and hope for and expect the Lord."

David knew the importance of waiting on the Lord. As a teenager he was anointed to be king but it didn't become a reality until many years later. He wrote in Ps. 37:7 (AMP), "Be still and rest in the Lord; wait for Him and patiently lean yourself upon Him." He then said in vs. 8, "Cease from anger and forsake wrath." People who don't like to wait often get angry and say and do harmful things. David is saying don't do that. The Message Bible says, "Bridle your anger, trash your wrath, cool your pipes - it only makes things worse." It's those who wait on God without murmuring and complaining that get blessed. These are the ones who grow spiritually and go on to do great works in the kingdom of God. Mature believers are those who know that seeking God and waiting on Him go hand in hand. As they wait on God and seek Him out, their expectations are high because Heb. 11:6 says, "He is a rewarder of those who diligently seek Him." The Message Bible says, "He cares enough to respond to those who seek Him." It will do you good to realize this heavenly response is worth waiting for.

God is not moved by need. He is moved by faith which is revealed by your willingness to wait on Him. Heb. 6:12 says to "imitate those who through faith and patience inherit the promises." Those who wait successfully are the ones who are always expecting something good to happen. This is why waiting is not a burden to them. It's a joy and a privilege to wait on God. He is good and He is faithful and He rewards those who diligently wait on Him. Ps. 37:9 says, "For evildoers shall be cut off; But those who wait on the Lord, they shall inherit the earth." Isn't that worth waiting for? Ps. 62:1 says, "Truly my soul silently waits for God; From Him comes my salvation." Vs. 5,6 says, "My soul, wait silently for God alone, for my expectation is from Him. He only is my rock and my salvation; He is my defense; I shall not be moved." Walking with God and waiting on Him will produce in you great expectations. The more you grow, the more you'll come to expect. Expectation is evidence of faith and you can have the confidence that God will do that which you're expecting Him to do.

You need to be careful not to set natural parameters around a supernatural God. Don't give Him a specific date and time in which He has to move. You trust Him with everything else, trust Him with time also. Believe the words of Eccl. 3:11, "He has made everything beautiful in its time." Trust God always and wait on Him for as long as it takes. If you'll do that, you will grow strong in the things of God for spiritual growth is taking place. Is. 40:31 says, "But those who wait on the Lord shall renew their strength; They shall mount up with wings like eagles, they shall run and not be weary, they shall walk and not faint." The Message Bible says, "But those who wait upon God get fresh strength." Waiting on God with joy and expectation will cause you to grow strong in your inner man. Those with little or no patience, those who get angry and frustrated all the time, are weak on the inside for they are spiritual babes. Is. 40:30 says, "Even the youths shall faint and be weary, and the young men shall utterly fall." Who are the strong in the Lord? Those who wait on the Lord, those "who expect, look for, and hope in Him" (AMP).

Those who struggle with waiting do so because they don't know what to do in the meantime. More times than not, they look at their circumstances that seem to be getting worse than better. This, in turn, causes them to get more and more frustrated and soon they begin to murmur and complain. On the other hand, those who wait cheerfully with great expectation are those who keep their eyes focused on God and not their circumstances. Ps. 25:15 says, "My eyes are ever toward the Lord, for He shall pluck my feet out of the net." Who gets delivered from the hardships of life? Those whose eyes are focused on the Lord, those who get alone with Him and say, "Show me Your ways, O Lord; Teach me Your paths. Lead me in Your truth and teach me, for You are the God of my salvation; On You I wait all the day" (vs. 4,5). You gave your life to God, now give Him your time also. If you do, victory will be yours. Vs. 2,3 says, "Let not my enemies triumph over me. Indeed, let no one who waits on the Lord be ashamed." Waiting on God should not be a burden. No, it's a blessing that will cause your life to flourish like never before.

Ps. 40:1,2 says, "I waited patiently for the Lord; And He inclined to me, and heard my cry. He also brought me up out of a horrible pit, out of the miry clay, and set my feet upon a rock, and established my steps." When you get alone with God and wait on Him with joy and expectation, a supernatural flow of divine life will be poured into you. You'll be like Adam before the fall when God "breathed into his nostrils the breath of life" (Gen. 2:7). God took what was inside Himself and breathed it into Adam. God gave him divine life and crowned him with glory and honor (Ps. 8:5). Adam was clothed with the atmosphere of heaven but he lost all that when he sinned. Jesus, "the last Adam" (1 Cor. 15:45), then came to earth and Heb. 2:9 says He also was "crowned with glory and honor." As you wait on God and get transformed into the image of Christ, you are now able to have that same divine life that the first Adam experienced as he walked with God in the cool of the evening. You can have the very thing that made Adam like God. You are in Christ and He is in you. That produces a life that is divine.

So much can be learned from the fall of Adam and Eve. Their downfall came about because they went to the wrong place and listened to the wrong voice. Don't go to bad places where God isn't glorified and don't listen to things that are contrary to the Word of God. Adam and Eve had a job to do and they weren't doing it. God told them to be fruitful and multiply and to have dominion on the earth (Gen. 1:28). If they were doing what they were called to do, they wouldn't have had time to wander around going places they shouldn't go. Because they missed the mark and sinned, they were now forced to live natural lives. No longer were they like God. Fellowship with the Almighty was broken and now they had to work by the sweat of their brow and suffer pain for the rest of their lives. Four thousand years went by and then Jesus came and changed the course of history. He paid the price for sin and now fellowship with God is restored. Man can now live supernatural lives in a natural world. He can meet with God in a quiet place and he can grow up to be like Jesus.

1 John 5:12 says, "He who has the Son has life; he who does not have the Son of God does not have life." It stands to reason that divine life comes from a divine God. Get in His presence and make Him your Lord today. Ps. 16:2 (MSG) says, "I say to God, 'Be my Lord!' Without You, nothing makes sense." Vs 5 (MSG) says, "My choice is You, God, first and only. And now I find I'm Your choice!" Vs. 8 (MSG), "Day and night I'll stick with you God; I've got a good thing going and I'm not letting go." A supernatural life doesn't happen on its own, it's got to be lived on purpose. You can't sit in your easy chair all day with your feet propped up and expect good things to just automatically happen to you. No, you've got to get alone with God, you've got to mediate in His Word, and you've got to wait on Him long enough to give you the divine direction you need. And then, when you do hear from Him, you've got to go out and do what He tells you to

do. This is all part of the growing up process. "First the blade, then the head, after that the full grain in the head" (Mark 4:28).

Ps. 16:11 says, "You will show me the path of life; In Your presence is fullness of joy; At Your right hand are pleasures forevermore." How can God show you the path of life if you don't get in His presence and wait for Him to do so? He can't and this is why you can never minimize the importance of waiting on God. One of the greatest things you can learn in life is that He is worth waiting for. Receiving divine life comes from knowing Jesus but flowing in that life comes from basking in His presence. It comes from waiting on Him to move no matter how long it takes. As you wait on Him, divine life is flowing into you. He is breathing into you the same life He breathed into Adam. Eph. 2:1 says, "And you He made alive." So blessed are you that it doesn't matter how long you have to wait. The longer the better. Your life is overflowing with the divine life of God. You are now seated with Christ in heavenly places (Eph. 2:6). Old things have passed away, behold, all things are becoming new. You are being changed from the inside out. Divine life is yours.

Make being in the presence of God the top priority of your life. It's here that divine life flows and it's the place where you grow up spiritually. When trials come and you don't know what to do, get in His presence and wait on Him. Jesus said, "If anyone thirsts, let him come to Me and drink. He who believes in me, as the Scripture has said, out of his heart will flow rivers of living water" (John 7:37,38). Jesus will show you the path of life and it's on that path where divine life flows. It's where you forever become mindful of the things of God and not the things of men (Matt. 16:23). It's where God has the final authority on everything you say and do. Jesus said in Matt. 16:24 (MSG), "Anyone who intends to come with Me has to let Me lead. You're not in the driver's seat; I am." This means you've got to die to yourself and your selfish wants and desires. To grow spiritually you've got to give God control of your life. Move over to the passenger seat and allow Jesus to be in the river's seat. He knows what's best so wait on Him to take you where you need to go.

Never become complacent when it comes to your relationship with God. Never be satisfied with where you're now at but crave Him more and more. It's those who hunger and thirst for righteousness that get filled. If you're satisfied, you won't hunger and thirst for anything. You won't draw closer to God and you won't grow spiritually. The good news is that once you taste and see that the Lord is good, you'll just naturally want to come back for more. Who wouldn't want more of the presence of God? It's wonderful, it's great, it's divine. Mary knew this and when Jesus came to her family's house she sat at His feet and heard His word (Luke 10:39). She had a hunger and thirst for more of Jesus and even her sister's complaining (vs. 40) couldn't pull her away from His presence. Martha was busy serving the Lord and in itself that is a good thing. Just don't allow yourself to get so busy that you don't have time to spend alone with Him. An hour in His presence is far more important than a full day of service. Always remember, if you're too busy for God, you're too busy.

Mary sat at the feet of Jesus and this was a sign of deep humility. She humbled herself, she heard the words of Jesus, and she grew up spiritually. James 4:10 says, "Humble yourselves in the sight of the Lord, and He will lift you up." When you humble yourself before the Lord, when you rely on Him for everything, He will lift you up to spiritual maturity. The Message Bible says, "Get down on your knees before the Master; it's the only way you'll get on your feet." Without humility you won't walk with God, you won't mature, and you won't fulfill your destiny. Moses was used by God in a mighty way and the reason for that is found in Num. 12:3, "Now the man Moses was very humble, more than all men who were on the face of the earth." Moses was humble and God lifted him up. Jesus said in Luke 18:17, "Assuredly, I say to you, whoever does not receive the kingdom of God as a little child will by no means enter it." Just as a child relies on its parents for everything, so must you rely on God for everything. That's humility. Humble yourselves and become totally reliant on God. Be like Mary and sit at the feet of Jesus.

Zeph. 2:3 (NLT) says, "Seek the Lord, all who are humble, and follow His commands. Seek to do what is right and to live humbly." Seeking the Lord and waiting on Him is a position of humility. It's when you realize you can't walk with God if you don't rely on Him. He rained bread down from heaven for the children of Israel and the people had to kneel down to pick it up. That's humility. Man's humility and God's provision go together. Stop relying on yourself and other people to meet your needs but rely on God for everything. No longer seek to do things your own way but get humble and say to the Lord, "Not my will but Your will be done." Pray to Him and say, "Give us this day our daily bread" (Matt. 6:11). Don't worry about Him meeting your needs tomorrow but trust Him to provide for you today. Jesus said, "For the bread of God is He who comes down from heaven and gives life to the world" (John 6:33). The people said, "Lord, give us this bread always" (vs. 34). Jesus responded, "I am the bread of life. He who comes to Me shall never hunger, and he who believes in Me shall never thirst" (vs. 35).

Humility is the key to God exalting you in your life. This is why you have to always sit at the feet of Jesus. 1 Peter 5:5,6 says, "Be clothed with humility, for 'God resists the proud, but gives grace to the humble.' Therefore humble yourselves under the mighty hand of God, that He may exalt you in due time." It is God's responsibility to lift you up, your responsibility is found in Jude 20,21, "But you, beloved, building yourselves up on your most holy faith, praying in the Holy Spirit, keep yourselves in the love of God, looking for the mercy of our Lord Jesus Christ unto eternal life."

Your responsibility is to keep your life in the love of God. The Message Bible says, "Staying right at the center of God's love, keeping your arms open and outstretched, ready for the mercy of our Master, Jesus Christ. This is the unending life, the real life!" If your relationship with the Lord is going to be a healthy one, then you're going to have to invest time and effort in making that happen. You're going to have to guard your heart and not allow yourself to be pulled away by the false passions of this world.

Jude is saying you need to be diligent to stay in the presence of God so you can experience and enjoy the love He has for you. As you do this, He'll give you whatever you need so you can grow up and become a mature and well-grounded believer. His love will equip you with what it takes to be successful in life. Getting alone with God and waiting on Him gives you the assurance that your relationship with Him doesn't become a cold, formal ritual. No, your relationship with Him is vibrant and alive. You're abiding in Him and He's abiding in you. An intimacy is taking place as you communicate and share with one another. You're keeping yourself in the love of God and you're growing up spiritually. Your faith and hope in Him is at an all-time high. Rom. 5:5 (NLT) says, "And this hope will not lead to disappointment. For we know how deeply God loves us, because He has given us the Holy Spirit to fill our hearts with His love." The Message Bible says, "In alert expectancy such as this, we're never left feeling shortchanged. Quite the contrary - we can't round up enough containers to hold everything God generously pours into our lives through the Holy Spirit."

Paul's prayer for spiritual growth is found in Eph. 3:14-21. Notice what he says in vs. 16-19 (NLT), "I pray that from His glorious, unlimited resources He will empower you with inner strength through His Spirit. Then Christ will make His home in your hearts as you trust in Him. Your roots will grow down into God's love and keep you strong. And may you have the power to understand, as all God's people should, how wide, how long, how high, and how deep His love is. May you experience the love of Christ, though it is too great to understand fully. Then you will be made complete with all the fullness of life and power that comes from God." Paul wants you to have a revelation that God loves you and that He has a plan for your life. You keep yourself in that love by staying in His presence all day long. As you do this, you'll grow strong in your inner man. You'll be filled with all the fullness of God. Think about that for a moment. The fullness of God was also in Jesus (Col. 1:19). This means that the greatness of God that was in Jesus is also in you. This happens when you keep yourself in the love of God.

Loving God is not what fills you with His fullness. It's when you realize how much He loves you that causes you to be supernaturally filled with His greatness. Several times a day say out loud to yourself, "God loves me. God loves me. God loves me." As you become more and more conscious of how much He loves you, the blessings of God will explode in your life. Eph. 3:20 says, "Now to Him who is able to do exceedingly abundantly above all that we ask or think, according to the power that works in us." The greatest of these blessings is that you'll grow spiritually. You'll be transformed into the image of Christ and can say what Jesus said in John 10:30, "I and the Father are one." He also said in John 14:9, "He who has seen Me has seen the Father." You can say these same things when you're filled with the fullness of God to the measure that Jesus was. Jesus is in you and His power is at work in your life. God's power and greatness is His fullness. You can experience all this when you're aware of how much He loves you. Say it again, "God loves me. God loves me. God loves me."

You are called to live a supernatural, divine life and this is why it's so important that you get alone with God and wait on Him. As you bask in His presence and give Him the time and honor He deserves, He in turn will give you wisdom and direction for everything that pertains to your life. Jesus said in John 15:5, "I am the vine, you are the branches. He who abides in Me, and I in Him, bears much fruit; for without Me you can do nothing." As you grow up in Christ, as you abide in Him, you can experience a life that is so divine that it goes beyond anything you can ask or imagine. John 1:4,5 says, "In Him was life, and the life was the light of men. And the light shines in the darkness, and the darkness did not comprehend it." The Message Bible says, "What came into existence was Life, and the Life was Light to live by. The Life-Light blazed out of the darkness; and darkness couldn't put it out." How would you like the divine life of Jesus to blaze out of you? Is this something worth waiting for? Indeed it is. Get alone with God and watch what happens.

Randall J. Brewer

-8-

"EARS TO HEAR"

Walking with God and knowing Him is what the Christian life is all about. Drawing near to God is progressive, it's something you should be constantly doing every day of your life. For sure, it's the most important thing you could ever do. Hosea 6:3 leaves no room for error when it says, "Let us pursue the knowledge of the Lord." The word "pursue" means to 'follow on, run after, attend to.' The Message Bible says, "We're ready to study God, eager for God-knowledge." Put yourself in the continual position of following God and getting to know Him better and better each and every day. Jesus is the good shepherd and He said in John 10:4, "And when he brings out his own sheep, he goes before them; and the sheep follow him, for they know his voice." Walking with God is about hearing the voice of God. As you walk with Him, He'll speak to you and give you direction for your life. He'll reveal to you your destiny and the wisdom you'll need to fulfill it. Prov. 19:21 says, "There are many plans in a man's heart, nevertheless the Lord's counsel - that will stand."

The mysteries of life will be revealed to you when you choose to continually walk with God. He'll speak to you but you've got to learn to slow down and be still in His presence. He is speaking, the question is, "Are you listening?" Prov. 3:5-7 (MSG) says, "Trust God from the bottom of your heart; don't try to figure out everything on your own. Listen for God's voice in everything you do, everywhere you go; He's the one who will keep you on track. Don't assume that you know it all. Run to God! Run from evil!" Those who hear from God are those who walk with Him and have a close, intimate relationship with Him. Ex. 33:11 says, "So the Lord spoke to Moses face to face, as a man speaks to his friend." The Message Bible says they spoke "as neighbors speak to one another." Friends and neighbors have conversations with one another. Both speak and both listen. Being close to God brings about the reality that He wants to talk with those He walks with. If you will walk with Him the same way a sheep follows its shepherd, you will hear Him speak.

It should be of great comfort to you to know you don't have to figure out on your own how to maneuver around the crazy maze of life this world offers you. All you have to do is constantly walk with God and He'll give you the direction you need. The Lord is your shepherd and Ps. 23:3 says, "He leads me in the paths of righteousness." The Message Bible says, "True to Your word, You let me catch my breath and send me in the right direction." God wants to lead you and direct you in every area of your life. He wants to guide you into all truth and tell you things to come (John 16:13). He wants to show you how to fulfill your destiny, how to raise your children, and how to manage your business. Ps. 32:8 says, "I will instruct you and teach you in the way you should go." God wants to lead you to freedom in whatever it is you are doing. He'll lead but it's your responsibility to follow. For that to happen, you have to believe that you can personally and directly hear from God. Millions of people scoff at the idea of hearing from God and this is why their lives are in the wretched condition it's currently in.

David has a word for those people who don't believe they can hear from God. Ps. 32:9 says, "Do not be like the horse or like the mule, which have no understanding, which must be harnessed with bit and bridle, else they will not come near you." A horse is led by a bit that's in its mouth and David is saying you don't need natural things and circumstances to direct your life. All you need is God. Vs. 8-10 (CEV) says, "I will point out the road that you should follow. I will be your teacher and watch over you. Don't be stupid like horses and mules that must be led with ropes to make them obey. All kinds of troubles will strike the wicked, but Your kindness shields those who trust You, Lord." It should take little or no persuasion to convince you that you are smarter than a horse or a mule. You were made in the likeness of God and are being transformed into the image of Christ. Jesus heard the Father speak and you can also. He wants to speak to you and tell you what His will is. Horses and mules have no understanding but Eph. 5:17 says, "Therefore do not be unwise but understand what the will of the Lord is."

The Lord admonishes those who don't listen to Him. Is. 42:18,19 (MSG) says, "Pay attention! Are you deaf? Open your eyes! Are you blind? You're My servant, and you're not looking! You're My messenger and you're not listening!" Vs. 23 (MSG) says, "But is anyone out there listening? Is anyone paying attention to what's coming?" Clearly, it is important to God that people listen when He speaks. Common sense will tell you that people speak for the sole purpose of being heard. So what's the problem? Why aren't people hearing the voice of God? Acts 28:27 says, "For the heart of this people has grown dull. Their ears are hard of hearing, and their eyes they have closed." The Greek word for "dull" means 'stupid, hardened, and calloused.' Those with a dull and hardened heart don't spend time alone with God nor do they meditate in His Word. They haven't grown up spiritually and for this reason they don't hear the voice of God. They don't have ears to hear and are paying a heavy price for their stupidity and blatant disobedience.

God is a speaking God who clothes His thoughts with words. The entire universe was created by the words God spoke. In Gen. 3:8 Adam and Eve "heard the voice of the Lord God walking in the garden in the cool of the day." Thankfully, the voice of God is active in the world today and this is why the Bible says you need ears to hear. Jesus said in Matt. 4:4, "It is written, 'Man shall not live by bread alone, but by every word that proceeds from the mouth of God.'" The Message Bible says, "It takes more than bread to stay alive. It takes a steady stream of words from God's mouth." You must stay close enough to God so that you can hear Him when He speaks. Get alone with God for it's in that quiet time where you'll most often hear His voice. Elijah was alone by a cave when he heard the still, small voice of God. Paul was alone in a jail cell when he heard from God and wrote the epistles. John was alone on the Isle of Patmos when he wrote the book of Revelation. Don't shun being alone with God, embrace it. If you'll do that, He'll be the voice that will give you the direction you need.

In Acts 9:11 the Lord spoke to a man named Ananias. He said to him, "Arise and go to the street called Straight, and inquire at the house of Judas for one called Saul of Tarsus, for behold, he is praying." Notice all the details involved in this conversation. The Lord told him what street and house to go to, the name of the man inside the house, and what this man was doing. God wants to direct you the same way. As you grow up spiritually and learn to hear His voice, He'll tell you who to marry, where to live, where to work, where to go to church, and how to fulfill your destiny. No detail will be left out as He leads you in the paths of righteousness. No question will go unanswered as you strive to follow God with all your heart and soul. Yes, He'll lead you in paths where goodness and mercy follow you all the days of your life (Ps. 23:6), but first there is one thing you need before you can hear the voice of God. Rev. 2:7 says, "He who has an ear, let him hear what the Spirit says to the churches." The Message Bible says, "Are your ears awake? Listen."

Jer. 33:3 says, "Call to Me, and I will answer you, and show you great and mighty things, which you do not know." God will answer you but you need ears to hear what He's saying. "If anyone has an ear, let him hear" (Rev. 13:9). You need to create an atmosphere where you can hear from God. The environment you're in can effect your ability to listen and hear from Him. People are just too busy and they need to slow down. Their lives are filled with all the trash that comes from social media. Their minds are littered with so much chaos and confusion they don't know if they're coming or going. Have a room that's not cluttered with things that will distract you. Find a place that brings you peace and is the type of room you would bring an invited guest. Set the mood by telling God how much you love and worship Him. Prov. 22:3 says God inhabits the praises of His people. Get still and allow the tranquility of the moment to be your invitation to God to come and have personal fellowship with you.

You need to put yourself in a position where you can hear from God. Jesus said in Matt. 11:28, "Come to Me, all you who labor and are heavy laden, and I will give you rest." Stop working so much and go off by yourself and get in His presence. Sit at His feet like Mary did and listen to what He has to say. God is not going to speak to you as you're watching that ungodly television program. Separate yourself from all that clutter and come to Him. He's there waiting for you. Rev. 3:20 says, "Behold, I stand at the door and knock. If anyone hears My voice and opens the door, I will come in to him and dine with him, and he with Me." People who dine together converse with one another. God is saying He wants to talk to you and He wants you to talk to Him. This is why you need to slow down in order to hear the knocking at the door of your heart. What happens when a person knocks on a door and nobody answers it? After a while they'll leave and go knock on another door. Don't let this happen to you. Is. 55:6 says, "Seek the Lord while He may be found, call upon Him while He is near."

God is not far away as some people would believe. He is not a distant God and for sure He is close at hand. Ps. 145:18 says, "The Lord is near to all who call upon Him, to all who call upon Him in truth." The Message Bible says, "God's there, listening for all who pray, for all who pray and mean it." God hears what you're saying, now it's time for you to hear what He's saying. He who has ears to hear, let him hear. You are called to do great things and this is why you've got to cultivate a close relationship with God every day of your life. Great things don't just happen on their own. No, you've got to rise up and make them happen. You do that by hearing from God and by doing the things He tells you to do. Get alone with Him and meditate on His Word. As you give Him the time and honor He deserves, He will speak to you. Inside of you will come an impulse that wasn't there before. A still, small voice is speaking to your heart and with that comes an inclination to go out and do something great for the kingdom of God. So wonderful is this conversation that you want it to happen over and over again.

The more time you spend with God, the better you'll recognize His voice. Jesus said the sheep know the voice of the shepherd. The sheep know his voice because they spend time with him morning, noon, and night. John 10:3 says, "He calls his own sheep by name and leads them out." The amount of time you spend alone with God determines how well and how often you'll hear Him speak. You will need little persuasion to do this once you realize that one word from God can change your life forever. Of course, that one word won't do you much good if you don't hear it being spoken. Never say that God doesn't speak to you. He speaks to you all the time. In fact, He calls you by name. If you don't hear Him speak then the problem is you're not listening. You don't take the time to get alone with Him and create an atmosphere where you can hear His voice and get that spiritual unction that comes to your inner man. But if you'll do what's needed, you can have the assurance that He'll come in and dine with you and you with Him.

You are a spiritual being and God designed you to live from the inside out. People who don't grow up spiritually and those who don't hear God speak are those who are too wrapped up in what's happening in the outside world. When God speaks to you, it will be to your heart and not to your outer ears. His still small voice will come as an inner witness down in your heart for He'll speak to you Spirit to spirit. Rom. 6:16 says, "The Spirit Himself bears witness with our spirit that we are children of God." The Good News Translation says, "God's Spirit joins Himself to our spirits to declare that we are God's children." The Message Bible says, "God's Spirit touches our spirits and confirms who we really are." When God speaks to you, your spirit takes what He said and turns it into a thought. Don't cast aside these thoughts thinking they're coming from you and not God. No, these thoughts are the result of your spirit hearing and being influenced by the Spirit of God. As you stay in the presence of God, you'll know that you know the prompting and direction inside of you came from the Spirit of God.

It is so important that you learn to hear the voice of God because, in truth, not everything you need to know will be found in the Bible. There is no chapter and verse that will tell you who to marry, what church to go to, and whether or not you should accept that job offer on the other side of the country. No, you need to seek the Lord and get direction from Him. A warning is given in Prov. 14:12, "There is a way which seems right to a man, but it's end is the way of death." Things that appear to be harmless on the outside may be the very thing that leads to your destruction. This is why you need to hear and obey the voice of God. In fact, God commands you to do so. He said in Jer. 7:23, "But this is what I commanded them, saying, 'Obey My voice, and I will be your God, and you shall be My people. And walk in all the ways that I have commanded you, that it may be well with you.'" It stands to reason that you can't obey the voice of God until you first hear Him speak. He knows this and is forever ready to speak to you and reveal to your heart what His will is.

Be aware that the devil will try to deceive you with things that seem right. It looks good on the outside but is it really? In Hebrew, the word for "seems" brings forth the idea of being 'convenient, straight, smooth, and prosperous.' The devil deals with outward appearances and will try to convince you that the easy way out is always the way of God. He wants you to not listen for that inward witness but to make your decisions based on how things look in the natural. You may be serving God in a mighty way at your local church and then comes an offer from a job in another city where you'll make twice as much money as you're making now. It looks good on the outside but is this what God wants you to do? Or is the devil using natural things to pull you away from fulfilling your destiny? In Gen. 13:1-13 Abraham and Lot parted ways and Abraham told his nephew he could have whatever land he wanted. Lot chose the good, well watered land to dwell in not realizing that the cities of Sodom and Gomorrah were also there. Vs. 13 says, "But the men of Sodom were exceedingly wicked and sinful against the Lord." In other words, best isn't always better.

Don't make your decisions based on what looks good on the outside. Doing this is what brought about the fall of man. Gen. 3:6 says, "So when the woman saw that the tree was good for food, that it was pleasant to the eyes, and a tree desirable to make one wise, she took of its fruit and ate. She also gave to her husband with her, and he ate." The world is in the mess it's in today because something looked good to Adam and Eve. They didn't realize that "Satan himself transforms himself into an angel of light" (2 Cor. 11:14). He'll take what's wrong and present it to you as something pleasing and beautiful to be desired. Millions follow his deceptions because they haven't learned yet how to hear the voice of God. Don't allow the devil to make a mess of your life. Get alone with God and get direction from Him. He who has an ear, let him hear. Yes, God "gives you richly all things to enjoy" (1 Tim. 6:17). Let Him lead you to these good things, not the devil. Jesus said in John 10:10, "The thief does not come except to steal, and to kill, and to destroy. I have come that they may have life, and have it more abundantly."

When God speaks, you will have inside of you a quiet assurance and a relaxed knowing that this indeed is the voice of God. The inward witness brings with it an awareness of peace. It's a peace that goes beyond human understanding and logic. As you grow up spiritually, you will be able to use the peace of God as a method of direction. If something isn't right, you won't have peace about it. If it is right, then peace will flood over your inner man. God is using peace to direct and govern your life. Heb. 12:14 says to "follow after peace." In Greek the word for "follow" is a hunting term that means 'to follow the tracks of the animal' or 'to follow the scent of the animal.' To follow after peace means you search for it, you hunt for it, you track it down. When God speaks to you, the scent of peace will be there and a strong conviction will come to your inner man. You'll just know that you know you've heard from Him. There is nothing peaceful about the devil and the absence of peace is a clear sign that what you heard was from him.

The closer you are to God, the more you meditate in His Word, the harder it is for the devil to deceive you. You're growing up spiritually and you've come to know the voice of God. Jesus said in John 10:5, "Yet they will by no means follow a stranger, but will flee from him, for they do not know the voice of strangers." The Message Bible says, "They won't follow a stranger's voice but will scatter because they aren't used to the sound of it." It really isn't hard to tell the difference between the voice of God and the voice of the devil. The voice of God brings peace and the voice of the devil brings unrest. All you have to do is follow after peace. If you're still not sure, then stay in the presence of God a little bit longer. Get still and listen for His still, small voice. He's not holding out on you and before long you'll have the confident assurance that, indeed, you have heard from God. A supernatural peace will rise up inside of you and you'll know without doubt that it is Him who is speaking to you. He is the good shepherd and Jesus says the sheep know His voice.

If you're ever in a situation where you don't know what to do, run to God and listen for His voice. Prov. 2:6 says, "For the Lord gives wisdom; from His mouth come knowledge and understanding." Vs. 7 (MSG) says, "He's a rich mine of common sense for those who live well, a personal bodyguard to the candid and sincere." The key to having a successful life is to hear the voice of God and do what He tells you to do. Those who do this is likened to a wise man who built his house on a rock. The rain fell and the wind blew but the house did not fall (Matt. 7:24,25). You need to act on what you hear. James 1:22 says, "But be doers of the word, and not hearers only, deceiving yourselves." Notice that it's not the devil deceiving you here. You're deceiving yourself if you don't do what God tells you to do. Much of the responsibility for your life is on your shoulders. It's up to you to create an atmosphere to hear God speak and it's up to you to do what He tells you to do. Don't always blame the devil for your hardship but first check up on yourself. Are you doing the things God told you to do?

In the parable of the two builders (Matt. 7:24-27), Jesus says you're wise if you do what He says and a fool if you don't. Obey God and be blessed in everything you do (James 1:25). Prov. 4:10 says, "Hear, my son, and receive my sayings, and the years of your life will be many." Isn't living a long, successful life the heart's desire of all people? It will happen if you'll only have ears to hear. Vs. 5,6 tells you what must be done, "Get wisdom! Get understanding! Do not forget, nor turn away from the words of my mouth. Do not forsake her, and she will preserve you; Love her, and she will keep you." Be a wise person and build your house on a rock. Hear the voice of God and be a doer of the Word. If you'll do that, you'll grow up spiritually and be blessed beyond your wildest dreams. You'll live an abundant life. Vs. 11-13 says, "I have taught you in the way of wisdom; I have led you in right paths. When you walk, your steps will not be hindered, and when you run, you will not stumble. Take firm hold of instruction, do not let go; Keep her, for she is your life."

Open your heart to God and say to Him, "Speak, Lord, for Your servant hears." You then prepare your heart to receive what He has to say to you. James 1:21 (AMP) says, "So get rid of all uncleanness and the rampant outgrowth of wickedness, and in a humble spirit receive and welcome the Word which implanted and rooted in your hearts contains the power to save your souls." Stop being so busy and slow down and rest. Humble yourself and sit at the feet of Jesus. With an open heart receive and welcome what He has to say to you. His words contain the power to change your life. This power gets activated when you rise up and do what He tells you to do. Have ears to hear and the courage to act on what you've heard. This is the key to a successful life. It's what helps you to grow up spiritually. The Message Bible says, "So throw all spoiled virtue and cancerous evil in the garbage. In simple humility, let our gardener, God, landscape you with the Word, making a salvation-garden of your life." How do you experience this wonderful life? By having ears to hear.

Randall J. Brewer

-9-

"BEACON OF LIGHT"

God doesn't want you to grow up spiritually just for the sake of doing so. No, there is a reason God wants you to grow up and become like Him. In the heart of God is the will and desire for you to live a godly life and to fulfill your destiny. He wants you to be abundantly blessed so you can turn around and be a blessing to others. Spiritual growth is a journey where God takes you by the hand and causes you to become greater than you already are. This journey begins when you develop on the inside of you a hunger for the deeper things of God. When it comes to God, you've got to get hungry and stay hungry. What does a person do when they are hungry for natural food? They go seeking for something to eat. The same thing is true when a person is hungry for spiritual things. You've got to seek God with everything that is in you. Jesus said, "Ask, and it will be given to you; seek, and you will find; knock, and it will be opened to you. For everyone who asks receives, and he who seeks finds, and to him who knocks it will be opened" (Matt. 7:7,8).

Everything you receive from God comes out of the hunger you have for Him. This is why you need to get hungry and expect God to give you more than you can think or imagine. It's those who are hungry that get filled, the ones who grow up spiritually. Dare to live differently. Dare to live by every word that proceeds out of the mouth of God (Matt. 4:4).

Clean up your cluttered life and make room so Jesus can come in and dine with you and you with Him. Pray and keep praying. Seek and keep seeking. Give your life to God and He'll give His life to you. Rom. 12:1 (MSG) says, "So here's what I want you to do, God helping you: Take your everyday, ordinary life - your sleeping, eating, going-to-work, and walking-around life - and place it before God as an offering." God sees this as an open invitation to come in and move in your life. Nobody goes where they're not made to feel welcome. Why would God go where He's not wanted? You draw near to God to make Him feel wanted in your life. Desire Him like that thirsty deer that pants for the water. Your hunger for Him, your desire, is what draws Him in.

What happens when God comes into your life? You get transformed into the image of Christ and that is what spiritual growth is all about. This is great and wonderful, but don't forget the purpose of growing up in the things of God. You grow so you can bear fruit in God's kingdom on the earth. That's the purpose for growing. God wants you to live a godly life and be a blessing to others. He wants you to run your race and do what you've been called to do. 1 Cor. 9:24 says, "Do you not know that those who run in a race all run, but one receives the prize? Run in such a way that you may obtain it." God wants you to possess everything He has for you. The Message Bible says, "Everyone runs; one wins. Run to win." You win your race by growing up and doing what God tells you to do. Jesus said in John 14:23, "If anyone loves Me, he will keep My word, and My Father will love him, and We will come to him and make Our home with him." It's seeds that are planted in good soil that grow up and bear much fruit. Pray and ask God to plant you in the soil of His kingdom.

Ps. 92:12-14 says, "The righteous shall flourish like a palm tree, he shall grow like a cedar in Lebanon. Those who are planted in the house of the Lord shall flourish in the courts of our God. They shall still bear fruit in old age; They shall be fresh and flourishing." The Hebrew word for "planted" means to be 'transplanted.' The Message Bible says, "Grow tall like Lebanon cedars; transplanted to God's courtyard." Being transplanted means to take a seed out of one type of soil and replant it in a different type of soil. Growing up spiritually helps you to be transplanted from your old way of life into the godly life God has planned for you. John the Baptist said, "Repent, for the kingdom of heaven is at hand!" (Matt. 3:2). He was saying that there is a better way to live. He told the people they had to be transplanted into the house of the Lord. The Father's house is the dwelling place of God. It's where He lives and He wants you to grow and flourish in His presence. When you are planted in His house, everything He has becomes yours.

The purpose of growing up spiritually is that you get so full of God and His Word that you can't hold it in any longer. You can't contain it all so you pour it out into the lives of those around you. Jer. 20:9 (MSG) says, "The words are fire in my belly, a burning in my bones. I'm worn out trying to hold it in. I can't do it any longer!" The CEV says, "But Your message burns in my heart and bones, and I cannot keep silent." Silence is not in the vocabulary of one who has grown up. God said in Jer. 23:28, "The prophet who has a dream, let him tell a dream; And he who has My word, let him speak My word faithfully." God put something inside of you that He wants the rest of the world to have. He wants you to grow up so you can tell these people what that something is. Matt. 13:32 says that small seeds can grow into big trees "so that the birds of the air come and nest in its branches." This is what God wants you to do. He wants you to grow up spiritually so others can come and find rest and comfort by listening to the things you have to say.

As you grow, you'll get changed from the inside out. God wants that same change to happen to other people and He'll use you as a living testimony to show how that can happen. Jesus said in Matt. 5:16, "Let your light so shine before men, that they may see your good works and glorify your Father in heaven." He said "you are the light of the world" (vs. 14) which means you are to live in such a way that your life reveals the love and goodness of God. God wants you to grow up so that you can be a beacon of light in a dark and hurting world. Your words and actions are to illuminate the pathway to salvation. Just as the heavens declare the glory of God (Ps. 19:1), so also does the light that's shining forth from within you. God wants to use you to help a darkened world find hope and eternal life through the Lord Jesus Christ. Jesus said you don't "light a lamp and put it under a basket, but on a lampstand, and it gives light to all who are in the house" (Matt. 5:15). The Message Bible says, "God is not a secret to be kept. We're going public with this, as public as a city on a hill."

The ultimate goal of your life is to become the type of person who brings glory to God. One way to do this is to touch the lives of others so they also will bring glory to God. By faith you become a child of God (2 Cor. 5:17) and after that you grow up and become transformed into the image of Christ and become more and more like Him (Rom. 8:29). Jesus touched the people of the world and as a beacon of light you can do the same thing. You're to live out who you are on the inside and "have a walk worthy of the calling with which you were called" (Eph. 4:1). That's why you're here. That's the purpose for growing up. The Message Bible says, "I want you to get out there and walk - better yet, run! - on the road God called you to travel. I don't want any of you sitting around on your hands. I don't want anyone strolling off, down some path that goes nowhere." Phil 1:27 says you are to conduct yourselves in a manner worthy of the gospel. You are to live differently than those in this fallen world. How can you be a beacon of light to others if you live like they do?

As a child of God you've got to know how to live your life in such a way that it becomes an example for others to follow.

In Titus 2, Paul speaks to both men and women at different stages of spiritual growth and what he has to say can help you on your spiritual journey. He begins by speaking about older men who are mature and over the age of fifty. Vs. 2 (NASB) says, "Older men are to be temperate, dignified, sensible, sound in faith, in love, in perseverance." To be temperate means to be 'clear-headed, to think correctly, to have a good understanding of what's right and what's wrong.' Older men are to live wisely and know how to conduct themselves in a dignified way. They need to be worthy of respect in everything that say and do. They've been faithful over the course of their life and have learned to be self-controlled no matter what life throws at them. He is sound in faith because he knows the scriptures and lives out its principles daily. This is where wisdom comes from. He walks in love always and in patience he perseveres and keeps going forward and trusting God.

Paul then speaks to the older women in vs. 3-5. An older woman is one who has raised her family, and her children are now grown and no longer living at home. Vs. 3 (NASB) says, "Older women likewise are to be reverent in their behavior, not malicious gossips nor enslaved to much wine, teaching what is good." An older woman needs to be holy in her behavior, set apart from those in the world. They don't slander other people behind their back but instead find something good to say about everybody. Neither are they in bondage to alcohol. Wine was a common drink in Biblical times so self-control had to be maintained at all times. Her children are grown up and living their own lives, so her responsibility now is to teach the younger women what is a good and acceptable way to live. They "encourage the young women to love their husbands, to love their children" (vs. 4 NASB). In the culture at that time many marriages were arranged by their parents and couples often got married without first falling in love with one another. It was the responsibility of the older women to teach the younger women the concepts of marital love.

Paul says the young women are "to live wisely and be pure, to work in their homes, to do good, and to be submissive to their husbands. Then they will not bring shame on the word of God" (vs. 5 NLT). Young women are to be discreet which means they're not always drawing attention to themselves. They're to be sexually virtuous and pure and are to keep busy taking care of their home. Placed inside of her is the heart and wisdom to manage her home in a godly way. A man can build a house, but it's the woman who makes it a home. The younger women are to be good, kind, and tender-hearted and she's raising her children to be the same way. A good wife is to be subject to their own husbands. This has nothing to do with superiority or inferiority. All are equal in the eyes of God when it comes to individual lives. In the home, however, God chose husbands to fulfill the role of leader. This is a great responsibility that is put on the shoulders of every husband. Wives can give their husbands support by willingly putting themselves under the authority that God had placed in the home.

All believers should live in such a way that God is glorified. Col. 3:17 says, "And whatever you do in word or deed, do all in the name of the Lord Jesus, giving thanks to God the Father through Him." In order to be a beacon of light to the world around you, you've got to continually do good deeds and proclaim good words. Paul now gives instructions to younger men. Titus is a young pastor and Paul uses him as an example. He says in Titus 2:6, "Likewise exhort the younger men to be sober-minded." This means they're to be sensible, self-controlled, and to live wisely. Young men are strong and can do things older men can't do. Paul is saying they need to know what's important in life and have sound judgment. They need a vision for the future and know what to do so their destiny gets fulfilled. Paul says to Titus in vs.7, "In all things showing yourself to be a pattern of good works." As a believer, know that other people are watching you. They'll notice what you say and how you behave. Paul is saying to set the pattern and be the example of what a young, godly man should be like.

People need role models. No matter how old you are or what gender, always live your life in such a way that God is glorified so others can see how a true believer is supposed to live. It's your responsibility to be their role model, a beacon of light in a dark world. People in the world don't want to be criticized for bad behavior. What they do want is somebody to show them the proper way to live. You need to grow up spiritually so God can use you to do just that. Titus 2:7,8 (NLT) says, "And you yourself must be an example to them by doing good works of every kind. Let everything you do reflect the integrity and seriousness of your teaching. Teach the truth so that your teaching can't be criticized. Then those who oppose us will be ashamed and have nothing bad to say about us." The Message Bible says, "Show them all this by doing it yourself, incorruptible in your teaching, your words solid and sane." Paul is saying that your words and actions are to be a reflection of a sound Christian lifestyle and the salvation message you've been sent to proclaim.

To be a beacon of light, you've got to watch what you say and watch what you do. Remember, the world is watching you. Then again, so is God. How you live is a key to your testimony. Actions speak louder than words. If your actions don't back up your words, you'll be called a hypocrite and people won't listen to you. More than that, they'll avoid you like the plague. Nothing turns a sinner away from God more than a Christian hypocrite. Don't let this happen, but every day strive to live out who you are on the inside. If you'll do that, you'll bear fruit everywhere you go. Titus 3:8 says, "Those who have believed in God should be careful to maintain good works. These things are good and profitable to men." Vs. 14 says, "And let our people also learn to maintain good works, to meet urgent needs, that they may not be unfruitful." Paul is saying that young men need to learn early in life to develop a pattern of good works and to have sound speech that cannot be condemned. They need to learn the Word and devote themselves fully to living by the principles contained therein.

The challenge for every believer is to learn how to live in a fallen world. You can do this if you'll allow your outward behavior to reflect the person you are on the inside. In other words, you're to live from the inside out. That's the way you become a beacon of light. Because the grace of God has been poured into your life, Titus 2:14 says you are now "His own special people, zealous for good works." Paul goes on to give further instruction for godly living in Titus 3:1,2, "Remind them to be subject to rulers and authorities, to obey, to be ready for every good work, to speak evil of no one, to be peaceable, gentle, showing all humility to all men." The Message Bible says, "Remind the people to respect the government and be law-abiding, always ready to lend a helping hand. No insults, no fights. God's people should be bighearted and courteous." Paul is saying to obey the laws of the land and don't argue with your boss at work when he tells you to do something you don't want to do. At church, your pastor is the shepherd of the local flock and you need to give him the honor and respect he deserves.

A beacon of light needs to come under the authority of those people God places over them. You need to drive the speed limit and stop at every stop sign. Wives should submit to their husbands and children should submit to their parents. Submission is not a bad word for there is even submission in the Godhead. The Holy Spirit submits to Jesus and Jesus submits to the Father. There should be no place for rebellion in the life of a believer. Rom. 13:1,2 (NLT) says, "For all authority comes from God, and those in position of authority have been placed there by God. So anyone who rebels against authority is rebelling against what God has instituted, and they will be punished." Don't rebel against paying taxes. Pay them and believe God to supply the means to do so. Don't go fishing without a license if one is required. Go get your license and then fish to your heart's content. Don't park your car in a no parking zone but park in the proper place as outlined by the city officials. You need to obey those in authority over you as if you were obeying God Himself.

You need to obey the laws of the land and be ready for every good work. Your life needs to be characterized by the good deeds you do for other people. It's these godly actions that will draw people into the kingdom of God. If you want sinners to come to know Jesus, then you must live your life that is worthy of your calling. Paul gets specific in what you should do. Titus 3:2 (NLT) says, "They must not slander anyone and must avoid quarreling. Instead, they should be gentle and show true humility to everyone." Don't gossip about other people and say bad things about them. Don't condemn the clothes they wear and don't criticize them based on what you think they should or shouldn't do. Get along with these people even if they rub you the wrong way. Rom. 12:18 says, "If it is possible, as much as depends on you, live peaceably with all men." The Message Bible says, "Don't hit back; discover beauty in everyone. If you've got it in you, get along with everybody." Be gentle with these people and be kind. Show consideration for all men.

Phil. 2:4 says, "Let each of us look out not only for his own interests, but also for the interests of others." You become a beacon of light by putting others above yourself. This is not a hard thing to do once you know that God is looking out for you. He'll take care of you as you strive to take care of others. Ask God to plant you in the lives of other people. Be willing to go where God tells you to so and stay where He tells you to stay. Be a light that shines brighter and brighter each and every day. Grow up and become a seed that flourishes to full maturity. The word "flourish" refers to a violent act. It means 'to break forth; to bud; to blossom; to enlarge; to spread out; to expand.' This is a description of what your life should be like once you've grown up spiritually. God is calling you to break forth and bud. Jesus said in Matt. 11:12, "The kingdom of heaven suffers violence, and the violent take it by force."

This means you've got to maintain good works and do the work of the ministry. Fulfill your destiny and flourish like the trees of Lebanon. Be a beacon of light to those around you.

When a flower blossoms, it becomes what it was created to be. It fulfills its destiny. This is why God wants you to grow up and become a beacon of light. Your life will blossom and you'll fulfill that which you were called to do. Understand that inside of you is the potential to touch the entire world. Believe that the possibilities God put inside of you will flourish and break forth. Don't limit God with small thinking. Think big and watch God move knowing that He'll move when you do. Put one foot in front of the other and go out and fulfill your destiny. Don't be satisfied where you're now at or with what you've done in the past. No, there's a great harvest of people out there waiting to be brought into the kingdom. Be like Paul who said, "I press toward the mark for the prize of the high calling of God in Christ Jesus" (Phil. 3:14). The Message Bible says, "I'm off and running, and I'm not turning back." Take up your cross daily and follow Jesus (Luke 9:23). If you'll do that, He'll lead you to a place where you'll blossom like never before. With His help, you'll reach your full potential.

Be prepared to do everything God has called you to do. Everywhere you go there will be opportunities to be a blessing to another person. Help somebody carry their groceries out to their car, mow the lawn of the elderly widow who lives next to you, help change the flat tire on the car that's pulled off to the side of the road. You don't have to preach to these people, just let the goodness of God shine through your actions. Don't be like Job who said, "My life drags by - day after hopeless day. I give up; I am tired of living. Leave me alone. My life makes no sense" (Job 7:6,16 TLB). Don't let another day drag by without realizing that God put you on this earth for a purpose. Time passes quickly so don't spend another moment feeling sorry for yourself thinking God couldn't possibly use a person like yourself. No, He can use you and He will use you. You're made in His image and this allows you to break forth and blossom in this fallen world. You're called to be a beacon of light so rise up and let your life be a reflection of the glory that's inside of you.

Believe that God has a plan for your life. Jer. 1:5 (ERV) says, "Before I made you in your mother's womb, I knew you. Before you were born, I chose you for a special work." Get alone with God and you'll hear His voice. He'll tell you what it is He wants you to do. Trust Him and He'll lead you step by step into His perfect plan for your life. No, it won't happen on its own. Destinies only get fulfilled through the power of positive expectancy. It's a proven fact, you get what you expect whether it be good or bad, positive or negative. Wake up every day expecting to grow, expecting to flourish, expecting to be used by God in a powerful way. If you will be faithful and loyal to Him, God says He will show Himself strong on your behalf (2 Chron. 16:9). With God on your side, there is no way the devil can stop you from breaking forth and fulfilling what you've been called to do. Now is the time to get out of your boat and start walking on the water. Now is the time for you to blossom, to leave your mark on this evil, sinful world. Expect it to happen and surely it will come to pass.

Randall J. Brewer

-10-

"GET THE PLAN"

Lives get wasted when people don't know why they're here, when they don't know the purpose for which they've been born. Life has no meaning if all you do is wander around like a vagabond seeking fortune and fame all the time. They say the rich get richer. Why is that? Because without Christ and a purpose for living, all the money in the world can't satisfy what their inner man is craving for. In fact, 1 Cor. 15:19 (CSB) says, "If our hope in Christ is good only for this life, we are worse off than anyone else." The Message Bible says, "If all we get out of Christ is a little inspiration for a few short years, we're a pretty sorry lot." So what do these rich people do? They keep making more and more money hoping to find what money can't buy. Their lives are miserable, their marriages fail, many commit suicide, and most die without having a relationship with the living God. It's when they breathe their last breath that they realize their money did them no good. Yes, money is a good thing if used properly, but never spend your life for the sole purpose of obtaining as much of it as you can.

James 4:14 (AMP) asks the question, "What is the nature of your life?" What does your life consist of? For what reason do you get up every morning? For what reason were you born? The problem for most people is that this is a question they ask themselves when, in truth, this is a question they should be asking God. Every believer needs to ask God this question, the sooner the better. "Lord, why am I here? For what purpose have You made me? What is Your plan for my life?" Life has no meaning for those who don't know the answers to these questions. You must grasp the reality that a good, successful life only happens when you fulfill God's purpose for your life. In fact, doing so should be the reason for everything you do. It's the reason you get alone with God, the reason you meditate in His Word, the reason you grow up spiritually. Your purpose in life is to do what God wants you to do. Jesus did not come to do His own will, but the will of the Father (Luke 22:42). Since you've been transformed into His image, you must do the same thing. Say to Him, "Not my will, but Yours, be done."

The devil is a thief and your assignment from God is the number one thing he's trying to steal. He'll do everything he can to distract you from doing what you've been called to do. He'll even make you rich in hopes you'll spend more time on your new yacht than you do serving God. The truth is, the devil really doesn't care about you personally. It's your assignment from God that concerns him most and he'll do everything he can to pull you away from it. Adam had an assignment and this is why the devil tempted him in the garden. Jesus also had an assignment and at His birth the devil caused the Romans to murder thousands of babies in hopes of killing the newly born Messiah. Don't let the devil steal your assignment. Rise up and don't let him take away your reason for living. Ps. 129:2 says, "Many a time they have afflicted me from my youth; Yet they have not prevailed against me." Not only will the devil try to steal your assignment from you, he'll also try to stop you from finding out what your assignment is. That is his number one ploy. How can you fulfill your assignment if you don't know what it is?

Two of the greatest days of your life are the day you were born and the day you discover why. Until you identify the gifts God has given you and learn of your purpose, life will feel empty to you. Never allow the devil to tell you you're not qualified to fulfill your heavenly call. Jeremiah thought he wasn't good enough to be the prophet he was called to be. He told God, "Behold, I cannot speak, for I am a youth" (Jer. 1:6). What did God do? "Then the Lord put forth His hand and touched my mouth, and the Lord said to me: 'Behold, I have put My words in your mouth'" (vs. 9). Rest assured, God will give you the power and the ability to do what He calls you to do. This is why you can't allow fear and intimidation to cause you to feel unimportant and not worthy. God wants you to know that you are important and very valuable to the world in which you live. So important are you that He has a specific purpose and plan for your life. Greatness is inside of you and it's waiting to be released. So what should you do? Get the plan, of course.

God will tell you what your assignment is and this is why it's necessary for you to spend time alone with Him and learn to hear His voice. God speaks to those who have ears to hear and it is life changing when He does. It's what God says that matters most in your life. Don't ever say you can't hear from God. If you know Him, you'll know His voice. Jesus said the sheep know the voice of the shepherd. Jer. 1:4 says, "Then the word of the Lord came to me." God also has a word for you. Listen for it. It's in His voice where your assignment will be found. It's where you find out you've been set apart, called for a specific purpose. It's where you realize that God will use you to do mighty things, to bring the answer to another person's prayer. Never make light of what God can do in you and through you. He's bigger than man's limitations and so are you. Fulfilling your destiny is one of the main reasons for spiritual growth. You'll live a good life and will do what God tells you to do. The more you grow, the more you'll be able to do for God and the more He'll be glorified.

You don't decide what God's plan is for your life, you discover it. Parents should never tell their children they can grow up and become whatever they want to be. No, they should tell them to grow up and become what God wants them to be. Tell them early that God has a plan for their life and it's their assignment from on high that they should seek to fulfill. You also need to do the same thing. Before all else, get the plan of God for your life. That plan will give you the direction in life you must go. The good news is that Jesus will be by your side, taking your hand and leading you all the way. God is the Great Provider and many times He provides for His own through the individual gifts He gives to each person. Your purpose for living, the reason God wants you to grow up spiritually, is so that He can use you to help meet the needs in the body of Christ, both uniquely and specifically. Somewhere in the world there is a hurting person who needs exactly what you have to give them. Allow God to use you to meet that need. After all, that's why you're here.

Your assignment is not about what you do, it's about who you are. Inside of you is a uniqueness that makes you different from anybody else in the world. You are unique for not everybody can do what you do, the way you do it. This is what will draw people in to receive what God is using you to give them. Never feel bad if you're not like everybody else for this is God's gift to you and to those around you. Identify what it is that makes you different and build on that. It is from here that the power of God flows. It's what gives you the ability to make a positive difference in a hurting world. Don't run from being different but cling to it. Hold on to it for it will take you to the fulfillment of your destiny. It's your passion and desire to be used by God. In Is. 6:8 there was a need in the land and God asked, "Whom shall I send, and who will go for Us?" Right away Isaiah stood up and said, "Here am I! Send me." You need to rise up and say the same thing. Get the plan of God and go after it with all that is in you.

You were born with great potential and that which you are able to do is what God wants you to do. God created you the way you are. It was He who put inside of you special desires that would draw you into His perfect plan for your life. What are you passionate about? What moves you? What stirs you up? What do you talk about all the time? Your answer to these questions is a clue to what your assignment is. There is a direct connection between your potential, your passion, and your purpose. The key to knowing God's plan is to know and focus on what your desires are. Do you like music? Perhaps God wants you to sing in the church choir or be a member of the praise team. Do you love children? For sure, there will be a place for you in the children's ministry. Your assignment from God is identified by what stirs up your passion and brings you the most joy. It's what you desire most that points you in the direction you should go. You get the plan by knowing what you truly love to do. You then grow up spiritually and build your life around that plan.

You were made for action. Once you find out what your assignment is, by all means, go out and do what you've been called to do. Rom. 12:6 says, "Having then gifts differing according to the grace that is given to us, let us use them." The Message Bible says, "Let's just go ahead and be what we were made to be, without enviously or pridefully comparing ourselves with each other, or trying to be something we aren't." The Bible leaves no room for confusion and doubt when it says that every believer has been given a gift from God which is to be used for the benefit of others. 1 Cor. 7:7 (GWT) says, "Each person has a special gift from God, and these gifts vary from person to person." Things that just come natural to you are in fact gifts God has given you. Your gift is the key to your success, both in life and in ministry. Prov. 18:16 (BSB) says, "A man's gift opens doors for him, and brings him before great men." Live your life by using your gift to build up and encourage those around you all for the purpose of bringing glory to God.

Paul told Timothy to "stir up the gift of God which is in you" (2 Tim. 1:6). The Message Bible says, "Keep that ablaze! God doesn't want us to be shy with His gifts, but bold and loving and sensible." Look around and you'll see problems all over the world. Your assignment is to solve one of those problems. Everything God makes is a solution to a problem. A dentist solves teeth problems and a lawyer solves legal problems. God created you which means you also are a solution to a problem. Find out what that problem is, find out what bothers you the most, and you will find what your assignment is. There are two things you must always do. You must maintain your communication with God at all times, and you must do what's best for others in every situation. 1 Cor. 10:24 says, "Let no one seek his own, but each one the other's well being." The Message Bible says, "We want to live well, but our foremost efforts should be to help others live well." Be motivated by what Jesus said in Matt. 25:40 (NIV), "Whatever you did for one of the least of these my brothers and sisters of Mine, you did for Me."

To fulfill your assignment, you must forever be ready for change. Be flexible and prepared to do what you've never done before and go to places you've never been. Jesus told the rich young ruler to sell everything he had and come follow Him. The young man walked away sad because he had great riches. What was his problem? He wasn't ready for change. It is a fact that God will send you to places if you're willing to go, places you've never thought of going. Don't be alarmed by this but welcome this God-given opportunity with opened arms. Isaiah was willing to go and he was used in a powerful way. Your assignment may also seem small and not very significant but do it anyway. Your obedience may be the link in a long chain of miracles. God may have you talk to a person who seems to be a worthless nobody but because of your words that person may go on to be the next Billy Graham. You may never know the end result of what God has you do but He knows. This is why you need to get the plan for your life and trust Him to do mighty things because of your obedience.

Get the plan! Seize the day! Unclutter your life and stay focused on what God has told you to do. Paul said, "But one thing I do, forgetting those things which are behind and reaching forward to those things which are ahead" (Phil. 3:13). The Message Bible says, "I've got my eye on the goal. I'm off and running, and I'm not turning back." Never minimize the importance of your assignment and do not despise the day of small beginnings (Zech. 4:10). A little boy had two small fish and five bread-like crackers and Jesus fed thousands of people with it. Believe you're making a difference even if you don't see it happen. Phil. 1:6 (NLT) says, "And I am certain that God, who began the good work within you, will continue His work until it is finally finished on the day when Christ Jesus returns." Paul also said in 1 Cor. 15:58, "Therefore, my beloved brethren, be steadfast, immovable, always abounding in the work of the Lord, knowing that your labor is not in vain in the Lord." The Message Bible says, "Don't hold back. Throw yourselves into the work of the Master, confident that nothing you do for Him is a waste of time or effort."

1 Cor. 12:27 (NLT) says, "All of you together are Christ's body, and each of you is a part of it." Paul is saying that you have a role to fulfill since all believers are part of the same body. The Message Bible says, "Only as you accept your part of that body does your 'part' mean anything." Every person has a place in the body and a role to fulfill. As each person does what they've been called to do, the church in turn will function supernaturally and God will be glorified. The problem is that the devil has blinded the eyes of many believers to the point that they don't know what their assignment from on high is. They don't know what role they're supposed to play. This is why it is so important to

spend time alone with God, talking and listening to Him. He who has ears to hear, let him hear. Remember, the devil is not after you, he's after your assignment. This is why he'll do everything he can to break the communication you have with God. If he can do that, he'll step back because you'll destroy your own life without much effort from him.

The journey you take in finding God's plan for your life is just as important as knowing what your purpose is. It's in the journey where you come to know God and learn how to hear His voice. It's in the journey where you meditate in and confess the Word of God which in turn will cause your faith to grow to an exceeding level. It's in the journey where you'll experience more of God as He takes you from glory to glory. It's in that experience where you'll be made aware of what your role is and how to fulfill it. It needs to be emphasized once again, never minimize the importance of spending quality time alone with God. It's the key to everything that relates to your life. It's the key to you getting to know God, it's the key to your spiritual growth, and it's the key to you finding your assignment and fulfilling your destiny. The journey begins by you giving all that you are as a living and holy sacrifice to God for His glory (Rom. 12:1). He gave His all to you, now you give your all to Him.

The NLT says, "This is truly the way to worship Him." The devil will try to blind your eyes to your assignment by bombarding your mind with the thoughts and ways of the world. Don't let that happen. Turn off that television and stay away from the poison of social media. Rom. 12:2 (NLT) says, "Don't copy the behavior and customs of the world, but let God transform you into a new person by changing the way you think. Then you will learn to know God's will for you, which is good and pleasing and perfect." In order to fulfill your destiny, you must forever strive to be faithful in all you do. Jesus said in Luke 16:10 (NLT), "If you are faithful in little things, you will be faithful in large ones. But if you are dishonest in little things, you won't be honest with greater responsibilities." In the early church, a need rose up and people were needed to meet the need. The disciples said in Acts 6:3 (NLT) "And so brothers, select seven men who are well respected and are full of the Spirit and wisdom. We will give them this responsibility."

God's direction was to find men who were faithful in what they were currently doing and put them in this new role. You also must be faithful whether it be at home, at work, or in the ministry. Understand that God is not as interested in what you're doing as He is in how you're doing it. Do you show up on time for work or are you always ten minutes late? Have you agreed to do something for somebody and forgot that the commitment was made? Do you go stomping off with a bad attitude when your spouse asks you to do something? Be aware that God is watching you. Your behavior shows Him how you will act and behave when it comes to spiritual matters and responsibilities. If, on the other hand, you are faithful where you're now at, no matter how trivial the task may be, then God knows you will be faithful where He places you. Be faithful where you're now at because it prepares you for what God has for you next.

All believers have the privilege of serving their Lord and Savior. Everyone has a call on their life and the key to successful ministry is faithfulness. 1 Cor. 4:2 says, "It is required in stewards that one be found faithful." The Message Bible says, "The requirements for a good guide are reliability and accurate knowledge." The devil will always seek to hinder the fulfillment of your destiny but God is telling you to be faithful and to run your race with endurance (Heb. 12:1). It's easy to start serving God, it's not easy to finish. Most people don't have the tenacity and perseverance to see their commitment through to the end. God takes your commitments to Him seriously. This is why you need to pray and think before you make such a commitment. Jesus said in Luke 9:62, "No one, having put his hand to the plow, and looking back, is fit for the kingdom of God." Let those words burn in your heart. Be faithful in all that you do. The Message Bible says, "No procrastination. No backward looks. You can't put God's kingdom off till tomorrow. Seize the day."

In 2 Tim. 2, Paul teaches about faithfulness by using as an example the actions of a soldier, an athlete, and a farmer. This passage of scripture deals with priorities, discipline, and rewards. As a soldier, you've got to have the right priorities. As an athlete, you need discipline. As a farmer, you've got to expect rewards for all your labor. He begins in vs. 3,4, "You therefore must endure hardship as a good soldier of Jesus Christ. No one engaged in warfare entangles himself with the affairs of this life, that he may please him who enlisted him as a soldier." This is a fallen world and a battle is forever raging between good and evil (Eph. 6:12). You must endure the hardship that comes as the devil tries to deviate you from God's plan for your life. This is why you can't get entangled with the affairs of this world. This is the top priority of a mature believer, one who has grown up and enlisted in the army of the Lord. Paul said in Col. 3:2, "Set your mind on things above, not on things on the earth." Jesus is the "Captain" of the army and it's Him that you've been called to please.

A faithful person is one who has their priorities in order. Jesus said in Matt. 6:33, "Seek first the kingdom of God and His righteousness." Paul said to not be conformed any longer to the pattern of this world but do the will of God (Rom. 12:2). A faithful person wakes up in the morning and says, "Lord, what is Your will for my life today? Use me for Your glory." Get the plan of God and then go out and do what He tells you to do. 2 Tim. 2:5 says, "And also if anyone competes in athletics, he is not crowned unless he competes according to the rules." It takes strict discipline to obey the rules of the game. You find out what the rules of life are by getting alone with God and meditating in His Word day and night. Paul is saying if you don't follow the rules, you're out of the game. If God tells you to do something, don't go off and do something else. Don't think your way is better than His way. Prov. 3:5,6 says, "Trust in the Lord with all your heart and lean not on your own understanding; In all your ways acknowledge Him, and He shall direct your paths."

Faithful believers live in obedience to the Bible. Jesus said, "You are My friends if you do what I command. If you love Me, keep My commands" (John 15:14,15). Discipline yourself and run in such a way that you may obtain the prize (1 Cor. 9:24-27). Paul then says you will be rewarded for faithful obedience. "The hard-working farmer must be first to partake of the crops" (2 Tim. 2:6). The Message Bible says, "It's the diligent farmer who gets the produce." When you work for God, when you serve Him diligently, you will be rewarded for all your labor unto Him, both in this life and the life to come (2 Cor. 5:10). You grow up and live for the purpose of one day hearing God say to you, "Well done, good and faithful servant; you were faithful over a few things, I will make you ruler over many things. Enter into the joy of your Lord" (Matt. 25:21). This will happen if you'll discipline yourself and play by the rules. It takes growth and maturity to do this, to have the right priorities, to have strict discipline, and to live a godly lifestyle.

Randall J. Brewer

-11-

"LIVING BY FAITH"

The purpose of your life is to please God and bring Him glory in everything you do. Spending time alone with Him brings great pleasure to His heart. He is also well pleased when you do those things that bring about spiritual growth. He is especially pleased when you take up your cross and follow Him, when you take on the responsibility of fulfilling your heavenly call. There is, however, one thing that pleases God more than anything else. The "frosting on the cake" of spiritual growth and maturity is to walk by faith on a daily basis. Faith is the foundation spiritual growth is built on. So important is this that Heb. 11:6 says, "But without faith it is impossible to please Him." Living by faith is the only lifestyle that pleases God and Rom. 1:17 says, "The righteousness of God is revealed from faith to faith; as it is written, 'The just shall live by faith.'" The Amplified Bible says, "For in the gospel the righteousness of God is revealed, both springing from faith and leading to faith, disclosed in a way that awakens more faith. As it is written and forever remains written, 'The just and upright shall live by faith.'"

The apostle Paul was used by God in a powerful way. The words God anointed him to write are the backbone of the gospel message. Still, everything Paul said and did would have been of little value if he didn't make living by faith his daily lifestyle. He knew how important faith is and wrote in

Gal. 2:20, "I have been crucified with Christ; it is no longer I who live, but Christ lives in me; and the life which I now live in the flesh I live by faith in the Son of God, who loved me and gave Himself for me." Faith is important to God, it was important to Paul, and it needs to be equally important to you as well. You can't grow up without faith and you certainly can't please God without it. Before you can grow, you need to understand that faith is not a doctrine you learn in some Sunday school class. Faith is a lifestyle, a way of life. It's what dominates your thoughts, words, and actions. It's how you deal successfully with all the situations that rise up in your life. You live by faith because that's how God lives. A child of God always mimics what they see their Father do.

God is a God of faith which means you should be a person of faith also. Back when time began as man knows it, God used faith to create the heavens and the earth. Heb. 11:3 says, "By faith we understand that the worlds were framed by the word of God, so that things which are seen were not made of things which are visible." How did all this happen? Ps. 33:9 says, "For He spoke, and it was done; He commanded, and it stood fast." Imagine you being able to do the same thing. It can happen if you'll grow up spiritually and learn to live by faith. You have been ordained by God to live the same way He does. You have been commanded to follow His example in everything you do. Jesus said in John 8:29, "I always do those things that please Him." Since it takes faith to please the Father, this means that Jesus lived by faith all the days of His life. Paul had a deep conviction that he had to follow Christ's example and live by faith also. He then turns around and tells you to do the same thing. He writes in 1 Cor. 11:1, "Imitate me, just as I imitate Christ." How are you to live? From faith to faith.

Amos 3:3 asks the question, "Can two walk together, unless they are agreed?" How can you and Jesus walk together unless you both agree on where you're going and how to get there? Jesus says faith is the vehicle that will take you to the fulfillment of your destiny and you must be in agreement with that. Jesus lived by faith and you also must make the same commitment to live by faith. God says "the just shall live by faith" (Heb. 10:38). This is not optional. It is mandatory that you "walk by faith, not by sight" (2 Cor. 5:7). Living by faith is the only way you can please God. He'll accept no substitute. In fact, you can't even approach God unless you first have faith and believe He exists. Heb. 11:6 says you "must believe that He is." Again, faith is not optional. There is no alternative. You must believe! You must live by faith! If what you do is not done by faith, it will not be acceptable to God. It won't be pleasing to Him. Why are you here? For what purpose were you born? You are here to glorify God. You are here to make Him happy. How do you do that? By living by faith every day of your life.

Living by faith is the only way to live. It's "the victory that has overcome the world" (1 John 5:4). The Message Bible says, "The conquering power that brings the world to its knees is our faith." It pleases God when you live by faith for it's what gives you access to all the blessings He has provided for you through the death, burial, and resurrection of His Son, Jesus Christ. Faith is the hand that receives all that God has given. It pleases Him when you're blessed, when you partake of all the riches of His goodness. He smiles when all your needs are met and you walk in divine health. If you want God's best in your life, if you want to make Him happy, then make the decision to live by faith. Allow faith to be in the fabric of who you are, the DNA of what makes you the person God created you to be. Walk in faith, talk in faith, act in faith. So important is this that Rom. 14:23 says, "Whatever is not from faith is sin." If the way you live isn't consistent with what you believe, if you're not living by faith, then your life is going in the wrong direction.

Put your life in the hands of Jesus and He'll take you down the road you should be on. He'll take you down the road of faith. If you're not living by faith, you're not pleasing God. If you're not believing for things you cannot see, you're not making Him happy. Gal. 2:21 says if you don't live by faith, you'll frustrate the grace of God. Remember, living by faith is a way of life. It's what you do. It should be as natural to you as breathing. It should be something you do without even thinking about it. God requires you to walk in faith because it's the conquering force that causes you to succeed in life. Faith contains the power of God that transforms darkness into light, bad into good. There is nothing you can do in the natural to bring these changes into your life. They come through faith and faith alone. Heb. 11:1 says, "Now faith is the substance of things hoped for, the evidence of things not seen." The Message Bible says, "The fundamental fact of existence is that this trust in God, this faith, is the firm foundation under everything that makes life worth living. It's our handle on what we can't see."

Faith is the foundation you stand on and it's all based on how well you trust God. Do you trust Him enough to believe He'll do everything He said He would do? Trusting God should not be a struggle for anybody. Nothing is impossible for Him. After all, He's God. The truth is, people don't doubt God's ability to help them, they doubt His willingness to do so. These people don't know God. They don't know He is a God of love and is forever ready to bless those who believe He will. He said in Jer. 31:3, "Yes, I have loved you with an everlasting love; Therefore with lovingkindness I have drawn you." The Message Bible says, "I've never quit loving you and never will. Expect love, love, and more love!" If you'll believe that, trusting God and living by faith will be the easiest thing you'll ever do. Faith is established on the character of God, which is love. He also said in Is. 54:10, "For the mountains shall depart and the hills be removed, but My kindness shall not depart from you, nor shall My covenant of peace be removed." Live by faith knowing that He is a kind God, a God of love.

Faith is found in your ability to trust God and to receive those things He has promised to give you. People often ask God to give them more faith but that is not what they need. What they really need is a greater revelation of how much God loves them. The most popular verse in the Bible tells of that love. "For God so loved the world that He gave His only begotten Son, that whoever believes in Him should not perish but have everlasting life" (John 3:16). 1 John 4:7 says, "God is love." God doesn't have love, He is love and because of that you can trust Him to help you in time of need. Is. 41:10 says, "Fear not, for I am with you; Be not dismayed, for I am your God. I will strengthen you, yes, I will help you, I will uphold you with My righteous right hand." People walk in fear when they don't believe God is with them. Those who live by faith, however, know there is nothing to fear because God is with them all the time. It's that trust in the love of God that will bring you through any hardship. It's what causes you to rise up and ask, "If God be for us, who can be against us?" (Rom. 8:31).

God wants you to trust Him just as much as He wants you to obey Him. For some people, obeying God is easy. It's trusting Him that they find difficult. When people don't know God, they obey Him for all the wrong reasons. They obey Him because they think He'll do something bad to them if they don't. This is also why they struggle trusting Him. How can you trust a bad God, a God who is ready to bring the hammer down on your head every time you fail? The answer is, you can't trust a God like that. The good news is that God is not that way at all. He is a good God, a loving and kind God. Ps. 103:3 says He forgives all your sins and heals all your diseases. Indeed, He is a good God and your faith will not fail when it's established on the fact that God loves you. Paul wrote in Rom. 8:38,39 (MSG), "None of this fazes us because Jesus loves us. I'm absolutely convinced that nothing - nothing living or dead, angelic or demonic, today or tomorrow, high or low, thinkable or unthinkable - absolutely nothing can get between us and God's love because of the way that Jesus our Master has embraced us."

In the Bible, Abraham is the preeminent example of a person who lived and walked by faith. Rom. 4:12 says you are to "walk in the steps of the faith which our father Abraham had." What made Abraham so special? He trusted God. Rom. 4:18 (MSG) says, "He dared to trust God to do what only God could do: raise the dead to life, with a word make something out of nothing. When everything was hopeless, Abraham believed anyway, deciding to live not on the basis of what he saw he couldn't do but on what God said He would do." Abraham became the patriarch of faith because he trusted God and walked by faith and not by sight. God wants you to walk in his shoes and do the same thing. He wants you to trust Him and believe He'll do the things He says He will do. Is. 55:11 says, "So shall My word be that goes forth from My mouth; It shall not return to Me void, but it shall accomplish what I please, and it shall prosper in the thing for which I sent it." In other words, if God said it, He'll do it. The Message Bible says His word will "not come back empty-handed."

Abraham was a great man of faith because he didn't look at the natural but at the supernatural. Strong was his confidence because he was "fully convinced that what He had promised He was also able to perform" (Rom. 4:21). He trusted God no matter what his circumstances told him. The Message Bible says, "He didn't tiptoe around God's promise asking cautiously skeptical questions. He plunged into the promise and came up strong, ready for God, sure that God would make good on what He had said." This is what it means to walk by faith and not by sight. 2 Cor. 5:7 (MSG) says, "It's what we trust in but don't yet see that keeps us going." Early in life are people programmed to walk according to what their senses tell them. They walk by what they see, hear, feel, and touch. God says to not live that way and it takes a renewing of the mind to walk by faith. It takes a strong determination to do this because daily you will be challenged to be pulled back into a lifestyle of walking by sight. Choose daily to walk by faith for there's far more out there than what you can see with the natural eye.

Faith is having confidence in God. It's knowing He is eternal and all your worldly trials are temporary. It's when you look to the One you cannot see instead of looking at the problems you can see. Faith sees what God can do instead of looking at what the devil has already done. God is on your side and He'll take care of you if you'll only believe He will. Heb. 3:6 (GNT) says, "But Christ is faithful as the Son in charge of God's house. We are His house if we keep up our courage and our confidence in what we hope for." The Amplified Bible says, "And we are His house if we hold fast our confidence and sense of triumph in our hope in Christ." Get a revelation that your body is the house God lives in. You take Him with you wherever you go. This is why with joyful expectation and confidence you can hold on to your hope in Christ until the very end. Deut. 31:6 says, "Be strong and of good courage, do not fear nor be afraid of them; for the Lord your God, He is the One who goes with you. He will not leave you nor forsake you." Look to Jesus for He is the author and finisher of your faith (Heb. 12:2).

When you live by faith, you live with confidence. Because you trust God, you just know that everything is going to turn out for your benefit. Rom. 8:28 (BSB) says, "And we know that God works all things together for the good of those who love Him, who are called according to His purpose." You know that God loves you and He is all powerful. 1 Cor. 2:5 says, "Your faith should not be in the wisdom of men but in the power of God." Confidence will come when you believe in the awesomeness of God and that He'll do whatever you believe He'll do. You've spent time alone with Him and you've meditated in His Word day and night. You've drawn near to Him and He's drawn near to you. You now have the assurance that He is your refuge and strength, a very present help in trouble (Ps. 46:1). You are living in faith and when calamity comes you rise up with confidence and boldly proclaim, "This too shall pass!" 2 Cor. 4:16-18 (MSG) says, "So we're not giving up. How could we? There's far more here than meets the eye. The things we see now are here today, gone tomorrow. But the things we can't see will last forever."

Paul said in 2 Tim. 1:12, "For I know whom I have believed." He didn't say what he believed, but the person he believed in. Faith comes when you seek His face and not His hand. This is why it's so important to spend time alone with God. You want Him more than the things He can give you. The better you know Him, the more you'll come to trust Him. It's that trust in God that faith is built on. It's what causes you to believe the words of Phil. 4:19, "And my God shall supply all your need according to His riches in glory by Christ Jesus." Notice that Paul didn't call Him "God," he called Him "my God." He knew God in a personal way and this is why he said he knew whom he believed. He had a deep rooted confidence that God would take care of him and be by his side every step of the way. David wrote in Ps. 20:6, "Now I know the Lord saves His anointed." The Message Bible says, "That clinches it - help's coming, an answer's on the way." Faith is not believing God will give you something, it's believing in the person doing the giving. You believe in the giver and not the gift.

Ps. 20:9 says, "Save, Lord! May the King answer us when we call." That's confidence, that's faith in the living God. David said in vs. 4,5, "May He grant you according to your heart's desire, and fulfill all your purpose. We will rejoice in your salvation, and in the name of our God we will set up our banners! May the Lord fulfill all your petitions." David could say these things because he was a man after God's own heart (Acts 13:22). He had absolute faith in God and was willing to do whatever God wanted him to do. He loved to meditate in God's Word (Ps. 119:47,48) and he never forgot to thank the Lord for everything he had (Ps. 100:4). Having a relationship like this with God gives you the confidence to believe that no weapon formed against you will prosper (Is. 54:17). David said before facing Goliath, "The Lord, who delivered me from the paw of the lion and from the paw of the bear, He will deliver me from the hand of this Philistine" (1 Sam. 17:37). Where did this confidence come from? It came because he was a man after God's own heart.

David saw the giant defeated before it happened. With faith, you can always see the end result of whatever it is you're going through. Faith has vision. It allows you to see into the realm of the supernatural, to see things not seen with the natural eye. Through faith you can see yourself doing what other people say can't be done. Through faith you can see yourself fulfilling your destiny. Faith allows you to think big and dream big for "all things are possible to him who believes" (Mark 9:23). Is. 54:2 (MSG) says, "Clear lots of ground for your tents! Make your tents large. Spread out! Think big!" You can do this when you're aware of God's presence in your life. It's what compels you to step out on the water while others stay in the boat. David ran toward his giant and you can run toward yours. Ps. 118:6 says, "The Lord is on my side; I will not fear. What can man do to me?" The spirit of faith is a spirit of victory and it's what allows you to step into your destiny. It causes you to press forward no matter what obstacles may be in your way.

A life fueled by faith causes you to leave fear and complacency behind. 2 Tim. 1:7 says, "For God has not given us a spirit of fear, but of power and of love and of a sound mind." The Message Bible says, "God doesn't want us to be shy with His gifts, but bold and loving and sensible." No longer are you limited by small thinking or the opinions of other people. The sky's the limit and you're going for it with everything you've got. Jesus walked on water and you can also if you know He's there beside you. Is. 43:2 (MSG) says, "Don't be afraid, I've redeemed you, I've called your name. You're mine. When you're in over your head, I'll be there with you. When you're in rough waters, you will not go down." Jesus said, "I am with you always, even to the end of the age" (Matt. 28:20). If you believe that, nothing will be impossible to you. You'll do things you've never done before, you'll go places you've never gone. It's time to trust Jesus and get out of that boat. It's time to put action to your faith. Step out on that limb and trust God to keep it from breaking.

Paul wrote to Timothy and said, "I remember your sincere and unqualified faith, the surrendering of your entire self to God in Christ with confident trust in His power, wisdom, and goodness" (2 Tim. 1:5 AMP). The Message Bible calls it "your honest faith - and what a rich faith it is." A rich faith is a faith that trusts in God at all times, in every situation. It's a faith that gets out of the boat with no fear of sinking. Abraham got out of the boat when he left his kindred not knowing where God was going to take him. David left his boat when he ran toward the giant. Jesus also got out of His boat when He allowed those large spikes to be driven into His hands and feet. Why did they get out of the boat? Because they trusted God to take care of them no matter how impossible the situation seemed to be. They had a deep-rooted conviction that God was on their side and He wouldn't allow anything bad to overcome and defeat them. They had faith in His ability and power, in His wisdom and in His goodness.

God wants you to fulfill your destiny. He wants to take you to a place you've never been before. In order to get there, you've got to get out of the boat and walk on the water. It takes faith to do that. It takes a knowing that God is with you every step of the way. People trust in the existence of God but do they believe in His ability and willingness to keep them from sinking? Some do, most don't. Why do people stay in the boat and not do anything significant in the kingdom of God? Because they don't understand that faith and the ability to believe is the most powerful force in the universe. This power is at their disposal but they won't get out of the boat and use it. In other words, they haven't grown up enough. They are still babes in Christ when by this time in their Christian walk they should be teaching others to walk on water. They need to know that all things are possible if they'd only believe. If the possibility is there, they'd step on the water and, with God's help and direction, they'd go out and find a way to do what they've been called to do.

Believing in the impossible is what the power of faith is all about. It's what causes you to climb the highest mountain and swim the deepest ocean. It's what causes you to run faster and go farther than anyone else. Faith causes you to see the manifestation of whatever it is you're believing for. If you're believing for good things in your life, you'll see good things in your life. If you'll believe for the best, you'll see the best. You'll always see what you believe. People who don't get out of the boat don't understand that God gave them the power to believe. God never tells anybody to do something without first giving them the power to do it. People can believe, they just have to choose to do so. Imagine your life without having the power to believe. Imagine not being able to look into the future and not having any dreams to reach for. Imagine not having a destiny to fulfill. Prov. 13:12 (NLT) says, "Hope deferred makes the heart sick, but a dream fulfilled is a tree of life." God gave you the power to believe because this is what He wants you to do. Why? Because without faith it is impossible to please Him.

Randall J. Brewer

-12-

"NEVER LET GO"

If you're going to live by faith, then it will be a good thing to know what faith is. God's definition of faith is found in Heb. 11:1 (YLT), "And faith is of things hoped for, a confidence of matters not seen, a conviction." Faith is having the assurance that something is true. This persuasion, in turn, will cause you to trust in who or what you're believing in. That being said, faith begins when you come to know God is faithful and is completely worthy of your trust. He is totally reliable and Heb. 6:18 backs this up when it says "it is impossible for God to lie." The Message Bible says, "When God wanted to guarantee His promises, He gave His word, a rock-solid guarantee - God can't break His word. And because His word cannot change, the promise is likewise unchangeable." Num. 23:19 says, "God is not a man that He should lie, or a son of man that He should change His mind. Does He speak and not act? Does He promise and not fulfill?" Not only is it impossible for God to lie, it is also impossible for Him to fail. This is the God in whom you are to put your trust.

Faith that is real is a faith in God. He is a loving Father who takes care of His children. This is who He is and this is what He does. It's your responsibility to believe that. If God says He'll do something, then you trust Him and expect it to happen. That's the type of God He is. He is faithful and He always keeps His word. Abraham was fully persuaded that what God had promised, He was also able to perform (Rom. 4:21). He believed in the faithfulness of God and this is why his faith was counted to him as righteousness (vs. 22). The Message Bible says, "Abraham was declared fit before God by trusting God to set him right." You live by faith when you have the assurance that God will keep His word. Vs. 16 says those who believe "are of the faith of Abraham, who is the father of us all." The Message Bible says, "He is our faith father." When you believe in the same God Abraham believed in, and believe the same way, you also will be set right with God. You'll please Him and, because you're living in faith, you can have the firm persuasion that there is nothing He won't do for you.

Rom. 4:20 says, "He did not waver at the promise of God through unbelief, but was strengthened in faith, giving glory to God." The Good News Translation says, "His faith did not leave him, and he did not doubt God's promise; his faith filled him with power, and he gave praise to God." God is honored and glorified when you trust in Him. How can you not trust a God who has never lied or failed? The persuasion that God will do what He promised is the very definition of faith. It's what faith is. Faith never doubts or wavers but is always convinced and assured. The more persuaded you are, the stronger your faith will be. God is glorified when you walk in faith because it allows Him to move mightily in your life. His will gets done when you trust in Him. It stands to reason, therefore, that if His will is to be done in your life, then you must know what His will is. How else will you know what to believe for? This is why it's so important to spend time alone with God and meditate in His Word day and night. It's here that you'll learn to hear His voice and discover what His plan is for your life.

Those who live by faith don't debate with God because they know what His will is. Knowing His will makes you stable and strong and puts you in a position to lay hold of His promises by faith. If you question His will, you're not persuaded and faith has nothing to stand on. Don't hesitate to ask Him if you're not sure what His perfect will is for your life or a certain situation you are in. James 1:5 says, "If any of you lacks wisdom, let him ask of God, who gives to all liberally and without reproach, and it will be given to him." God is on your side and He'll tell you what you need to know. He'll give you wisdom that will direct your steps, wisdom that sees the end from the beginning. Vs. 6,7 says, "But let him ask in faith, with no doubting, for he who doubts is like a wave of the sea driven and tossed by the wind. For let not that man suppose that he will receive anything from the Lord." When you ask God something, do so in faith. The Message Bible says, "Ask boldly, believingly, without a second thought." Ask in faith being persuaded that He'll give you the answer you're looking for.

People who waver are not persuaded and their faith won't work. Check up on yourself. Are you sure you know what God's will is? If so, then stand on that. If not, get alone with God until you know that you know what His plan for your life is. Faith begins where the will of God is known. It's only when you are fully persuaded of what His will is that you'll be able to exercise your faith. James 1:8 says "a double-minded man is unstable in all his ways." The NLT says, "Their loyalty is divided between God and the world, and they are unstable in everything they do." This is the opposite of what faith is. Instability is the result of wavering and this is the condition most of the world is in. They don't know who they are, why they're here, or where they're going. Like a wave on the sea, they're being tossed to and fro by the wind. They don't know if they're coming or going. Don't let this describe you. Read your Bible for contained in its pages is the will of God. Be convinced that God will perform His Word, then stand back and watch what He will do for you.

Walking by faith is the greatest adventure you'll ever have. It pleases God and it's what causes you to fulfill your destiny. In faith you'll overcome all adversity and receive every blessing. It's what causes you to hold on and never let go. You have this confidence because God is in you directing every step you take. Heb. 3:6 (NLT) says, "And we are God's house, if we keep our courage and remain confident in our hope in Christ." The Message Bible says, "Christ as Son is in charge of the house. Now, if we can only keep a firm grip on this bold confidence, we're the house!" You trusted God when you got born again, now trust Him for everything else. Heb. 10:23 (MSG) says, "Let's keep a firm grip on the promises that keep us going. He always keeps His word." Vs. 35 says, "Therefore do not cast away your confidence which has great reward." The Message Bible says, "But you need to stick it out, staying with God's plan so you'll be there for the promised completion." Never let go of the promises of God.

The Bible teaches that the just shall live by faith. You do this by holding on to the promises of God and never letting go. Heb. 10:38,39 (NLT) says, "'And My righteous ones will live by faith. But I take no pleasure in anyone who turns away.' But we are not like those who turn away from God to their own destruction. We are the faithful ones, whose souls will be saved." Those who live by faith are the faithful believers who never let go even when the waters rage and the winds blow. They have confidence in, are convinced of and forever committed to, the revealed will of God. They hold fast to their confession of faith without wavering. They never, never give up because they know God is not a man that He should lie. Hold on to the promises of God and don't let go. Have confidence in the God who calms the storm and raises the dead. Be convinced of His desire to bless you and be committed to His plan for your life. Mature believers don't let go and this causes them to grow up even more. Yes, if you want to grow up spiritually, never let go.

God's will is for your spirit to grow stronger and that you learn how to rise up and be an overcomer in this hostile world. This only happens when you walk by faith and not by sight. You'll trust God to the point where you can always be positive in a negative world. When you never let go, you'll have the deep conviction that when the dust settles, you'll still be standing strong. Your faith is built on the rock of your salvation and there is nothing, by any means, that can hurt you. In spite of what you see and feel, you know that God will never leave you or forsake you. That's the power of faith. What's more, your positive attitude will cause people to flock to you in groves. They'll listen as you tell them about Jesus and how much He loves and cares for them. They'll want what you've got and, because you didn't let go, you'll be able to usher them into the kingdom of God. Is. 52:7 (MSG) says, "How beautiful on the mountains are the feet of the messenger bringing good news, breaking the news that all's well, proclaiming good times, announcing salvation, telling Zion, 'Your God lives!'"

Faith is a lifestyle and you need to grow in it as much as you can. The Bible tells you how but first it asks a couple of questions in Rom. 10:14, "How then shall they call on Him in whom they have not believed? And how shall they believe in Him of whom they have not heard?" Paul is saying that you can't believe in something unless you hear about it first. To believe in Jesus, you must first hear about Jesus. To believe the Word, you must first hear the Word. Hearing results in believing. That being said, Paul then writes in vs. 17, "So then faith comes by hearing, and hearing by the Word of God." The CEV says, "No one can have faith without hearing the message about Christ." The Message Bible says, "Before you trust, you have to listen. But unless Christ's Word is preached, there's nothing to listen to." Faith comes by hearing. This is so simple that it's amazing how the enemy is able to confuse people about this. He deceives people into praying for faith and asking God for it. This they do all the time when clearly the Bible does not say faith comes by asking for it. It only comes by hearing what you want to believe in.

Notice that the Bible doesn't say faith comes by reading the Word of God. As important as reading and meditating on the Word of God is, it's only when you hear what you're reading that faith will come. Those who want to have faith need to look no further than their own two ears. Faith only comes by hearing yourself speak out loud that portion of scripture that you're believing for. Faith doesn't come by hearing the pastor at church speaking the Word or the preacher on the radio. Faith only comes when you hear your own voice saying out loud what the Bible says. There's a reason for this. You're going to believe yourself more than anybody else. A deeper conviction comes when you hear yourself say something than when you hear somebody else say it. You just automatically believe your own words more than the words of others. You'll believe yourself more when you say "By Jesus' stripes I'm healed" than if you hear your pastor say it. Your own words go straight to your heart where there will be a strong conviction that what you're hearing yourself say is true.

Heb. 4:12 (NLT) says, "For the Word of God is alive and powerful." There is an anointing that comes with every word of the Bible you hear yourself speak. Faith doesn't come just because of sound waves bouncing off your eardrums. The power of God is involved which causes anointed speaking to turn into anointed hearing. This power goes into your inner man and causes you to be fully convinced that what you heard yourself say is true. You believe that the Word you spoke is true and this is called faith. You spoke the Word, you heard the Word, you believed the Word. This is how faith comes and remains. So powerful is this that the faith you receive is a measure of God's own faith. It's the same faith He used to create the heavens and the earth. The power that said "Light be" is now inside of you. You've been created in His likeness and image and you're to function the same way He does. The words you speak are designed to bring change to the world around you. God turned darkness into light, you can do the same thing.

The words you speak are powerful so watch what you say. People bring havoc into their lives because they don't realize they'll receive whatever they hear themselves say. If they say they'll never get a good job, they'll never get a good job. If they say they're always sick, they'll always be sick. People believe and receive the words that come out of their mouth so be careful what you say. If need be, pray the words of David in Ps. 141:3, "Set a guard, O Lord, over my mouth; keep watch over the door of my lips." If you can't say something good, don't say anything at all. When you do speak, make sure it lines up with the Word of God. The truth is, you can have faith for bad things just as much as you can have faith for good things. Fear is when people say and believe the words of the devil, faith is when people confess and believe the words of God. People are always going to believe in something. Why not believe the things God said? It's the Word that brings life to your inner man. It's what causes light to shine in a dark place.

There is no Word of God that is void of power or incapable of being fulfilled. Is. 55:11 (GWT) says, "My word, which comes from My mouth, is like rain and snow. It will not come back to Me without results. It will accomplish whatever I want and achieve whatever I send it to do." The Message Bible says, "They'll complete the assignment I gave them." Imagine having this much power at your fingertips. You have this power and it's called faith. Even Jesus said in Mark 9:23, "If you can believe, all things are possible to him who believes." Have you considered that maybe one day God would use you to raise somebody from the dead? It's possible. Jesus said it was in John 14:12 (NLT), "I tell you the truth, anyone who believes in Me will do the same works I have done, and even greater works, because I am going to be with the Father." Smith Wigglesworth was used by God to raise fourteen people from the dead. It's not unheard of that He wants to use people today to do the same thing. Could you be one of these people?

Faith is when you believe that God is who He says He is and have the confidence that He will do what He says He will do. Without confidence there is no faith. This is why Heb. 10:35 says, "Therefore do not cast away your confidence, which has great reward." There are many benefits for those who trust God. Heb. 11:6 says, "He is a rewarder of those who diligently seek Him." The Message Bible says, "He cares enough to respond to those who seek Him." God has a plan for your life that far exceeds anything you could ever imagine. The only way for this plan to become a reality in your life is for you to keep a firm grip on your confidence in the reliability of God. That's what faith is and that is what faith is all about. To live by faith you must hold on to this confidence and never let go. Heb. 3:14 (MSG) says, "If we can only keep our grip on the sure thing we started out with, we're in this with Christ for the long haul." Faith is the confidence of things hoped for, the conviction of things not seen. You also need to be steadfast in what you believe in. You can't believe one day and doubt the next.

Stay in faith at all times. You do this by being sure of what you're believing in. Uncertainty is what causes doubt to come in, it's what causes you to be double-minded. Those that waver in their faith will not receive anything from the Lord (James 1:6,7). This is why you need to seek God and study the Bible continually. This is what causes you to know His will and to be sure of His plan for your life. Confidence removes all doubt and defeats the devil every time. People who say "you never know what God is going to do" haven't read their Bible. Amos 3:7 says, "Surely the Lord God does nothing, unless He reveals His plans to His servants the prophets." God will tell you what He's going to do and believing that eliminates all wavering. You trust in Him and this confidence is what causes faith to work. It causes you to receive whatever it is you're believing for. Why is that? Because you're confident God will give it to you. He said it, that settles it. Never let go of that. God does not lie and He cannot fail. 1 Peter 1:25 says, "The word of the Lord endures forever."

Those who struggle with faith do so because they're not sure what the will of God is. This is not the case with you. 1 John 2:20 says, "But you have an anointing from the Holy One, and you know all things." God is saying He will cause you to know everything you need to know. The answer to all your questions is inside of you and this means you have access to unlimited knowledge and understanding. This knowledge comes from the Holy One who lives inside of you. People who are not saved do not have this knowledge and is the reason they have no direction for their lives. The more you grow up spiritually, the more you are able to tap into this knowledge and the easier it will be to fulfill your destiny. Remember, faith is built on the foundation of knowing God's will. You must be sure of what His will is before faith will work. People who pray "if it be Thy will" are willfully ignorant of what the will of God is. They don't read their Bible and neither do they tap into the anointing of the Holy One inside of them.

People who pray without knowing the will of God automatically believe that whatever happens after their prayer must be the will of God. It's because of these faithless prayers that God gets blamed for many things He did not do. They pray, "Lord, if it be Thy will, don't let my sick grandmother die." She then passes away and they think it was God's will that she died of her illness. No, it wasn't His will but He got blamed for it anyway. Faith works only when the will of God is known. 1 John 5:14,15 says, "Now this is the confidence that we have in Him, that if we ask anything according to His will, He hears us. And if we know He hears us, whatever we ask, we know that we have the petitions that we asked of Him." The requirement for confident praying is to know the will of God. These are the prayers God hears and answers. Mark 11:24 says, "Therefore I say to you, whatever things you ask when you pray, believe that you receive them, and you shall have them." Never let go of that promise.

Walking by faith brings with it a great reward and 2 John 8 (MSG) says, "I want you to get every reward you have coming to you." Heb. 11:6 says you must believe that God rewards those who diligently seek Him just as much as you believe that He exists. These two beliefs go together. God is real and He rewards those "who make a serious search for Him" (BBE). Faith is not passive. You can't sit back and wait for things to happen on their own. No, faith is an action. It steps out, it seeks, it searches, it moves forward. It causes you to draw near to God believing He'll draw near to you. Most Christians will tell you who God is but few by comparison will tell you what God does. They won't tell you that He rewards those who do something, those who step out and search for Him. Yes, God will reward you. He'll bring results into your life if you'll get alone with Him and seek Him out. You must believe that! Every time you talk to Him and every time you read your Bible, you must believe that a great reward is coming your way. The Message Bible says, "He cares enough to respond to those who seek Him."

Jesus said, "Seek, and you will find" (Matt. 7:7). God will reward your faith by causing you to find what you're searching for. Matt. 5:6 says, "Blessed are those who hunger and thirst for righteousness, for they shall be filled." Are you seeking for health in your body? Through faith you'll find it. Are you looking for a new job? Walk by faith and God will reward you with one. He'll open doors that no man or devil can close. He'll provide everything you need to accomplish what He wants done in your life. Remember, faith is an action. When you act on what you believe, when you trust and obey, you will receive the petition asked of God. It all starts with you. You act first, and then God will act. At the Red Sea, God told Moses, "Why do you cry to Me? Tell the children of Israel to go forward" (Ex. 14:15). Before the waters were divided, the people had to do something first. They had to go forward. They had to get out of the boat. They acted first and then a great miracle happened. They were rewarded for their actions. They crossed through the sea on dry ground and on that day they saw the salvation of the Lord (vs. 13).

People who are grown up spiritually don't ask God to move the mountain in their life. No, they speak to the mountain and move it themselves (Mark 11:23). They do that because they know inside of them is a measure of the same faith God used to create the universe. Babes in Christ need to understand that God will not do what He told them to do. It's their responsibility to grow up, to step forward and speak to the mountain. Never beg God to do something He's already done or something He told you to do. Speak to your problem and believe what you say will come to pass. Mark 11:22 says, "Have faith in God." The Aramaic Bible in Plain English says, "May the faith of God be in you." God spoke things into existence and, when you have the God-kind of faith, you can do the same thing. The Message Bible says, "Embrace this God-life. Really embrace it, and nothing will be too much for you." Stand on the foundation of faith. Never let go of the things God said you can have. Speak to your mountain and watch it be cast into the sea.

What if you speak to the mountain and it doesn't move? First of all, you can't move a mountain with molehill faith. You need to first speak to and remove the molehill. You then grow up spiritually until you reach the point where you have mountain-moving faith. Faith is a lifestyle, a journey, and along the way you need to do what Paul said in 2 Cor. 13:5 (NLT), "Examine yourselves to see if your faith is genuine. Test yourselves." You say you're living by faith but are you really? The Message Bible says, "Test yourselves to make sure you are solid in the faith. Don't drift along taking everything for granted. Give yourselves regular checkups. You need firsthand evidence, not mere hearsay, that Jesus Christ is in you. Test it out. If you fail the test, do something about it." People say "I believe" all the time but that doesn't mean they're in faith. Faith comes by hearing the anointed

Word of God, not by hearing you say "I believe." Don't say "I believe I'm healed" but instead confess the Word and say "By Jesus' stripes I'm healed" (1 Peter 2:24). See the difference? Confessing the Word brings faith, saying what you believe doesn't.

2 Tim. 1:5 talks about a faith that is real and genuine. There is a real faith and there is a pretend faith. Just because a person says they're in faith doesn't mean they really are. Paul said to examine yourself to see if your faith is real or pretend. If you say you're believing something, what is it based on? Faith is always built on a firm foundation. Faith in God is based on what you have heard from Him. Babes who think they can believe for whatever they want have misinterpreted the meaning of scripture. 1 John 5:14 says, "If we ask according to His will, He hears us." Faith comes by hearing what God wants you to have. You must have a personal word from God or a scripture to stand on in order to rightfully believe for something. Just because the Bible says you can have whatever you say (Mark 11:23) does not mean you can believe for your neighbor to give you his car. What is that belief based on? Certainly not the Word. No, that is a pretend faith, a faith built on one's foolish desires and not the Word of God. Paul said you need to examine yourself. If you're believing for something, what is it based on? The answer determines if your faith is real or genuine.

-13-

"JOY IN BELIEVING"

Everybody faces challenges in this world and this is why people need to grow up and have a faith that is alive and active. Nobody can deny that problems are inevitable. They come to everybody. They come to the good and bad, the strong and weak, the rich and poor. People in generations past were more adapt to confront and handle their problems than those living in today's world. People today are squeamish when problems arise and they go around complaining that life isn't fair instead of rising up and doing something about it. Phil. 2:12 says to "work out your own salvation with fear and trembling." People today are too spoiled with their smart phones and remote controls and microwaves that the word "work" is a foreign concept to them. The young millennials of today are not being trained to work hard but instead are being programmed to take the easy way out, to take the path of least resistance. Sad to say, these are the same people who will be running this world in a very short time. God help us.

Believers who want to grow up spiritually need to step away from this type of thinking. Maturing in the things of God is like going to the gym and working out. It takes hard work and effort for muscles to grow big and strong. Any bodybuilder will tell you that "no pain, no gain" is a truth that cannot be denied. And so it will be for those who want to grow up spiritually. For the born again believer, growing up is not an option. You are commanded to do it and, yes, it will take hard work. 2 Peter 3:18 (TLB) says, "But grow in spiritual strength and become better acquainted with our Lord and Savior Jesus Christ." You must learn at the start of your spiritual journey that you'll get out of your walk with Jesus what you put into it. Little effort brings little reward whereas great effort brings great reward. 1 Tim. 4:7 (CEV) says, "Don't have anything to do with worthless, senseless stories. Work hard to be truly religious." The NLT says, "Train yourself to be godly." The Living Bible says, "Spend your time and energy in the exercise of keeping spiritually fit."

The Greek word for "spiritually fit" is "gymasia" and is where the word "gymnasium" comes from. Paul is saying to exercise yourself spiritually for it will help you grow strong in faith and character. The stark reality of life is that not everybody who grows old, grows up. Some people are lazy and don't want to put in the work and effort that spiritual growth requires. There are others, however, who want to grow up but don't know how. It is for these people that God devoted an entire book in the New Testament to the subject of spiritual maturity. This vitally important requirement for godly living is the central theme of the book of James. God wants you to grow up in your walk with Him and James tells you how to do it. As you read this book and apply its principles to your life, James 1:4 (Phillips) says, "You will find you have become men of mature character, men of integrity with no weak spots." This should be the goal and desire of every born again believer."

Jesus had four half-brothers of whom James was the youngest. He was raised with Jesus but at first he did not recognize Him for who He was (John 7:5). He saw many of the miracles Jesus did but still he did not understand the nature or the destiny of his older brother. It was not until after the resurrection that James accepted Jesus as his Lord and Savior (1 Cor. 15:7). James was in the upper room on the day of Pentecost when all who were there were filled with the Holy Spirit. He succeeded Peter as pastor of the church in Jerusalem for he had become a man of profound wisdom and maturity. James literally called himself the servant of the Lord, as did Peter and Paul in their writings. He was saying that he no longer had the right to think or act independently of his Master. He surrendered his will to the will of God and was now a golden vessel through which the Holy Spirit could flow. His life is a testimony to the transforming power of God.

The book of James was written a few short years after Jesus ascended into heaven, somewhere between 45-49 A.D. It's the first book written in the New Testament and is one of the most practical books in all the Bible. It's purpose is to get believers to grow up and have a faith that works, a faith that brings transformation into your life, a faith that makes an impact on the things you say and do. It's down to earth and the good thing about this book is that it doesn't leave you guessing. James is a pastor and fifty-four times in only a hundred and eight verses he uses his spiritual authority to tell you to do something. He commands you to do things that will cause you to grow up and be mature, the result being that you will have a genuine faith that works in your life. Faith is not passive. It doesn't sit in an easy-chair all day. No, faith is aggressive. It does something, it works to bring positive changes into your life. If you are truly living by faith, then it should be evident to those around you.

Col. 2:6 says, "As you have therefore received Christ Jesus the Lord, so walk in Him." You received Jesus by faith and you are to continue to walk by faith all the days of your life. Vs. 7 (NLT) says, "Let your roots grow down into Him, and let your lives be built on Him. Then your faith will grow strong in the truth you were taught, and you will overflow with thankfulness." All people need to be instructed on how to live life successfully. James is not a very long book but it contains some of the greatest treasures of wisdom found anywhere in the Word of God. James shows you how to have a living faith, a faith that works and produces good things in your life and the lives of other people. The evidence that a person is living by faith is righteous living and godly behavior. You must do more than just go to church on Sunday morning realizing that this alone goes not guarantee you a free trip to heaven. No, you must walk the walk and talk the talk. What you do must match what you say.

You can grow up spiritually but you'll have to roll your sleeves up and be ready to work. No, life is not fair but nobody ever said it was. Good people struggle while evil people flourish beyond comprehension. The psalmist wrote about this in Ps. 73:1-5 (NLT), "Truly God is good to Israel, to those whose hearts are pure. But as for me, I almost lost my footing. My feet were slipping, and I was almost gone. For I envied the proud when I saw them prosper despite their wickedness. They seem to live such painless lives; their bodies are so healthy and strong. They don't have troubles like everyone else." Interesting enough, the book of James was written to believers who were mostly poor with some of them being oppressed by the rich. James 1:1 says, "James, a servant of God and of the Lord Jesus Christ, to the twelve tribes which are scattered abroad: Greetings." The word "greeting" means 'to greet with a wish of joy and happiness.' James is writing for the purpose of giving his readers joy and happiness in the midst of their trials.

The book of James was a letter written to a group of Jewish believers who were living in a world ruled by the strong forces of Rome. When James wrote to these people, none of the four gospels had yet been written nor had the epistles of Paul. People were hearing about Jesus only from the disciples who had lived and walked with Him. This letter was the first epistle ever written and it was to these Jews who were living outside the land of Palestine. They had been persecuted and scattered throughout the regions of Judea and Samaria (Acts 8:1). This scattering took place after Stephen was stoned to death. The Greek word used here refers to the scattering of seed, a sowing of lives in many places. These human seeds later bore much fruit (Acts 11:19) proving once again that what the enemy meant for evil, God meant for good (Gen. 50:20). These believers were having great difficulties and James knows they have to take responsibility for their spiritual growth. What follows is one of the greatest letters ever written.

After his short introduction, James jumps right into the situation at hand. He pulls no punches when he says, "My brethren, count it all joy when you fall into various trials, knowing that the testing of your faith produces patience. But let patience have its perfect work, that you may be perfect and complete, lacking nothing" (James 1:2-4). The Message Bible says, "So don't try to get out of anything prematurely. Let it do its work so you become mature and well-developed, not deficient in any way." The first command James tells you to do seems a bit irrational but he says it anyway. The NLT says, "When trials come your way, consider it an opportunity for great joy." This is his way of saying, "Don't worry, be happy!" In order for this to make any sense to you must first come the realization that God is not as interested in fixing your problems as He is in fixing you. God can and will use your trials to help you grow up spiritually and become a person of strength and godly character.

How many people do you think consider this their favorite verse in all the Bible? Probably none, the reason being that the culture of today's world has crept in and impacted the church. People are taught to run away from trials and to avoid anything that even looks like a trial. This is even more true of the born again believer. They think they're entitled to a trial-free life, a life that brings nothing but comfort and ease. When trials come, the first thing they do is pray to God and ask Him to remove the problem and make it go away. That makes sense, doesn't it? After all, that's His job. Right?

The problem with that is there is no such thing as a trial-free life. Even Jesus said in John 16:33, "In the world you will have tribulation." The problem in today's church is that people put comfort too high up on their priority list. They don't realize that God has something for them that is far more valuable than their comfort. His plan goes far beyond the fixing of life's temporary problems.

You've got to stop making God your fix-it-up handy man. He'd be a small God if that is all He's here for. No, He's bigger than that and you need to realize He's not here to serve you, you're here to serve Him. James says when trials come to consider it an opportunity for great joy. The word "consider" means to make a decision not based on how you feel but on the grounds of who God is. He's your Heavenly father, your strong tower, the lover of your soul, your shepherd and provider. Your decisions are deliberate and they're based on who He is and not on what you can see with your physical eyes. God's promise is not that you won't have any problems but, in Christ, you can overcome them. David said, "Yea, though I walk through the valley of the shadow of death, I will fear no evil; For You are with me" (Ps. 23:4). God didn't take David out of the valley but He did walk with Him through it. With God by your side, it really doesn't matter where you are.

You are living a supernatural life and you've got to look at the big picture. You have to see things from God's perspective and not your own. He never promised you an easy life. He did promise that if you'll grow up and trust in Him, you could live a victorious life. If you'll allow Him to direct your steps, if you submit your will to His will, you will reach your destination. Understand that trials and chaos is a normal part of life. It's only through struggle that growth and development take place. No pain, no gain. Those who seek to live an easy life never grow up and mature in the things of the Lord. It's only in the storm where faith can grow. Faith that is tested by fire becomes a pure faith, a faith that won't let you down. It's in the storm where you discover God's power to deliver you, that He is an ever-present help in time of need (Ps. 46:1). Overcoming one trial gives you the confidence and capacity to overcome bigger trials. David was sure he could defeat the giant because God had already delivered him from the lion and the bear.

Every trial brings with it the opportunity to advance in life. It's what pushes your full potential to the forefront of whatever it is you're doing for God. Don't focus on your difficulty but rejoice because of where it's taking you. Look at all the opportunities that are being presented before you. Don't look at what you're going through but set your sights on where you're going to. Above those dark clouds the Son is shining brightly. He has answers you haven't even thought of. He'll cause you to stand strong when the waters rage and the winds blow. Trust Him and lean not on your own understanding. God still does the impossible and He's the One you put your trust in. He wants you to use your faith and enter into His rest, to reach a point in your life where you trust Him so much that you know that you know everything in your life is going to be okay. Allow this place of rest to become your dwelling place. Jesus is called Savior because He can save you when you can't save yourself. You may not always see Him in your circumstances but, rest assured, He is always there.

Jesus is not the light at the end of the tunnel, He's the light in the tunnel. During your darkest hour you can say with confidence, "The Lord is my light and my salvation; Whom shall I fear?" (Ps. 27:1). Run to Jesus and He'll give you joy unspeakable. You may have problems but that doesn't mean problems have to have you. No matter how dark your circumstances may be, no matter what you're going through, you can still rejoice in the Lord and enter into the rest of God. Heb. 12:1,2 (NLT) says, "And let us run with endurance the race God has set before us. We do this by keeping our eyes on Jesus, the champion who initiates and perfects our faith." The words "count it all joy" is a command and not an option. In Greek it means to "command with official authority; to govern; to have the rule over." You're not being told to be happy because of your hardship but to command the force of joy to fight against any trial. You must put joy to work for you and rule your situation with godly authority. You can do this if you'll keep your eyes of Jesus.

Being joyful in the midst of your trials bring stability to your hardship. It's what causes you to face up to the challenge, to be strong and never give up. It gives God the freedom to do the work in you that needs to be done, work that enables you to cross the finish line in first place, work that allows you to fulfill your destiny. Run away from the idea that the Christian life is an easy one. Paul said in Acts 14:22, "We must through many tribulations enter the kingdom of God." The good news is that like diamonds that are formed under great pressure, trials present circumstances that in time can bring out the best in you. This can happen if you have the right mindset for your outlook will always determine your outcome. James is saying you can have joy in the midst of your trials if you'll consider first the fact that God has a bigger plan for your life, a plan that goes beyond the fixing of all your problems. God sees "the end from the beginning" (Is. 46:10) and you must do the same.

The word "trial" means 'a piercing; an experience or test of evil; adversity; enticement.' Trials come to all people at all times. They always have, they always will. 1 Peter 4:12 (NLT) says, "Dear friends, don't be surprised at the fiery trials you are going through, as if something strange were happening to you." He goes on to say, "Stay alert! Watch out for your great enemy, the devil. He prowls around like a roaring lion, looking for someone to devour. Stand firm against him, and be strong in your faith. Remember that your Christian brothers and sisters all over the world are going through the same kind of suffering you are" (1 Peter 5:8,9 NLT). How do you stand firm against the devil? With joy! Neh. 8:10 says, "Do not be grieved, for the joy of the Lord is your strength." James is not talking about being happy here. Happiness is the attitude of the soul while joy is a supernatural force in the born again human spirit. True joy finds its pleasure and delight in the Lord and not in people or things in this world. Ps. 16:11 says, "In Thy presence is fullness of joy."

Counting it all joy is like reading the last chapter of a book before you read the first chapter. That way, if the hero of the story gets into any type of danger, you'll know ahead of time he survived and went on to defeat the enemy. In the book of life, you're the hero and by faith you can read the last chapter and see the glorious ending of your walk with the Lord. You win, the devil loses, God is glorified. You can't write a better ending than that. You can have steadfast joy if you know the ending of the story, if you know that God is at work in the midst of what you're going through. For that to happen, you must take your eyes off your problems and put them on God and the plan He has for your life. Is this easy? No, of course not. If it were easy, everybody would do it. It's those who are grown up and mature who are able to laugh in the devil's face when the world seems to be crashing in around them. It's the strong in the Lord who don't worry because they know God is with them.

Paul wrote in 2 Cor. 7:4, "I am filled with comfort. I am exceedingly joyful in all our tribulation." How could Paul say this considering everything he went through? He had his eyes on God and His purpose for his life. He wasn't consumed with his circumstances but with his God. This is why he was able to write in Phil. 1:21, "For to me, to live is Christ and to die is gain." Paul's only aim in life was to bring glory to Jesus, and this he did continually. You also can make a decision to have joy in your trials if you're aware of the victory that's yours. 1 Peter 1:6 (NLT) says, "So be truly glad. There is wonderful joy ahead, even though you have to endure many trials for a little while." This is exactly what Paul is saying. This is what motivated him to write in Rom.

8:18 (MSG), "That's why I don't think there's any comparison between the present hard times and the coming good times." The ESV says, "The sufferings of this present time are not worth comparing with the glory that is to be revealed in us." Paul knew the victory was his so he wrote in vs. 21 (MSG), "The joyful anticipation deepens."

Is. 43:2 says, "When you pass through the waters, I will be with you; And through the rivers, they shall not overflow you. When you walk through the fire, you shall not be burned, nor shall the flames scorch you." The Message Bible says, "When you're between a rock and a hard place, it won't be a dead end." Believing that will put a smile of confidence on your face and the sound of joy in the words you speak. Those who walk by faith do so with great joy. Rom. 15:13 (NLT) says, "I pray that God, the source of hope, will fill you completely with joy and peace because you trust in Him. Then you will overflow with confident hope through the power of the Holy Spirit." King James says "the God of hope will fill you with joy and peace in believing." Most people got this backwards. They only have joy when their problems go away but Paul says God will fill you with joy and peace as you believe. This means that if the problem is still there, you can be filled with joy and peace anyway. This will compel you to be faithful in all that you do knowing it takes persistence to overcome resistance.

There's joy in the journey because there is so much God has for you on the way to your destination. Don't allow the devil to use some silly trial to blind your eyes to the truth. Believing God is fun. There's joy in believing He'll do what He says He will do. Atheists have nothing to believe for and this is why they're always sad. There is joy when you allow your imagination to soar above the clouds. Your faith is up there for you know God will do exceedingly, abundantly above all that you could ask or think (Eph. 3:20). God's not lazy. He's a working God and it's your faith that puts Him to work. This is why He'll always have you believe for something that is bigger than yourself. If you could do something on your own, you wouldn't need God. He wants you to give Him something to do. It's your job to believe and have fun doing it, it's God's job to bring it to pass. It brings God great joy whenever you believe Him for something. It's what pleases Him most. Wake up every day and tell God what you're believing Him for. You'll have great joy if you do, and so will He.

Believing gives you the power to enjoy what's around you. Being cheerful is a duty you owe God. You have a responsibility before Him to have joy in your believing. This is why you should always walk around with a smile on your face. You're believing God for something and it shows. Being excited is a sign your faith is working. Jesus said, "Be of good cheer, I have overcome the world" (John 16:33) and you're doing it. Don't tell people what your problems are, tell them what the answer is. Tell them what you're believing for and smile when you do it. There is joy in believing. You can have joy because you know the day you believe for something is the day you receive it. By faith you always receive something before the manifestation comes. That's how faith works. You can believe for anything if you'll only stop thinking about your problems all the time. Stop thinking and start believing. Then smile about it for there is joy in believing. Yes, there is more joy in believing than there is in receiving. The journey is more fun than the destination. Far more fun!

-14-

"BEYOND THE TRIAL"

Christianity is a way of life and believers are to act in such a way that sets them apart from other people. Those who are born again act one way, or at least they're supposed to, and sinners act another way. Christianity is by far the best life you could possibly live but it's not always the easiest life. Problems will come that sinners don't have to deal with and it's how you handle these trials that will separate you from the rest of the world. Yes, life can sometimes be quite difficult but the good news is that God is still a good God and He is forever on your side. James starts his letter by saying how believers are supposed to react to the trials of life. Trials include adversity, inconvenience, personal suffering, and injustice. Problems can make you or break you. They can make you better or they can make you bitter. It's how you respond to them that makes the difference. You can get frustrated or you can choose to have an attitude of joy. You're not joyful for the trial, you're joyful in the trial.

Believe it or not, problems do have a purpose. By themselves they will not make you a better person but responding to them properly certainly will. God is not the author of these trials but He'll use them to produce in you endurance that will cause you to stand strong through anything. The Greek word used here is "hypomone" which means 'hyper-stand.' When problems come you don't turn to the left or the right.

No, you hyper-stand on the Word of God. Thayer's Greek Lexicon says it's "the characteristic of a man who is unswerved from his deliberate purpose and his loyalty to faith and piety by even the greatest trials and sufferings." Doing this is the greatest mark of spiritual maturity. When you hyper-stand, you keep doing what God called you to do no matter what roadblocks come your way. You keep your eyes fixed on Him at all times. You stand your ground. You become the person God wants you to be. Problems are not good but your benefit from them surely is.

The truth be told, people who moan and groan about all their problems, those who constantly struggle with the pressures of day to day living, have got a serious priority problem. God wants people to focus on their eternal future but all they want to do is worry and talk about what Paul calls "our light affliction, which is but for a moment" (2 Cor. 4:17). The Message Bible says, "These hard times are small potatoes compared to the coming good times, the lavish celebration prepared for us. The things we see now are here today, gone tomorrow." The Bible says your life is like a mist that appears for a little while and then vanishes away (James 4:14). What's your micro-second of a problem compared to all eternity? Why focus on your temporary trials when you should be putting all your time and effort into your eternal future? Your entire life is like the blink of an eye and God wants to use that blink of time to transform you for all eternity. Those who have their priorities set right will allow Him to do just that.

For Christians, there is always more than just the trial going on. There is a work happening that goes beyond the trial you're currently going through. James 1:2,3 (CSB) says, "Consider it a great joy, my brothers and sisters, whenever you experience various trials, because you know that the testing of your faith produces endurance." James says your faith is being examined. God is taking your life and examining your faith. How well you do is found in the way you respond to your trials. Faith is examined in the storms of life, in how well you handle temptation, and how you respond when nobody seems to care what you're going through. The testing of faith through trials is what produces endurance, the ability to remain steady under pressure. You don't give up, you don't lose hope, you don't complain. Endurance is a wonderful thing but its virtue is only produced by going through the storms of life.

When you become an overcomer, inside of you will be developed the character of perseverance. Jesus said, "But he who endures to the end shall be saved" (Matt. 24:13). You need to be steadfast in order to be victorious in this world. James is saying it's the testing of your faith that produces in you staying power, heroic endurance, and spiritual toughness. Stop whining about how tough life is and let the trial do what it's supposed to do. Let it develop in you a trust in God and a steadfastness that never quits. James 1:4 (CEV) says, "But you must learn to endure everything, so you will be completely mature and not lacking in anything." It's by going through trials that you grow up spiritually and develop the character to be an overcomer in this world. Like a giant puzzle, all the pieces of your life will be in its perfect place. J.B. Phillips says, "But let the process go on until that endurance is fully developed, and you will find you have become men of mature character with the right sort of independence."

Deliberately have a different outlook on life when hard times come. Ps. 43:1 says, "I will bless the Lord at all times. His praise shall continually be in my mouth." This is what it means to consider it all joy when trials come. You can rejoice because you know God will give you the supernatural ability to endure and overcome any trial if you'll join Him in what He's doing. This endurance will keep you on the right path when the devil puts detour signs in front of you. The end result of endurance is peace in the inner man, a calm delight that comes from knowing you're being molded and shaped into the image of Christ. You'll have the confidence that you and Jesus can overcome anything the devil throws your way. You've overcome in the past, you can overcome today. You've killed the lion and the bear; you can now defeat the giant that's standing in front of you. You just need to understand that God wants to produce something in you beyond the trial that is of far greater value than Him removing the trial from your life.

God loves you enough to allow trials into your life that will increase your faith. He is a loving Father and He won't let something happen to you that you can't handle. 1 Cor. 10:13 (NLT) says, "And God is faithful. He will not allow the temptation to be more than you can stand. When you are tempted, He will show you a way out so that you can endure it." The Message Bible says, "He'll never let you be pushed past your limit; He'll always be there to help you come through it." Remember, no pain, no gain. Strength only comes by going through difficulty. This is why you never help a butterfly break out of its cocoon. It needs strength to fly and it's developed through the struggle of getting out of the cocoon. You also need struggle to get the strength that allows you to be victorious in this world. Don't complain when a trial comes but endure it with gladness. This trial won't last forever but you'll be a better person because you went through it with joy and thankfulness.

Rom. 5:3,4 (MSG) says, "We continue to shout our praise even when we're hemmed in with troubles, because we know how troubles can develop passionate patience in us, and how that patience in turn forges the tempered steel of virtue, keeping us alert for whatever God will do next. In alert expectancy such as this, we're never left feeling shortchanged." God can use suffering to bring good into your life if you will allow Him to. He sees something you don't see and He's using what you're going through for your good. Don't be a sissy when trials come but stand strong and let God's work be perfected in your life. It's being steadfast that causes you to grow up and be fully mature. Trials don't cause you to grow up but your endurance does. As you meet with God and join Him in the work He's doing in your life, it is then that your trials will bring spiritual maturity and completeness to your life. If you'll remain steadfast, God will refine you like gold and give you a special joy that goes beyond all your trials.

The unspeakable joy and supernatural confidence that James is talking about doesn't come from you being in a trial, it comes from you depending on God in the trial. It comes when you remain steadfast when the storms of life blow your way. None of this is automatic. In order for your trial to make you stronger, you must go through it with God's wisdom and genuine faith. James 1:5 (GNT) says, "But if any of you lack wisdom, you should pray to God, who will give it to you; because God gives generously and graciously to all." There is a connection between your trial and a desperate need for God's wisdom. God is doing a good work in the midst of your difficulty and you'll need His wisdom if you're to join Him in the work He's doing. He is a giving God and He'll give you the wisdom you're asking for. The Amplified Bible says, "If any of you is deficient in wisdom, let him ask of the giving God, who gives to everyone liberally, and it will be given him."

Pray and ask for wisdom. Ask God to tell you what He wants you to learn from this. Ask to see things from His perspective, to see His plan for you through all that is going on. Ask for direction so you can navigate through this maze of problems, for His will to be done and not your own. God does not want you to fail and He gives help to believers so they can successfully face their trials. He gives wisdom that is connected to the trial itself. He'll give you the ability to see the good and the truth in the situation you are experiencing and not just the pain and inconvenience of it all. You must be able to look beyond the trial and see the bigger picture of what's going on. It takes spiritual insight to perceive the true nature of what's happening to you. God will give you the wisdom to do that if you'll ask for it in faith. It is through the prayer of faith that you'll receive godly wisdom and insight. If you'll ask for this wisdom, God says He'll give it to you.

Trials don't bring you eternal blessings but being steadfast through them does. For that to happen, you'll need God's wisdom. Without it, you'll never be able to make a deliberate decision to hold on to the joy God brings in the midst of your trial. The problem most people have is they ask for deliverance from the trial instead of wisdom to go through it. Nobody ever got stronger by having their problems taken away. No, you grow up spiritually by asking for God's wisdom which will give you the endurance to go through it. If you don't have this wisdom, ask for it. The ESV says, "God gives generously, without reproach." The NLT says, "He will not rebuke you for asking." God wants to generously give you wisdom for your trial but He won't force it on you. You must ask for it. You must seek and desire it with all your heart and soul. With that asking comes the assurance He'll give it to you. Rom. 8:32 (NLT) says, "Since He did not spare even His own Son but gave Him up for us all, won't He also give us everything else?"

Asking for and receiving godly wisdom will result in you having joy in the midst of your trial. God wants to bring you to the next level of spiritual maturity through the trial you're in. You rejoice because you know you'll be stronger when you come out on the other side. People who struggle are not asking for God's wisdom. The word "ask" in Greek is a 'continual, purposeful action.' It's the same word used in Matt. 7:7 (NLT) where Jesus said, "Keep on asking, and you will receive what you ask for." You need to ask and keep asking God for His wisdom to bring you through your trial with steadfastness and joy. Get alone with God and meditate in His Word day and night. Ps. 62:1,2 (NLT) says, "I wait quietly before God, for my victory comes from Him. He alone is my rock and my salvation, my fortress where I will never be shaken." Wait on God until He uses your trial to transform you into the person He wants you to be. Be steadfast in your waiting and have joy while you're doing it. Ask for wisdom with focused intent and He'll give it to you.

God is well pleased when you ask Him for His wisdom. In 1 Kings 3:5, He told Solomon he could ask Him for anything he wanted. Instead of asking for a long life and riches, Solomon asked for wisdom and an understanding heart. Vs. 10 says, "And the speech pleased the Lord, that Solomon had asked this thing." Ask for wisdom and believe He'll lead you to that portion of scripture that will tell you precisely what you need to do. For things more personal, be still in His presence and listen for His still, small voice. He'll speak if you'll take the time to listen. In order to receive His wisdom, you must approach God in total and complete surrender. Ps. 111:10 says, "The fear of the Lord is the beginning of wisdom." The CEV says, "Respect and obey the Lord! This is the first step to wisdom and good sense. God will always be respected." The second step is found in James 1:6, "But let him ask in faith, with no doubting, for he who doubts is like a wave of the sea driven and tossed by the wind." God will give you His wisdom but not without your genuine faith.

Heb. 11:1 (NET) says, "Now faith is being sure of what we hope for, being convinced of what we do not see." God will give you what you confidently expect Him to give. If you are going to receive God's wisdom for the trial you're in, you must go to Him in faith that is genuine with no doubting. To those who doubt, James 1:7,8 says, "For let not that man suppose that he will receive anything from the Lord; he is a double-minded man, unstable in all his ways." James is talking about a person with divided loyalties, a person who is not looking to God alone as his source of supply. You can't trust God on Sunday and consult with ungodly friends on Monday. If your loyalty is divided between God and the world, you're unstable in everything you do. This is why you must be sure that your faith is in God and God alone. This is genuine faith, a faith that is real, a faith that works and gets the job done. It's a faith that will bring God's wisdom into your life so you'll know what to do when the storms of life blow.

Don't allow negative circumstances to cause you to doubt the goodness of God or His willingness to give you the wisdom you need. Are you a believer only in good times or can you stand up and trust God when the floor falls out from under you? How you respond during trials is what reveals if you're in or if you're out. Are you a true believer or aren't you? Asking for wisdom is the first step of faith you must take even when you don't know what the second step will be. God will reward you for your faith and many times it's the revelation of what your second step should be. This is how He operates. Ps. 37:23 says, "The steps of a good man are ordered by the Lord, and He delights in his way." Never gamble when it comes to believing God. Don't roll the dice thinking maybe He'll answer your prayer and maybe He won't. People who gamble with God are double-minded and unstable in all their ways. These type of people ought not to expect that they will receive anything from the Lord.

James then tells how wisdom will exalt the poor man and humble the rich man. It is good news that God gives wisdom to both. James 1:9,10 (NIV) says, "Believers in humble circumstances ought to take pride in their high position. But the rich should take pride in their humiliation." What is James saying here? He is saying down is up and up is down. This is called a paradox and the Bible is full of them. 2 Cor. 12:10 says, "When I am weak, then I am strong." The Bible says you are blessed when you are cursed (Matt. 5:11), the slave is free (1 Cor. 7:22), and to die is gain (Phil. 1:21). Even Jesus said in Matt. 10:39, "He who finds his life will lose it, and he who loses his life for My sake will find it." The book of James is a letter telling all people that in Christ they're supposed to live an upside down life. Everything about living for Jesus and growing up spiritually is a paradox. What the world calls down is the way up and what the world calls up is actually the way down.

James is telling you to have an upside down perspective in everything that happens to you. Telling you to have joy in the midst of your trials is an example of this. He is saying you need to see things from God's perspective. How you see the things that are happening to you is what determines if you'll have joy in the midst of your trials. Perspective is everything for it's what impacts who you are, what you do, and whether or not you'll grow up spiritually. Still speaking of joy, James 1:9 (NLT) says, "Believers who are poor have something to boast about, for God has honored them." The wisdom of God helps the poor person see how rich he truly is. James 2:5 says, "Has God not chosen the poor of this world to be rich in faith and heirs of the kingdom which He promised to those who love Him?" James is saying that when you're in a dark valley, you can rejoice because you'll have an experience with Jesus that you won't have on the mountain of success.

A life-changing opportunity comes with every trial you face. During hard times you can have a perspective that far outweighs whatever you're going through. Col. 3:2 says, "Set your mind on things above, not on things on the earth." J.B. Phillips says, "Give your heart to the heavenly things, not to the passing things of earth." This new perspective will cause you to see the unseen and this is what faith is all about. You're clinging to Jesus and you know everything is going to work out in your favor. You don't see like the world sees. You see what God is doing and not what the devil is doing. You're holding onto eternal realities over temporal circumstances. You've got the right perspective and this is what will carry you to victory. There is no way to lose if you'll set your mind on things above, if you'll see things from God's perspective. In this portion of scripture, James is contrasting the financially poor with the financially rich. He is making it very clear that your financial condition should never determine your perspective on life, and especially your life with God.

God is God whether you're rich or poor, high or low. People think He's a good God if their needs are met and a bad God if they're not. This should not be. This is a worldly perspective and not a heavenly one. The Bible says you can be blessed beyond measure no matter what your financial condition may be. Jesus said in Matt. 5:3, "Blessed are the poor in spirit, for theirs is the kingdom of heaven." Being "poor in spirit" means to be humble-minded. It's what drives you into the arms of a loving Savior during times of need. The NLT says, "God blesses those who are poor and realize their need for Him, for the Kingdom of Heaven is theirs." James says it's a blessing when your life is in shambles and all you have is Jesus to lean on. So often it's when your life is out of order that you'll seek Christ with all your heart and soul. This is a good thing and you're blessed when that happens. You're poor in spirit and you recognize your need for Jesus. He'll exalt you when you maintain your desperate dependence on Him.

In order to grow up spiritually, you must be consumed with the things of God. Take your eyes off your problems and set your sights on the realities of heaven. Think about the things of heaven and not the things of the earth. This is the perspective you must have in order to be the person God created you to be. Living in this world is not what your life is all about. Heb. 11:13 says God's people are "strangers and pilgrims on the earth." J.B. Phillips says you're "on the earth as exiles and foreigners." Col. 3:3 (NLT) says, "For you died to this life, and your real life is hidden with Christ in God." What you're going through compares not to sharing in the glory of Christ and His rich inheritance. 1 Peter 2:9 says you are God's own possessions and Rom. 8:35 says nothing can separate you from the love of Christ. This should impact how you feel in the midst of your circumstance. 1 Peter 1:3,4 (MSG) says, "Because Jesus was raised from the dead, we've been given a brand new life and have everything to live for, including a future in heaven."

Many of the trials you'll face are because of poverty or they'll lead to poverty. Recognizing one's true wealth in Christ is the wisdom that helps the person suffering with poverty to have hope. The truth be told, poor people often have a zeal for God that rich people will never have. Why is that? Because it's in the depth of the valley that God's presence changes who you are, and that is something to take glory in. By faith you see Him taking your hand and leading you out the other side. This causes you to draw closer to God and for that you greatly rejoice. If you're struggling financially, then rejoice because all the promises of God are yes and amen (2 Cor. 1:20). This same wisdom also helps the rich man see how poor he is without Jesus in his life. Both poor and wealthy Christians need to pray in faith in order to possess the wisdom needed to deal with their particular life circumstance. Without this wisdom the poor may be discouraged and quit and the rich may be blinded by their wealth and lose their soul.

James next talks about those who are well off financially. James 1:10 (NLT) says, "And those who are rich should boast that God has humbled them." The NCV says, "Those who are rich should take pride that God has shown them that they are spiritually poor." Why should those who are rich have the perspective of being humbled by God? Because when they were poor they needed God but now that they're rich they don't. It is the strong tendency of the rich to trust in their money and not in God. Paul warns against this in 1 Tim. 6:17 (NLT), "Teach those who are rich in this world not to be proud and not to trust in their money, which is so unreliable. Their trust should be in God, who richly gives us all we need for our enjoyment." The Amplified Bible says the rich person gets humbled "by being shown his human frailty." You can't hide behind your riches "because as a flower of the field he will pass away" (James 1:10).

If your perspective in life is determined by how wealthy you are, you may be in serious eternal danger. If you're not careful, trusting in money can prevent you from seeing your need of a Savior. Money can become a god to you and Ex. 20:3 explicitly says, "You shall have no other gods before Me." Jesus told the rich young ruler to sell everything he had and come follow Him. Mark 10:22 says, "The man went away sad because he had many possessions." Jesus responded and said in vs. 24 (AMP), "How hard it is for those who trust (place their confidence, their sense of safety) in riches to enter the kingdom of God!" Having plenty of money is a good thing but trusting in those riches can blind your eyes to your need of Jesus. If you're not careful, great riches can lead to eternal destruction. You need to put your trust in God and God alone. Allow God to humble you, to show you that He is all you need. Boast in your humility, in your desperate need for God. It's all a matter of perspective.

Randall J. Brewer

-15-

"READY TO RUN"

At the start of his letter, James talks about trials, tests, and temptations. These all come from the same Greek word. A trial may be a test that comes in the form of a temptation. This is a fallen world and temptations are everywhere. Jesus knew this and He told people to go to the Father and pray, "And lead us not into temptation, but deliver us from the evil one" (Matt. 6:13 NIV). The Message Bible says, "Keep us safe from ourselves and the devil." A large part of spiritual growth and your success as a believer is going to be based on how you handle the temptations that come your way. Like a magnet, a temptation pulls on your life to do what is wrong. It's purpose is to get you to follow your own desires rather than the desires of God. It was a temptation acted upon that brought about the fall of man. Trials expose what's inside of you. Like a tea bag, it's when you get in hot water that you realize what's inside your inner man. A temptation is a test you must respond to in a proper way if you're to please God and grow up spiritually.

Trials in a Christian's life are very important because it's through trials that a person's faith is proven genuine. James 1:12 (ESV) says, "Blessed is the man who remains steadfast under trial, for when he has stood the test he will receive the crown of life, which God has promised to those who love Him." J.B. Phillips says, "The man who patiently endures the temptations and trials that came to him is the truly happy man. For once his testing is complete he will receive the crown of life which the Lord has promised to all who love Him." James told you to make a deliberate decision to have joy in the midst of your trials, to believe that you are blessed no matter what is taking place. Here he says that the blessing will come when you endure temptations when they come and remain steadfast under trial. This is no ordinary blessing. It's the receiving of God's favor which brings with it inner joy and contentment, things which only God can give.

You will receive God's favor when you persevere during times of trial. You'll be blessed beyond measure when you continue to be strong in the Lord and remain faithful when the storms of life blow. God is smiling on you and that takes you to a higher level than your circumstances. You've stood the test and you are now perfect and complete, lacking nothing. The Greek word used here is "dokimos" and it means 'proven by testing' or 'proven as genuine.' As fire tests and refines gold, so do trials test and refine your faith. It's in the refining fire where faith is proven to be genuine or counterfeit. 1 Peter 1:6,7 (NLT) says, "So be truly glad. There is wonderful joy ahead, even though you have to endure many trials for a little while. These trials will show that your faith is genuine. It is being tested as fire tests and purifies gold - though your faith is far more precious than mere gold. So when your faith remains strong through many trials, it will bring you much praise and glory and honor on the day when Jesus Christ is revealed to the whole world."

God wants to be more to you than a person who can fix your problems. He wants you to draw near to Him because of who He is and not because of what He can do for you. He wants you to seek His face and not His hand. If you'll do that, you'll have the assurance that He will never leave you or forsake you. The two of you will walk together through the valley of the shadow of death. Ps. 91:10 (NIV) says, "No harm will overtake you, no disaster will come near your tent." The

Message Bible says, "Evil can't get close to you, harm can't get through the door." Vs. 13 (MSG) says, "You'll walk unharmed among lions and snakes." With Jesus by your side, you've got nothing to worry about. James says if you'll remain steadfast under trial, you will receive the crown of life. This is a victor's crown as opposed to a royal crown. James is encouraging you to hold on to your faith with your eyes firmly set on receiving God's promised reward. Is this crown worth enduring temptations when they come? Absolutely, positively yes!

Most people don't recognize the opportunity for growth that a trial brings. Their craving for comfort blinds their eyes to the potential before them. They run from trials instead of embracing them and the growth they bring. They don't realize that trials are needed for spiritual growth. Like the growth of a muscle lifting weights, so does faith grow when you stand and face your trial head on. David ran toward the giant and you should too. This will produce in you maturity, godly character, and a genuine faith. Paul said he would glory in his infirmities so that the power of Christ would rest upon him (2 Cor. 12:9). Paul had just asked God to remove a trial from his life, a thorn in the flesh, and God said, "My grace is sufficient for you, for My strength is made perfect in weakness." God was telling Paul to trust Him in the storm. Genuine faith does not always remove the trial but it will carry you through the trial. This is what makes you strong and allows you to give God glory. Growth comes no other way.

God doesn't need to know if your faith is real or not, you do. Wouldn't you like to know how strong your faith is before you run out to face your giant? How you go through trials reveal the condition of your faith. Many people talk the talk but run away when it's time to walk the walk. This means their faith is counterfeit and not real. A trial came and they cried out asking God to take it away. How many people have said, "Please, God, I can't take it anymore"? That's not true. Scripture says God will not let you be tempted beyond what you can bear. 1 Cor. 10:13 (Phillips) says, "No temptation has come your way that is too hard for flesh and blood to bear. But God can be trusted not to allow you to suffer any temptation beyond your powers of endurance. He will see to it that every temptation has a way out, so that it will never be impossible for you to bear it." God still governs human experience. If He says you can remain steadfast in your trials, then believe Him and do what you have to do.

If you're serious about your walk with the Lord, then you must understand that He will take you where you never intended to go in order to produce in you what you can't achieve on your own. That's what a trial is. Your response determines if this is a test you pass or a temptation you give in to. How you handle temptation will either make you or break you. The choice is yours. Unfortunately, getting born again does not remove the ever-present temptation to sin. The sin nature is there and will always be there as long as you're alive on this planet. Notice what Paul said in Rom. 7:22,23 (MSG), "I truly delight in God's commands, but it's pretty obvious that not all of me joins in this delight. Parts of me covertly rebel, and just when I least expect it, they take charge." The reason sin is so rampant in the world today is that most people discover early in life that it's easier to give in to the temptation than it is to resist it. People want to grow up spiritually but they don't want to suffer the fleshly pain of resisting temptation that causes maturity to take place.

The Irish poet Oscar Wilde once said, "I can resist anything but temptation." Most people in the world, Christians included, can relate to that. They feel like they're in bondage with the every day temptations to do the very thing they don't want to do (Rom. 7:15). The word "temptation" means 'to seduce, solicit, encourage to sin.' It also means 'to be tested, examined.' It is not a sin to be tempted to do wrong. People know that but sometimes it's hard to accept and grasp emotionally. They are ashamed and feel guilty because of what the temptation is asking them to do. This is all part of the wicked schemes of the devil so don't be surprised when these temptations come to you. It's all part of living in this sinful world. James is saying to be realistic when it comes to temptation. They're going to come and there is nothing you can do about it. Don't beat yourself up because you were tempted to do something wrong. Jesus was tempted and you'll be also. All people are tempted to sin so don't be shocked when it happens to you.

James has been encouraging his readers to remain strong in trials that come from the outside. He now switches gears and gives a very clear warning about temptations that rise up from the inside. Thoughts of sinning will rise up within you in response to the outward trials you are now facing. You might get angry and do something you'll later regret. That is an inner response to an outer trial. Perhaps somebody hurt you in a deep, personal way and suddenly you want to hurt them back. This also is an inner response to an outer trial. James warns against this type of behavior because he knows there is a tendency to be tempted into sin when trials come. Notice what he says first in James 1:13 (ESV), "Let no one say when he is tempted, 'I am being tempted by God,' for God cannot be tempted with evil, and He himself tempts no one." How foolish it is to say God has a role in a person's temptation to sin. Sad to say, this happens all the time. Prov. 19:3 (NLT) says, "People ruin their lives by their own foolishness and then are angry at the Lord."

Since the fall of man, people have been blaming anybody and everybody for their sin. In fact, they blame everybody but themselves. Some even cross the line like Adam did and say it was God's fault they sinned. James is literally getting in your face and saying don't you dare blame God for your temptation to sin. Don't remotely or indirectly think God is the source of your temptation. God and sin exist in two totally separate realms that can never meet. James turns the tables on those who would blame God and puts the blame where it should rightfully be. James 1:14 says, "But each one is tempted when he is drawn away by his own desires and enticed." James makes it perfectly clear that the origin of a person's temptation to sin is their own sinful desire. James is saying that you must take responsibility for your sin. Your friends didn't make you sin, the devil didn't do it, and certainly God is not to blame either. The person responsible for you missing the mark is you and you alone. Deal with it.

There are three adversaries you will contend with all the days of your life here on earth. The enemies of your soul are the devil, the world system, and your own stinking flesh. Make no mistake about it, the devil is out to get you. Like a roaring lion, he walks about seeking whom he may devour (1 Peter 5:8). He's the accuser of the brethren (Rev. 12:10), a liar and the father of lies, and a murderer (John 8:44). His ultimate plan is to stop a believer from believing and stop a servant from serving. Sin and the temptation to sin are the weapons he uses most. The world around you is controlled by the devil and the evil therein is pulling at your flesh every day. Everywhere you go, the pull to sin is there. However, not all trials come from the world around you. Most times they come from within and this is why people struggle so much with temptation. Rom. 7:18 (ESV) says, "For I know that nothing good dwells in me, that is, in my flesh. For I have the desire to do what is right, but not the ability to carry it out." It's in the flesh where the pull is to do wrong.

When temptations come, you don't have to fall because God has made a way of escape for you (1 Cor. 10:13). This being true, why then do people give in to the temptation and fail? Why do people sin? They sin because they want to. They choose a different path than the way of escape God has provided for them. J.B. Phillips says, "A man's temptation is due to the pull of his own inward desires, which can be enormously attractive. His own desire takes hold of him, and that produces sin" (James 1:14). Sin is attractive to the person who is self-centered while being righteous looks silly and old-fashioned. Sin satisfies the flesh and the problem in the world today is that people are too consumed with themselves. They have the "what's in it for me" attitude and it's this way of thinking that determines the path they travel on. The world says you've got to look out for yourself because nobody else will. This is why people go around wanting to get their own way all the time. They're selfish and they want to appear important in the eyes of others.

Here's what you need to understand. If you're not consciously being transformed by the Word of God, you will unconsciously be conformed to the world. Rom. 12:2 (Phillips) says, "Don't let the world around you squeeze you into its own mold, but let God re-mold your minds from within." Paul is saying to stop allowing the world to dictate how you think, act, and talk and allow the Word to change you from the inside out. What a backward place this world is. They say nice guys finish last and only the good die young. This world is a sinful place because it's been corrupted by the fall of man. Rom. 8:22 (GNT) says, "For we know that up to the present time all of creation groans with pain, like the pain of childbirth." J.B. Phillips say, "All created life groans in a sort of universal travail." This is the world the born again Christian lives in, a world filled with sin and the temptation to sin, a world where people center on themselves and not on God. As a born again believer you can't let yourself get caught up in all of this.

To overcome temptation you must see the world for what it truly is. 1 John 2:15-17 (Phillips) says, "Never give your hearts to this world or to any of the things in it. A man cannot love the Father and love the world at the same time. For the whole world-system, based as it is on man's primitive desires, their greedy ambition and the glamour of all that they think splendid, is not derived from the Father at all, but from the world itself. The world and all its passionate desires will one day disappear. But the man who is following God's will is part of the permanent and cannot die." John is saying the temptation to sin comes from "the lust of the flesh, the lust of the eyes, and the pride of life" (NKJV). Temptations come from the craving for physical pleasure and the desire for physical gratification. It comes through the lust for worldly possessions, a deep craving for everything you see, and through pride and worldly arrogance in your achievements and the things you own.

All three of these were present when man fell in the Garden of Eden. Gen. 3:6 says, "So when the woman saw that the tree was good for food, that it was pleasant to the eyes, and a tree desirable to make one wise, she took of its fruit and ate. She also gave to her husband with her, and he ate." This story shows that there is a progression to sin. You see something, you want it, you take it. After realizing you did wrong, you then try to hide what you did. Gen. 3:8 says, "And they heard the sound of the Lord God walking in the garden in the cool of the day, and Adam and his wife hid themselves from the presence of the Lord God among the trees of the garden." The same thing happened to David when he saw Bathsheba bathing on the rooftop. He saw her, he wanted her, he took her, he later tried to hide what he did. Why did David sin? Because something inside of him wanted to. There was a desire that was being activated by the circumstance he found himself in.

James 1:14 (MSG) says, "The temptation to give in to evil comes from us and only us. We have no one to blame but the leering, seducing flare-up of our own lust." People sin because they want to sin. This is what James is telling you. Temptations awaken inner desires and those who sin follow after them. This is not a normal desire one might have but rather an intense desire, a desire that causes you to want something too much. This ungodly desire consumes you. You're obsessed with what you want to the point that you'll sin to get it. David was so consumed with his desire for Bathsheba that he had her husband killed in order to get her.

The devil uses these desires like bait on a hook in an effort to draw you into a life of sin. He'll get you to be so fatally attracted to what you want that eventually this desire takes the place of God in your life. James 1:15 says, "Then, when desire has conceived, it gives birth to sin; and sin, when it is full-grown, brings forth death."

Temptation is the grandmother of death. It gives birth to sin and sin gives birth to death. That which was so enticing to you has now robbed you of everything of value in your life. It will cause you to lose your family, your ministry, your job, and even your very life. Rom. 6:23 says, "For the wages of sin is death." J.B. Phillips says, "Sin pays its servants: the wages is death." The devil will try to seduce you with things that look very good on the outside, something fun and very exciting. He is trying to lure you away from the safety of self-restraint. These things are very desirable to the flesh but the truth is they are evil and immoral. Sin will control you if you'll let it. Once that happens, it produces death which is separation from God. If you allow the bait of sin to draw you in, you'll fall into its power to control you. If you don't control sin, sin will control you. It's always easier to give in to sin the second time you're tempted if you don't resist it the first time.

God said to Cain in Gen. 4:7 (NLT), "You will be accepted if you do what is right. But if you refuse to do what is right, then watch out! Sin is crouching at the door, eager to control you. But you must subdue it and be its master." The Message Bible says, "Sin is lying in wait for you, ready to pounce; it's out to get you, you've got to master it." Instead of controlling his anger and hostility, "Cain rose up against Abel his brother and killed him" (vs. 8). He was carried away into the bondage of sin because he left the safety of self-restraint. The desire to satisfy his deep anger was the bait the devil used to get him to do this diabolical act. He chose to commit murder over admitting he was wrong in his attitude and behavior. One sin led to another and before long he was snared in its ugly grasp. He spent his life allowing sin to control everything he said and did. One of his descendants also committed murder and boasted of his sin to his two wives (Gen. 4:23,24).

What should you do? Recognize the presence of temptation which means the enemy is near. Satan's ultimate goal is to separate you from God and other believers and that is what sin and temptation is all about. Sin separates, it pulls apart the best of relationships. The devil will entice you to sin and then he'll lie to you in an effort to cover up the consequences of your wrong doing. Acknowledge the reality of what's happening. Realize that Christians usually fall into sin when they fail to take action at the point of temptation. This is why you can't sit still and do nothing when temptation comes. Take action. Pray for strength and wisdom. Seek help from God and other believers. 1 Tim. 6:11,12 (MSG) says, "But you, Timothy, man of God: Run for your life from all this. Pursue a righteous life - a life of wonder, faith, love, steadiness, courtesy. Run hard and fast in the faith. Seize the eternal life, the life you were called to, the life you so fervently embraced in the presence of so many witnesses."

When temptation comes, be ready to run. Remember, God always provides a way of escape. Joseph ran away from the lustful advances of Potipher's wife because he was determined not to sin against God. 2 Tim. 2:22 says, "Flee also youthful lusts; but pursue righteousness, faith, love, peace with those who call on the Lord out of a pure heart." J.B. Phillips says, "Turn your back on the turbulent desires of youth." Always be prepared for a temptation when it comes. Know the circumstances under which you are most likely to commit a particular sin. Perhaps you criticize your boss in a negative way whenever you sit with your coworkers at lunch break. Be aware of this and, if necessary, sit someplace else. Don't risk sinning for the sake of being "one of the guys." Or maybe you're a married man and you've begun to flirt with the petty young female attendant at the local gas station.

Don't destroy your life and that of your family because you can't control the lusts of your flesh. Run from sin and get your gas at a different station. You'll be glad you did.

At the moment when the temptation to sin is at its strongest, God can become unreal to you. The devil doesn't try to get believers to hate God, he tries to get them to forget Him. At the moment of sin, all believers become temporary atheists. God is no longer a reality in their lives and the only thing real to them is that fleshly craving that is so consuming it's eating them up on the inside. In their weakness they succumb to the temptation and moments later everything comes crashing down on them. They weep and say, "What have I done?" while the devil backs away laughing because he claimed another victim. Recognize that sin and temptation is the devil's attempt to pull you away from God so run away from it as fast as you can. Accept responsibility for the times you failed and missed the mark. Stop blaming God and other people for the wrong you consciously and willingly did. You sinned so take responsibility for it. If you don't, you won't be able to resist the next temptation and you'll remain in the same lifestyle of sin until it kills you.

Randall J. Brewer

-16-

"THE BOTTOM LINE"

James is building a solid foundation on the ins and outs of the Christian life. Throughout his letter, James shares and develops the characteristics of spiritual growth and maturity. His words describe the behavior which is indicative of the life that has been conformed to the image of Christ. He covers a variety of subjects that when put together constitute the bottom line of what it means to be a disciple of Jesus Christ. He tells you what to do and what not to do, what to say and what not to say. The description of practical Christianity is found here in these five chapters. He makes these instructions for godly living and spiritual growth easy to understand for which there can be no disagreement or dispute. Christianity is a way of life that goes way beyond the keeping of moral rules and regulations. The primary mark of the Christian life is how one responds to the Word of God. It's the bottom line where one's attitude and conduct is concerned. It's what determines the level of your spiritual growth in the things of God.

James begins his letter by laying a firm foundation on what to do in times of testings and trial. In order to impact your life to the fullest measure, he concludes this portion of scripture with one of the greatest truths you will ever learn. James 1:16,17 says, "Do not be deceived, my beloved brethren. Every good gift and every perfect gift is from above, and comes down from the Father of lights, with whom there is no variation or shadow of turning." James knows that people have a tendency to blame God during times of trial and he wants his readers to know that God is good all the time. The Message Bible says, "There is nothing deceitful in God, nothing two-faced, nothing fickle." James tells you to not be deceived and he then reminds you of the goodness of the Heavenly Father. There is no shadow of turning with Him, never the slightest variation or shadow of inconsistency. He's the same yesterday, today, and forever. He always has been good, and forever will be.

Mark Twain once said, "It is easier to deceive a person than to convince that person they're already deceived." People don't like to admit they're capable of being deceived but it happens all the time. 2 Cor. 11:3 (NLT) says, "But I fear that somehow your pure and undivided devotion to Christ will be corrupted, just as Eve was deceived by the cunning ways of the serpent." At its core, deception comes when you believe the lies of the devil. He told Eve she wouldn't die if she ate of the forbidden fruit when God said she would. She believed the serpent more than God and was deceived. Never listen to and believe the words of the devil. He is a liar and the father of lies. If he says something, it's a lie. 2 Cor. 2:11 (MSG) says, "After all, we don't want to unwittingly give Satan an opening for yet more mischief - we're not oblivious to his sly ways!" James is saying don't be deceived, don't allow yourself to "get thrown off course" (MSG). Draw near to God and He'll draw near to you.

To overcome temptation, you've got to change your focus. Don't focus on what you shouldn't do, focus on God and what you should do. Phil. 4:8 (NLT) says, "Think about things that are excellent and worthy of praise." Run from sin but, more than that, run to God. Flee youthful lusts and follow after the Lord. To overcome temptation, you must be reminded of the goodness of God. Allow the good to push out the bad. Thankfully, He understands the frailty of man and He'll remain by your side even when you blame Him for something He didn't do. He's a good God and He doesn't run away during times of human weakness. No, God won't leave but if you doubt His goodness long enough, it will take root in your heart and disbelief will set in. If you're not careful, you'll soon be running from God rather than running to Him. That's the danger when you question the goodness of God. James is on a mission to make one thing perfectly clear. He is saying that God is good and all good things come from Him.

You must have a rock-solid belief in the unchangeable goodness of God. People who don't have this faith blame Him for the mess their life is in. To these people James is saying, "Do not be deceived." Don't be deceived about where temptations come from and don't be deceived about where good things come from. Temptations come from your own evil desires and all good things come from God. The Amplified Bible says, "Every good thing given and every perfect gift is from above; it comes down from the Father of lights, the Creator and Sustainer of the heavens, in whom there is no variation, no rising or setting, or shadow cast by His turning for He is perfect and never changes." All goodness comes from God. If something is truly good, it originated first in the heart of God. If you believe that wholeheartedly, doubt and blame will flee when the storms of testing and trial appear on the radar screen of your life. Rom. 8:28 (Phillips) says, "Moreover we know that to those who love God, who are called according to His plan, everything that happens fits into a pattern for good."

Be careful what you ask for. What may appear to be good to you may not be good in the eyes of God. You may think it is a good thing to be taken out of a trial while God thinks it's a good thing for you to go through the trial. Seek God's will above your own knowing that only good things come from Him. Trust Him to give you what you need more than what you want. Trust Him knowing He only gives good and perfect gifts that will never wear out, break down, or go out of style. He gives you enduring peace, unspeakable joy, and abundant love. God's nature is to always give that which is right, true, and excellent. Ps. 100:5 (NLT) says, "For the Lord is good. His unfailing love endures forever, and His faithfulness continues to each generation." David invites you to "taste and see that the Lord is good" (Ps. 34:8). Doing this will give you the assurance that something good will come out of your trial because God is good all the time. This is life changing. This is what causes you to grow up and be spiritually mature.

God is good but bad things happen to God's people. Consider Job. He was a just and righteous man yet he suffered pain beyond measure. Still, God put a limit on what the devil could do to him and in the end Job had twice as many blessings as he had before. In the midst of your trial, you must believe that God is good and that He is at work in your life. Join Him in what He is doing. Set aside your own will and submit to His perfect plan for your life. James calls God "the Father of lights" meaning that He "created all the lights in the heavens" (NLT). If God can do that, then surely He is big enough and powerful enough to bring good and perfect gifts into your life, even in the midst of your trials. James is saying to look around you and see how good God has been. He then tells you to look within. James 1:18 says, "Of His own will He brought us forth by the word of truth, that we might be a kind of firstfruits of His creatures." J.B. Phillips says you will be "the first specimens of His new creation."

Salvation is the ultimate good and perfect gift. "For God so loved the world that He gave His only begotten Son, that whoever believes in Him should not perish but have everlasting life" (John 3:16). If eternal life was the only thing you received from God, that would be enough. Thankfully, He doesn't stop there. Rom. 8:32 (ESV) says, "He who did not spare His own Son but gave Him up for us all, how will

He not also with Him graciously give us all things?" How wonderful is that? This is the God you serve, the God from whom all good things come. Eph. 1:13 says, "You were sealed with the Holy Spirit of promise." The word "sealed" means 'a sign of authentic ownership.' This means you belong to God. He saved you, gave you new life in Jesus, and sealed you as His own with the Holy Spirit. If He did all that for you, how can you doubt that He'll bring good to you in the midst of your trials? The pinnacle of all truth is to know that God is good all the time and that all good things come from Him.

James then says, "Therefore, my beloved brethren, let every man be swift to hear, slow to speak, slow to wrath; for the wrath of man does not produce the righteousness of God" (James 1:19,20). These two verses apply to every area of your life, including how you respond to God and His Word and how you interact with other people. James is saying this is what it looks like to be a Christian. J.B. Phillips says, "In view of what He has made us then, dear brothers, let every man be quick to listen but slow to use his tongue, and slow to lose his temper. For man's temper is never the means of achieving God's true goodness." The bottom line is to listen more and talk less. So many times the pressures of life can cause you to do the opposite of what you're supposed to do. Your frustration boils up inside of you and you don't want to hear anything from anybody, including God. You're saved but you're not acting like it. You're mad at everybody and say things you shouldn't be saying.

It should come as no surprise that one of the recurring themes of the book of James is the control of the tongue. In the Old Testament, the book of Proverbs laid the foundation for what James is saying here. Prov. 10:19 (NLT) says, "Too much talk leads to sin. Be sensible and keep your mouth shut." Consider also Prov. 13:3 (NLT), "Those who control their tongue will have a long life; opening your mouth can ruin everything." And then there's Prov. 29:20 (NLT), "There is more hope for a fool than for someone who speaks without thinking." The Greek word James uses to introduce this portion of scripture means literally to "Know this!" or "Understand this!" He's being very exuberant and forthcoming with his words. "Understand this! Be swift to hear, slow to speak, slow to wrath!" This is not a casual word of advice for his readers. No, he's forcibly driving home a point with deep conviction. He is saying to wake up so you'll know and understand what he's saying.

If you're born again, be quick to hear. Listen proactively and have a God-like quality to the way you hear what's being said. Be anxious to hear, have a genuine desire to listen to the speaker with an eagerness to truly hear with understanding. What's being said to you is valuable and worth listening to. If you care enough about God and have a deep desire to grow up spiritually, you'll put down that smart phone and pay attention to what's being said. If you're more concerned about yourself, you won't be a good listener. Know also that people who talk all the time have not perfected the art of listening. This is why James says next, "Understand this! Let every person be slow to speak." Prov. 17:27,28 (NLT) says, "A truly wise person uses few words; a person with understanding is even-tempered. Even fools are thought wise when they keep silent; with their mouths shut, they seem intelligent." The Message Bible says, "The one who knows much says little. Even dunces who keep quiet are thought to be wise."

The more you keep your mouth shut, the less chance you'll have of putting your foot in it. Turn your brain off for a second. While the other person is still speaking, stop thinking about ways to interrupt them so you can give them a piece of your mind. Slow down so you can thoughtfully evaluate what's being said to you. You can't multitask. You can't speak and listen at the same time. So often people speak out before they fully comprehend what's going on. James is saying, "Understand this! Listen more, talk less!" That's the bottom line! He then says, "Know this! Let every person be slow to anger." In Greek, he is saying "to be inactive in preparing your anger." Most outbursts of anger don't happen instantaneously. No, there's something eating at you and slowly but surely feelings of hostility accelerate on the inside. The more you think about it, the angrier you get and the more you prepare to blow off steam. The pressure mounts and like a tea kettle you blow your top not caring who you hurt with your words and actions.

James is saying don't do this for the wrath of man does not produce the righteousness of God. The Amplified Bible says, "The resentful, deep-seated anger of man does not produce the righteousness of God, that standard of behavior which He requires from us." Human anger does not produce the right kind of living that should be evident in all believers. Eccl. 7:9 (ESV) says, "Be not quick in your spirit to become angry, for anger lodges in the heart of fools." The Message Bible says, "Don't be quick to fly off the handle. Anger boomerangs. You can spot a fool by the lumps on his head." You've got to be very careful because if anger is not dealt with quickly, it can lodge in your heart for the rest of your life. Countless people are angry and bitter today because of something that happened forty years ago. This is why Paul said in Eph. 4:26,27 (NLT), "And 'don't sin by letting anger control you.' Don't let the sun go down while you are still angry, for anger gives a foothold to the devil."

The Message Bible says, "Don't use your anger as fuel for revenge." People say hurtful things when they're angry. They're out for revenge and use words to deliver the punishment they believe the other person deserves. James later says the uncontrolled tongue "is set on fire by hell" (James 3:6). David knew this and prayed in Ps. 141:3,4 (ESV), "Set a guard, O Lord, over my mouth; keep watch over the door of my lips. Do not let my heart incline to any evil." David did not want to dishonor God in the midst of his trial. Sometimes the hardest step to take in any endeavor is the first step. When anger wants to erupt out of you like a fiery volcano, the first thing you must do is stop speaking.

Yes, it will be hard but do it anyway. James wants you to understand the need to listen more and talk less. Stop talking and saying you've got the right to speak your mind. You don't. Stop defending yourself and then pray until the anger is gone and God sets you back on the path you should be on.

What should you do next? First of all, admit you were wrong and stop justifying your sin of anger. James 1:21 (NLT) says, "So get rid of all the filth and evil in your lives, and humbly accept the word God has planted in your hearts, for it has the power to save your souls." James is saying to aggressively reject the sin of the world and purposefully receive the Word of God. The ESV says to "receive with meekness the implanted word." A grown up believer is a person who has a living relationship with God and His Word. The pages of their Bible are torn and worn out. Verses are underlined and notes fill the margins. These believers hunger for spiritual food more than physical food. Their Bible is not a book that sits on a shelf collecting dust but is one they honor and respect, a book that determines their thoughts, words, and actions every day of their lives. J.B. Phillips says, "And humbly accept the message that God has sown in your hearts, and which can save your souls." The power is in you but you've got to receive it and put it to work in your life.

Put off your anger and put on speaking the truth in love. Receive the implanted Word of God until it changes the way you react to the trials and difficulties of life. Believe that the Holy Spirit will take the holy Word and give you a holy life. He makes you "a kind of firstfruits of His creatures" (James 1:18). This means you belong to Him for you were bought with a price (1 Cor. 6:20). Jesus is your Lord and Savior which means it is He who determines the direction your life will take. You no longer live the way you used to. James is saying to meekly submit to the Word that has been planted in your heart. For that to happen, you must lay aside all sin from your life. Only you can do this. Repent and stop doing the sin you're doing. Examine your heart and see what's stopping you from hearing God when He speaks. Asking God to reveal your sin to you is one prayer that always gets answered. As you do this, the Word will renew your mind so you'll think differently and, in turn, you'll act differently as well.

The Bible is to direct your steps all the days of your life. In James 1:25 the Word is called "the perfect law of liberty." James is being intentional when he says this. He is saying the Word governs and leads and guides. 2 Tim. 3:16,17 (NLT) says, "All scripture is inspired by God and is useful to teach us what is true and to make us realize what is wrong in our lives. It corrects us when we are wrong and teaches us to do what is right. God uses it to prepare and equip His people to do every good work." The mark of a mature believer is they want God to tell them what to do. The evidence of being grown up spiritually is that you want God to direct your steps daily, to tell you what to do, where to go, and what to say. You want Him to govern everything that pertains to your life. Change is what you're looking for. You want more from God than mere inspiration and good advice. What you want is to be changed from the inside out and this is precisely what the Word of God will do for you.

James has made it very clear that you need to be quick to hear. He now takes this a step further and says to beware of being a hearer only. James 1:22 says, "But be doers of the word, and not hearers only, deceiving yourselves." The Message Bible says don't let "the Word go in one ear and out the other. Act on what you hear!" This may be hard for some people to admit, but there are those who deceive themselves and they do it on purpose. They pat themselves on the back for going to church and hearing a godly message preached from the pulpit. They think they've accomplished something really important but if this is all they do, they are deceiving themselves. James says you must act on what you hear. Then there are those people who go to church because they enjoy the social gathering that's taking place. They go for the fellowship and not to hear instructions on how they're to live their lives. God doesn't want you to just hear the Word, He wants you to obey the Word you've heard. Jesus said in John 8:31 (NCV), "If you continue to obey My teaching, you are truly My followers."

It's not enough to just hear the Word, you must do what it says. People who don't live it out are only deceiving themselves. You can know how to drive a car but, unless you do it, the car won't do you any good. Likewise, knowing the Bible also isn't good enough. You must do what it tells you to do. Your life must be shaped by the content within its pages. There must be some evidence that you are who you say you are, a child of the living God. That evidence is found in your obedience to God and His Word. It's not important how much you mark your Bible, what matters is how much your Bible marks you. It's not about you getting into the Word of God; it's about the Word of God getting into you. Rom. 2:13 (NLT) says, "For merely listening to the law doesn't make us right with God. It is obeying the law that makes us right in His sight." J.B. Phillips says, "It is not familiarity with the Law that justifies a man in the sight of God but obedience to it." People deceive themselves when they think their hearing is the same as doing.

James 1:23,24 says, "For if anyone is a hearer of the word and not a doer, he is like a man observing his natural face in a mirror; for he observes himself, goes away, and immediately forgets what kind of man he was." The person who is a hearer only forgets things very quickly. In a church service, when the minister ends his sermon, most people have forgotten what he said at the beginning of the message. They weren't listening for the purpose of learning how to act properly in day to day living. No, they want to feel good because they fulfilled their obligation to go to church and listen to the pastor for a few minutes. Not only do these people forget what they've heard, what's worse is they forget intentionally. On purpose they set their minds on something other than the Word that's being taught. Their minds are on what they're going to eat for Sunday dinner and which ballgame to watch afterward. Who are these people fooling? Certainly not God.

The bottom line in Christianity is that God's Word has both the power to save and transform you if you'll respond to it and eagerly do what God tells you to do. Sitting in the pew at church only is not enough to satisfy the demands of Christianity and spiritual growth. You must allow the Word to be a mirror to you and not walk away without making the appropriate changes that need to be made. You must be a doer of the Word and not a hearer only. The answer to forgetful hearing is found in James 1:25, "But he who looks into the perfect law of liberty and continues in it, and is not a forgetful hearer but a doer of the work, this one will be blessed in what he does." The Greek word for "looks into" means 'to stoop to look.' It means to stop what you're doing and stoop down to closely examine the details of what you're looking at. It's the same Greek word that described Peter when he arrived at the empty tomb of Jesus. He went inside and looked intently. He saw the grave clothes lying there as he took in the significance of what it all meant.

James is talking about a determined examination in order to absorb the details of God's Word. To look intently and habitually into the Word means you continue in it day after day, year after year. You meditate in it morning, noon, and night. A casual glance will do you little good. You won't grow up spiritually and you'll remain a babe all the days of your life. Just remember that you also must go out and do what the Bible says to do. A hearer hears but a doer acts. The power of God is activated in your life when you do what the Word of God tells you to do. Don't just hear the Word, do the Word. Don't be like those who are hearers only, those who reject God's Word so they can live only for themselves. Your freedom from the bondage of sin comes only when you choose the joy of being willfully obedient to God and His

Word. If you'll do that, James says you'll be blessed in whatever you do. You'll know the truth and the truth will make you free. To know and obey the Word of God is to know what real freedom truly is.

-17-

"GO AND DO"

Many Christians don't like the word "religion" to be used to describe their relationship with God. Still, James says there is a religion that is pure and undefiled before God. James 1:26 says, "If anyone among you thinks he is religious, and does not bridle his tongue but deceives his own heart, this one's religion is useless." The Message Bible says, "This kind of religion is hot air and only hot air." James continues in vs. 27, "Pure and undefiled religion before God and the Father is this: to visit orphans and widows in their trouble, and to keep oneself unspotted from the world." James is writing to believers and is attempting to drain the poison of deception from the hearts of his readers. Jer. 17:9 says, "The heart is deceitful above all things, and desperately wicked." Three times in this first chapter James warns believers about being deceived. Here he is telling the people there is a religion that is worthless and offensive to God. It's when people do good deeds when their hearts have not yet been transformed by the saving power of God.

Jesus was talking to people like this in Matt. 23:27,28 when He said, "Woe to you, scribes and Pharisees, hypocrites! For you are like whitewashed tombs which indeed appear beautiful outwardly, but inside are full of dead men's bones and uncleanness. Even so you also outwardly appear righteous to men, but inside you are full of hypocrisy and lawlessness." These people were putting on a show in the name of religion for the sole purpose of looking good in the eyes of other people. This is the external religion that God has no use for. James does say, however, that there is a religion that is pure and undefiled before God. He is referring to the outward expressions of a life that has been truly transformed by Jesus Christ. He then gives three examples of a life that has been genuinely changed by God. He starts by saying a person needs to bridle their tongue. The power of the tongue is strong and bridling the words you say is like holding back a stampeding horse.

James is saying that your tongue reveals your true spiritual condition. It reveals whether or not you're deceiving yourself and if your religion is useless. Stay away from people who slander and criticize others. Some people never have a good word to say about anybody. If necessary, ask them to leave and not talk to you again. The second example James gives is to visit orphans and widows in their affliction. Don't just visit them but care for them. God is calling you to care for those who are unable to care for themselves. Even more, get down on their level and help them carry their burden right where they're at. Show these people how important they are when the world turns their back on them. Treat them as if they were Jesus who said in Matt. 25:40 (NLT), "I tell you the truth, when you did it to one of the least of these My brothers and sisters, you were doing it to Me!" How you treat these people whom society has discarded reveals the level of your transformation in Christ. It reveals if your religion is worthless or authentic.

The third example is your refusal to let the world corrupt you. Don't allow the fleshly desires of the world to become your desires. Walk away from the love of money and the lusts of the flesh. You're in the world but not of the world. That's the bottom line. That's what pure and undefiled religion is all about. It's when your relationship with Jesus is so real and authentic that every area of your life is transformed. You've presented your life to God as a living sacrifice and are no longer being conformed to this world. No longer do you hurt people with harmful words and no more do you pass by a homeless beggar as if he wasn't there. You've been transformed from the inside out and it shows in your words and actions. You're not like those who go through the motions and living in self delusion. No, you have an authentic religion that is pure and undefiled, a religion that is genuine and acceptable to God, one that is an outward expression of an authentic relationship with the Lord Jesus Christ.

In Luke 10:29-37 Jesus told the parable of the good Samaritan. A man had been beaten up and wounded by thieves and left for dead. A Jewish priest and a Levite came by, saw the man, and passed by on the other side. A Samaritan then came by, a man hated and despised by the Jews, and he took care of the man and helped him receive the treatment he needed, not thinking of the cost. This Samaritan showed mercy on this Jewish man and Jesus said, "Go and do likewise" (vs. 37). He is saying to be a doer of the Word and not a hearer only. Jesus never asks, "How are you doing?" He does ask, "What are you doing?" You know the Word but are you living the Word? Are you doing what it tells you to do? Is your life radically different from the world around you? If you're a Christian, it should be. That's the bottom line, the purpose for which James writes this letter. As the pastor of a huge church, James had a heart for all people, showing no partiality whatsoever. Therefore, he could not keep quiet when he heard that the sin of favoritism was taking place in the lives of fellow believers.

There was virtually no middle class during the time in which James lived. There were a very small percentage of people who were rich and everyone else was poor. Because of their wealth, this small remnant of rich people were almost always treated like royalty and held in high esteem. They received preferential treatment wherever they went and James is shocked that the sin of favoritism had made its way into the local church. So appalled was he that he asks forcefully in James 2:1 (NLT), "My dear brothers and sisters, how can you claim to have faith in our glorious Lord Jesus Christ if you favor some people over others?" The Greek language indicates this question was asked in shock and dismay. James can't believe what's happening because the charge to show no partiality is one of the oldest commands in the Bible. Lev. 19:15 says, "You shall do no injustice in judgment. You shall not be partial to the poor, nor honor the person of the mighty. But in righteousness you shall judge your neighbor." A mere three verses later God said, "But you shall love your neighbor as yourself: I am the Lord" (vs. 18).

God takes this very seriously. He shows no favoritism and neither should you. Deut.10:17-19 (NLT) says, "For the Lord your God is the God of gods and Lord of lords. He is the great God, the mighty and awesome God, who shows no partiality and cannot be bribed. He ensures that orphans and widows receive justice. He shows love to the foreigners living among you and gives them food and clothing. So you, too, must show love to foreigners." In the New Testament, the chief priests and scribes recognized that Jesus intensely followed this command. They said to Him in Luke 20:21, "Teacher, we know that You say and teach rightly, and You do not show personal favoritism." Peter said in Acts 10:34,35 (NLT), "I see very clearly that God shows no favoritism. In every nation He accepts those who fear Him and do what is right." The Greek word for "favoritism" means 'to receive the face.' It means to make a judgment about a person based on external appearance. James is saying if you show favoritism to someone because of their wealth, it proves your actions are guided by evil motives.

James 2:2-4 says, "For if there should come into your assembly a man with gold rings, in fine apparel, and there should also come in a poor man in filthy clothes, and you pay attention to the one wearing the fine clothes and say to him, 'You sit here in a good place,' and say to the poor man, 'You stand there,' or 'Sit here at my footstool,' have you not shown partiality among yourselves, and become judges with evil thoughts?" Vs. 4 (NLT) says, "Doesn't this discrimination show that your judgments are guided by evil motives?" Notice that this rich man came into the church wearing gold rings and fine apparel. He was making a show openly about how rich he was and he wanted to be recognized for his wealth. He came into the church expecting to be shown favor. Sad to say, he wasn't disappointed proving that money still does the talking in far too many churches. It is an offense to God when you honor the rich man hoping to win his favor while you dishonor the poor man because he can do nothing for you.

It is a sad day when the church favors the rich person who is not saved but in truth is an unrepentant sinner. Favor is not what these people need. They need somebody who doesn't care how rich they are to stand up and show them how lost they are without Jesus. God is not against people being wealthy but He is against people showing favoritism to a person because of their wealth. James says when you favor one person above another, you become evil "judges who can't be trusted" (MSG). Those who show partiality are manipulating people for their own benefit. They're being nice to a rich person in hopes that maybe they're return the favor and do something nice for them. A poor person does not have the means to give these people anything of financial value so why be nice to them? As disgusting as this behavior is, the truth be told, it happens all the time. How many men sweet talk their boss at work but talk down to their wives at home? What people don't realize is those they favor most are the very ones who will one day do them the most harm.

James 2:5-7 (NLT) says, "Listen to me, dear brothers and sisters. Hasn't God chosen the poor in this world to be rich in faith? Aren't they the ones who will inherit the kingdom He promised to those who love Him? But you dishonor the poor!

Isn't it the rich who oppress you and drag you into court? Aren't they the ones who slander Jesus Christ, whose noble name you bear?" James is saying you honor the rich man when all he wants is to take you to court and take from you everything he can. The person you want to be your best friend is in fact your worst enemy. Don't judge people based on their wealth or background, their race or gender, their age or education. People hold in high esteem actors and professional athletes based on their achievements and not on who they are on the inside. People are mesmerized and influenced by famous people who have attained success and high social standing, people who don't care if you're dead or alive. Don't worship rich people and definitely don't despise poor people. The truth be told, everybody puts on their pants the same way.

Why do you want to favor someone who wants to make your life miserable? Why honor someone who openly and without shame blasphemes the name of Christ? Why think highly of the rich celebrity who supports abortion and same-sex marriage? These are the very people who want to remove all Biblical principles from the modern day culture. Stop idolizing these people who are lost in sin and trying to damage the kingdom of God on the earth. The solution to all this is to consider Jesus Christ and His glory. Jesus identifies Himself with the lost and the hurting and the broken. He left the glories of heaven to come to earth and walk among the outcasts of the world, those who were the poorest and most pitiful of all sinners. Jesus gave priority to the lowest in His midst and so should you. 1 Cor. 1:27, 28 (NLT) says, "God chose things the world considers foolish in order to shame those who think they are wise. And He chose things that are powerless to shame those who are powerful. God chose things despised by the world, things counted as nothing at all, and used them to bring to nothing what the world considers important."

If you don't treat the poor person the same way you treat a rich person, you are not a doer of the Word and are self-deceived. So serious is this that even your faith in Jesus is brought into question over it. If Jesus is truly the Lord of your life, then you will relate and interact with people the way He wants you to. James 2:8 (NLT) says, "Yes indeed, it is good when you obey the royal law as found in the Scriptures: 'Love your neighbor as yourself.'" Love is more than a sermon you hear on Sunday morning, it's a way of life. Loving your neighbor as yourself is when you consider the needs and concerns of others as important as your own. This is the royal law, the law of the King of kings who said in John 14:15, "If you love Me, you will keep My commandments." Favoritism is a direct violation of God's royal law of love. You can't favor one person without mistreating another. James 2:9 (NLT) says, "But if you favor some people over others, you are committing a sin. You are guilty of breaking the law."

The way you treat people should be an overflow of the relationship you have with Jesus on a continual basis. The time you spend alone with God is more important than anything else you do. It changes you on the inside and as you grow up spiritually it overflows out of you into the lives of other people. You can always tell where a person is in their relationship with God based on how they treat other people. Do they favor the rich man over the poor man or do they treat everybody the same loving way? Micah 6:8 says, "He has shown you, O man, what is good; And what does the Lord require of you but to do justly, to love mercy, and to walk humbly with your God?" The Message Bible says, "But He's already made it plain how to live, what to do, what God is looking for in men and women. It's quite simple: Do what is fair and just to your neighbor, be compassionate and loyal in your love, and don't take yourself too seriously - take God seriously." If you'll do that, you will fulfill the royal law of love.

Make no mistake about it, it is a sin to favor the rich man above the poor man. James says people do this because their motives are evil. They're trying to get something from the rich man and they'll mistreat the poor man to get it. What these people don't realize is that they'll lose more than they could ever hope to gain. Sin separates you from God and this is what happens when you discriminate anybody for any reason. Sin is sin and showing partiality is the same as adultery and murder (vs. 11). Don't show favoritism but love your neighbor, even if he is poor, as yourself. Don't treat your fellow brothers and sisters as being common but as royalty which they truly are. James calls Jesus "the Lord of glory" (vs. 10) and all believers are made in His image. These people are a reflection of the Lord Jesus Christ and their lives have great significance here in this world. God's hand is upon them and they are worthy of your respect and honor no matter how rich or poor they may be. Look at their heart and not the size of their bank account.

What is sad about this show of favoritism is that it took place inside the church (vs. 2), the one place where discrimination should never happen. James wants his readers to know they're all part of the same family, the family of God. Over and over again, James addresses these people as "my brethren" and in James 2:5 he calls them "my beloved brethren." He is saying that family members don't discriminate against one another. All believers are brothers and sisters in Christ and God loves all His children the same, and so should you. The next time a poor man walks into your church, remember that he is your brother in the Lord and treat him in a loving, caring way. He's an heir of the kingdom so see the person and not what he can or cannot give you. This same man has been chosen by God to be rich in faith, the very thing you as a believer should value and treasure the most. In regards to faith, you don't have what he needs, he has what you need, a total trust and dependency on God. Honor the poor man, give him justice and mercy. Treat him as if he was the Lord Himself.

James wants you to feel the weight of sin that is taking place when you favor one person above another. "For the person who keeps all of the laws except one is as guilty as a person who has broken all of God's laws. For the same God who said, 'You must not commit adultery,' also said, 'You must not murder.' So if you murder someone but do not commit adultery, you have still broken the law" (James 2:10,11 NLT). It is a very serious sin to show favoritism in order to get what you selfishly want from people. It is a breach of the royal law of love to favor someone for selfish motives and to disregard others if they have nothing to offer you. Don't let the devil fool you into thinking you can get away with this. No, God will hold you accountable for these selfish actions. "So whatever you say or whatever you do, remember that you will be judged by the law that sets you free" (Vs. 12 NLT). James is saying your motives and actions should be driven by the fact that one day you will stand before Jesus and give an account of everything you have done during your lifetime as a believer.

2 Cor. 5:10 (NLT) says, "For we must all stand before Christ to be judged. We will each receive whatever we deserve for the good or evil we have done in this earthly body." This is a judgment for believers only. You're born again and have passed from death to life. The "judgment seat of Christ" is not about whether or not you're saved, it's about being judged on how you lived your life after getting born again. James is using this judgment as a motivation to get you to deal with your sin. You will one day have to give an account to Christ for your actions and at this judgment there will be both rewards and loss. Every day you should live your life in the light of one day facing Jesus. The Message Bible says, "Sooner or later we'll all have to face God, regardless of our conditions. We will appear before Christ and take what's coming to us as a result of our actions, either good or bad." What you do in your life significantly impacts what will happen to you in heaven. Did you produce good fruit or fruit that was worthless? Did you favor one person above another or did you treat everybody the same?

1 Cor. 3:8 says, "Now he who plants and he who waters are one, and each one will receive his own reward according to his own labor." The Greek word for "reward" means 'just due recompense' and has equal positive and negative uses. You will receive what you deserve based on whether your actions were of value or whether they were worthless. You are going to get back exactly what you are due when you stand before the judgment seat of Christ. Think about that the next time a rich man and a poor man enter your church at the same time. James 2:13 (NLT) says, "There will be no mercy for those who have not shown mercy to others. But if you have been merciful, God will be merciful when He judges you." Instead of giving favor to those you can benefit from, you need to show mercy to those who are in need. You need to learn very quickly that if you're not showing mercy to those around you, there will be no mercy for you when you stand before the judgment seat of Christ.

Jesus said in Matt. 7:1,2 (NLT), "Do not judge others, and you will not be judged. For you will be treated as you treat others. The standard you use in judging is the standard by which you will be judged." How can the body of Christ ignore such a stern warning as this? The Message Bible says, "Don't pick on people, jump on their failures, criticize their faults - unless, of course, you want the same treatment. That critical spirit has a way of boomeranging." How you treat others directly impacts how God is going to treat you. Gal. 6:7-10 (Phillips) says, "Don't be under any illusions: you cannot make a fool of God! A man's harvest in life will depend entirely on what he sows. If he sows for his own lower nature his harvest will be the decay and death of his own nature. But if he sows for the Spirit he will reap the harvest of everlasting life by that Spirit. Let us not grow tired of doing good, for, unless we throw in our hand, the ultimate harvest is assured. let us then do good to all men as opportunity offers, especially to those who belong to the Christian household."

Jesus said you are the salt of the earth and the light of the world (Matt. 5:13,14). This means you've been called to influence in a positive way the world you live in. Inside of you is something other people need. God designed it that way and this is why you are to live in such a way that you are a credit to the Christian life you've been called to live. Phil. 1:27 (NLT) says, "Above all, you must live as citizens of heaven, conducting yourselves in a manner worthy of the Good News about Christ." What is vitally important for you to understand is that you may have what that poor person needs. God may want to use you to be the answer to that person's prayer. The sadness of the situation is that God won't be able to use you if you discriminate that person and want nothing to do with him. Be like that good Samaritan and show mercy to those in need around you. Be fair without partiality and demonstrate by your actions what the kingdom of God is really like. Go and do to others what Jesus has done for you.

Randall J. Brewer

-18-

"FAITH THAT WORKS"

In the field of medicine, it is a common practice for a patient to be given a harmless pill prescribed more for the mental relief of the individual than for its actual effect on a physical disorder. A placebo pill has no therapeutic value and is given merely to calm or please someone who thinks they have to have a particular pill in order to get better. A placebo is given in a clinical context in order to deceive the recipient into thinking it's an active treatment. They think it's real but in reality it's not. And so it is in the Christian world when it comes to faith. Every believer thinks they have faith but do they really? Is the faith they think they have real or is it a placebo faith? Will their faith be there when they need it most or does it lack the power to do what it's supposed to do? People with placebo faith are deceived and will sadly learn when it's too late that what they thought was real was in fact fake. What they thought would help them in time of need is not there and this is what James writes about next in his letter to these scattered believers.

James is a pastor and he cares deeply for the people he's writing to. He knows how the people are living, he's heard the stories, and he's compelled by the Holy Spirit to write this "in your face" type of letter to stir them up. The main theme of this letter, the one thing James wants people to grasp and hold onto the most, is to be doers of the Word and not hearers only (James 1:22). He is saying that if you are truly a doer of the Word, then your faith should be noticed by others. You need a faith that works, a faith that is lived out through your words and actions. If your faith is not producing good works, James gets in your face and says your faith is dead and not real. He really does tell it how it is. Notice that he doesn't say you have to do good works to get saved. Titus 3:5 (NLT) says, "He saved us, not because of the righteous things we have done, but because of His mercy. He washed away our sins, giving us a new birth and new life through the Holy Spirit." Salvation comes by grace through faith and this is what sets Christianity apart from every belief system in the world.

Jesus provided everything you need to get saved by dying on the cross for your sins. He did the work so you wouldn't have to. Eph. 2:8,9 (NLT) says, "God saved you by His grace when you believed. And you can't take credit for this; it is a gift from God. Salvation is not a reward for the good things we have done, so none of us can boast about it." The work of salvation is finished and now that you're born again, you need to become a doer of the Word. A faith that works will cause you to love people more than the physical pleasures this world offers. You'll reach out and help the poor man even when he can't give you anything in return. You'll mow the lawn of the elderly widow who lives next to you and you'll help the single mother with five children buy some groceries. You've been changed from the inside out and it shows in the things you do. 2 Cor. 5:17 says, "Therefore, if anyone is in Christ, he is a new creation; old things have passed away; behold, all things have become new." No longer do you live for yourself but rather for the benefit of others. That's what a working faith does.

James is driving home a point that a genuine faith, a faith that works, is noticeable. People will see by your words and actions that you really have been changed from the inside out. Jesus said in Matt. 7:17-20, "Every good tree bears good fruit, but a bad tree bears bad fruit. A good tree cannot bear bad fruit, nor can a bad tree bear good fruit. Every tree that does not bear good fruit is cut down and thrown into the fire. Therefore by their fruits you will know them." it is so important that you understand you'll be recognized by the fruit you bear, by that which is produced in your life. Jesus also said in John 15:5, "I am the vine, you are the branches. He who abides in Me, and I in him, bears much fruit; for without Me you can do nothing." He then said in vs. 8, "By this My Father is glorified, that you bear much fruit; so you will be My disciples." A disciple is a believer under the discipline of God, a person who does what God tells him to do. If God says to bear much fruit, he'll do everything he can to bear much fruit. It's as simple as that.

James has been very serious as he came down hard on those believers who favored the rich man over the poor man. He made it very clear that the sin of favoritism has no place in the local church and in the lives of individual believers. The point he was forcefully making is that faith in God removes all discrimination. He then decides to remain just as serious as he tells his readers that faith always proves itself by works. Your actions, he says, is an outward expression of an inward faith. Your good works prove that you are who you say you are, a child of God. It is wrong to believe you have to do good things in order to earn God's favor. Learn quickly that your actions don't earn you anything from God. They do prove, however, that you have already received something from Him. True faith will show forth in how you live your life, in the choices you make, and in how you treat other people. James is saying that real faith will show in your actions and the works you do.

James asks, "What does it profit, my brethren, if someone says he has faith but does not have works? Can faith save him?" (James 2:14). If a person says they have faith, James says, "Prove it!" Notice that he is not saying this person has faith but that this person is saying he has faith. There is a difference between having faith and saying you have faith. People everywhere think they're saved when really they're not. Anybody can raise their hands at church and say they believe in Jesus. Is this profession of faith validated by the appropriate behavior of such a claim? Are their words backed up by obedience to the Word, a changed life, and good works? They call themselves a Christian but there is no Christlikeness in their lives. Where's the proof that these people are truly saved? James bluntly declares that without works there is no such thing as saving faith. How about you? Do you have works that prove you're a Christian? What would your neighbors say if asked this question about you?

James' objective is to answer the question, "What is genuine, saving faith?" This portion of scripture is vitally important because it deals with a person's eternal destiny. The most frightening deception of all is to think you have a living faith when in fact you don't. A living faith will be proven authentic in the production of good works. You don't do good works to get saved or to stay saved, you do good works because you are saved. James is saying that if you don't do good works people won't be able to see that you're a Christian. A living faith is a working faith and you are to show others that you're saved by the good works you do. Faith is an action and you're called by God to live out your faith in a fallen world, to "have a walk worthy of the calling with which you were called" (Eph. 4:1). You've been called to take the truths of God's Word and live them out. You are to put into practice what you believe in your heart, to be doers of the Word and not hearers only.

Good works are an essential expression of faith and James is challenging the validity of a faith that does nothing. Is your faith alive enough to show? Do your actions prove that your faith is real, that Jesus Christ is living inside of you, that He is truly Lord of your life? If you have a faith that is not real, if you have a placebo faith, James wants you to know it and be convicted in your heart. He wants your eyes to be opened to the point where you'll do something about it. He wants you to get to where you know that you know your faith is real and that it will be there when called upon. A faith that is real and genuine is a faith that works. 1 John 2:4-6 (MSG) says, "If someone claims, 'I know Him well!' but doesn't keep His commandments, he's obviously a liar. His life doesn't match his words. But the one who keeps God's word is the person in whom we see God's mature love. This is the only way to be sure we're in God. Anyone who claims to be intimate with God ought to live the same kind of life Jesus lived."

Your faith is not determined by what you do, it is demonstrated by what you do. It's an outward response to an inward work. Faith in God and His Word will cause you to act like Jesus, the same way Jesus acted like the Father. Faith must be active in order to be alive. It's conceived in the heart but without action it is never brought to life. Real faith is alive toward others. It helps the orphans and widows in their trouble and turns not its back on the person who is poor. It sees the needs of others and does something about it. Faith is the basis for everything and is the foundation for all work done in the kingdom. It reaches out expecting nothing in return from the person being helped. 1 John 3:16-18 says, "By this we know love, because He laid down His life for us. And we also ought to lay down our lives for the brethren. But whoever has this world's goods, and sees his brother in need, and shuts up his heart from him, how does the love of God abide in him? My little children, let us not love in word or in tongue, but in deed and in truth."

Paul made it clear in his writings that you can't earn salvation by doing good deeds. You are saved by grace through faith. James takes this a step further and says you can't be saved by a carnal belief in God that shows no evidence of this transformation in the things you do. There is no conflict in scripture between faith and works. They work in unison and go together hand in hand. Your actions are the proof of your faith, not the path to salvation. If a person is truly saved, it will have a visible impact on how they live their life. If faith doesn't produce good works then "you believed in vain" (1 Cor. 15:2). Faith is not based on how much you believe but on how well you behave. James asks, if a person does not have works, can faith save him? The Greek word for "save" means 'rescue from great peril, to protect, keep alive, preserve life, deliver, heal, be made whole.' It's the same Greek work the Philippian jailer asked Paul and Silas, "Sirs, what must I do to be saved?" (Acts 16:30).

James is not saying you have to do good works in order to be born again. He is saying that faith alone will not save you from the judgment that comes when you don't do good works and discriminate other people (vs. 11-13). Prov. 3:12 says, "For whom the Lord loves He corrects, just as a father the son in whom he delights." J.B. Phillips says, "No true son ever grows up uncorrected by his father. Can we not much more readily submit to a heavenly Father's discipline, and learn how to live?" (Heb. 12:7,9). The Message Bible says, "This trouble you're in isn't punishment; it's training, the normal experience of children. Only irresponsible parents leave children to fend for themselves. Would you prefer an irresponsible God? We respect our own parents for training and not spoiling us, so why not embrace God's training so we can truly live?" James was saying that if you favor one person above another, God will discipline you. Can faith without works save you from this discipline? The answer is no! You're saved but yet you did wrong. You will be disciplined.

The fact that God disciplines His children is often ignored by most believers. People complain about the negative circumstances their sin brought into their life not realizing that this is part of the Lord's loving discipline. This is not punishment, it's discipline that is a response of God's love for you and His desire for you to live a holy life. God uses these predicaments to bring you back to Himself in sincere repentance. This will strengthen your faith and cause you to have a closer and renewed relationship with Him. 1 Peter 1:14-16 (NLT) says, "So you must live as God's obedient children. Don't slip back into your old ways of living to satisfy your own desires. You didn't know any better then. But now you must be holy in everything you do, just as God who chose you is holy. For the scriptures say, 'You must be holy because I am holy.'" The Message Bible says, "As obedient children, let yourselves be pulled into a way of life shaped by God's life, a life energetic and blazing with holiness."

A faith that works will cost you something. It will cost you time, effort, material resources, and personal investment. It's true, words are cheap. Promises made are worthless unless they are fulfilled. If you speak a blessing over someone, be willing to be the one to bring forth that blessing. When a believer has a need, that need should be supplied by another believer who has the ability to give what is lacking. Sad to say, many sinners refuse to come to Christ because the Christians they know are hypocrites. They talk about God and faith but do little to demonstrate it. With this in mind, James gives an example of faith without works. "If a brother or sister is naked and destitute of daily food, and one of you says to them, 'Depart in peace, be warmed and filled,' but you do not give them the things which are needed for the body, what does it profit?" (James 2:15,16). Faith without works is compared to words of passion without acts of passion. You can say all the religious words you want but without good works to back them up, what you say is meaningless.

Real faith, a faith that works, shows mercy to the less privileged. Notice that these are not unknown strangers who are naked and without food. No, these are your fellow brothers and sisters in the Lord. James is saying there are Christians in the local church who are without food and clothes and other Christians won't help them. It is a despicable thing to think that a well-off believer won't stop to help a fellow believer in need. God feels the same way about faith that has no action. James puts the nail in the coffin in vs. 17, "Thus also faith by itself, if it does not have works, is dead." The Greek word for "dead" is "nekios" and means 'a corpse, one who is spiritually dead.' Strong's dictionary says those who are spiritually dead are "destitute of a life that recognizes and is devoted to God." The Message Bible says, "Isn't it obvious that God-talk without God-acts is outrageous nonsense?" Just as Adam lay helpless on the ground until God breathed life into him, so also faith lies helpless until you act upon what you believe.

Breathing doesn't bring life to a person but it is proof that a person is alive. Likewise, James is saying that good works don't earn you eternal life but are proof that you have life, that your faith is not dead. Another definition for the word "dead" in Greek is 'to be rendered inactive.' The person has faith but it's not working. A dead faith doesn't grow and it doesn't change anything. It's not alive, it's static and not dynamic. It is worthless to the individual because it's dead and doesn't do anything. Faith without works is like a car with a dead battery. You may have a car but it's not working, it's not doing you any good. In other words, nice words with no action is the mark of a dead faith. James is stressing the point that it's good works that gives life and power to your dead battery. It's what causes your faith to work. A living faith accompanied by good works is moving and growing. It's alive and working in your life. The proof that you've been born again is that your actions confirm and validate your faith.

A student of Martin Luther named Philip Melanchthon understood what James was saying and wrote, "You're saved by faith alone but not by a faith that remains alone." He knew that works won't save you but they are proof that you have been saved. When you see a lightning bolt flash across the sky, you automatically expect the roar of thunder to follow. If there were no lightning, there would be no thunder because one causes the other. That's how it is with faith. Just as thunder always follows lightning, good works always follow true faith. James 2:18 says, "But someone will say, 'You have faith, and I have works.' Show me your faith without your works, and I will show you my faith by my works." Faith and works go together like a hand in a glove and James is saying, "I will show you my faith by the good deeds my faith provokes me to do in the name of Christ." Ps. 1:3 says the godly man "shall be like a tree planted by the rivers of water, that brings forth its fruit in its season, whose leaf also shall not wither; and whatever he does shall prosper."

You were created to bear good fruit, to produce something good with your life. 1 Thess. 1:3 (Phillips) says, "We never forget that your faith has meant solid achievement, your love has meant hard work, and the hope that you have in our Lord Jesus Christ means sheer dogged endurance in the life that you live before God, the Father of us all." The New King James Bible calls it "your work of faith, labor of love, and patience of hope." Out of faith rises love. Paul says that faith works and love labors. Labor involves toil, fatigue, difficulty, and persistence. The Christian life is not a walk in the park on a cool, summer evening. No, it's a life of work, toil, and labor. Faith and love take delight when given something hard to do. Eph. 2:10 says, "For we are His workmanship, created in Christ Jesus for good works, which God prepared beforehand that we should walk in them." The Message Bible says, "He creates each of us by Christ Jesus to join Him in the work He does, the good work He has gotten ready for us to do, work we had better be doing."

The Greek word for "workmanship" is "poiema" and is the same word from which comes the Greek word for "poet." A poet has the extraordinary ability to create a literary masterpiece and Paul uses this word to describe what God did to you. On the day you got saved, God put forth His most powerful and creative effort to turn you into a new person. "Old things have passed away; behold, all things have become new" (2 Cor. 5:17). You are a child of the living God and the goal of every believer is found in Titus 2:12 (NLT), "And we are instructed to turn from godless living and sinful pleasures. We should live in this evil world with wisdom, righteousness, and devotion to God." When you asked Jesus into your heart you become a masterpiece, skillfully and artfully created in Christ Jesus. God gave you a new identity. His intelligent genius went into your transformation and there is nothing negative about the new you. God turned you into something spectacular for His best effort went into making you into the person you now are.

You are His workmanship created in Christ Jesus and have been made worthy to bear His name. You are a "poetic masterpiece" and you must now put forth your best effort to do those good works that correspond with you being a new creature in Christ. You are abiding in the Vine and your works are being initiated and energized by the Holy Spirit. Phil. 2:13 (Phillips) says, "For it is God who is at work within you, giving you the will and the power to achieve His purpose." Paul also said in 2 Cor. 9:8 (NLT), "And God will generously provide all you need. Then you will always have everything you need and plenty left over to share with others." Titus 3:1 says, "Remind them to be subject to rulers and authorities, to obey, to be ready for every good work." Always be in a state of readiness to help a person in need. Be prepared to respond when called upon without delay or hesitation. This attitude helps equip you for every good work, to "be a vessel for honor, sanctified and useful for the Master, prepared for every good work" (2 Tim. 2:21).

Never forget, you were created in Christ Jesus to do good works which is a reflection of the new life you now have. Good works are not the root of salvation but they are the fruit of one's born again experience. Faith is the root of salvation and action is the fruit of being saved. Good works make faith visible and useful for God. Still, there are people who think believing in God is enough and that a person can have faith without works. To these people James writes, "You believe that there is one God. You do well. Even the demons believe - and tremble" (James 2:19). Some people have dead faith, others have demonic faith. Believing right things about God is not enough to have a saving faith. Demons believe in the same Jesus you do and they shudder with fear. That's what a cat does when it is afraid. It hunches its back and the hair on its neck stands up. That cat believes he is in danger and that's what this verse says about demons. They know who Jesus is and they know He'll one day be their eternal judge. The truth be told, what the local church needs today are some trembling believers.

Yes, Christians believe there is one God and this is what they should believe (Deut. 6:4). The Message Bible says, "That's just great. Demons do that, but what good does it do them? Use your heads!" Satan and his demons believe in God but have no commitment to Him. They are faithless rebels committed only to themselves. They know who God is but they don't love Him nor do they serve and honor Him. This belief in God will not save them and neither will it save you. If a person says they believe in God and it does not impact their actions in any way, then they are believing the same way demons do. James asks, "But do you want to know, O foolish man, that faith without works is dead?" (vs. 20). He is literally saying, "Pay attention to this! You are a foolish person who seriously lacks understanding." J.B. Phillips says, "For, my dear short-sighted man, can't you see far enough to realize that faith without the right actions is dead and useless?" Having faith in God is supposed to produce actions in your life. James next gives examples of two people who did.

Heb. 11 tells of great faith exploits by people in the Old Testament and fourteen times it said it was "by faith" that they did these things. Their faith was demonstrated by the things they did. Two of these people, Abraham and Rahab, are listed as examples by James to prove "that a man is justified by works, and not by faith only" (vs. 24). Abraham was a male Jew and Rahab was a female Gentile so these two examples cover everybody. Abraham was willing to obey God in offering up his son because of the incredible faith he had in God. He believed that even if Isaac did die that God would raise him from the dead in order to fulfill His promise. Abraham's obedience was a validation of his faith (vs. 21) and his faith was completed by his works (vs. 22). You will not know the depth of your faith until it is tested. If you do stand strong, the testing of your faith will mature your faith. You can talk all you want but if this is all you do, James says your faith is dead.

True faith creates action, it makes things happen. Rahab was a prostitute who hid the spies Joshua sent into Jericho to scout it out before the battle. She believed in the God of Israel enough to take action and risk her life for her belief (vs. 25). Abraham and Rahab both had a faith that works. Do you? Realize that the quality of your life is determined by the quality of your faith. As your faith is, so are you. James 2:26 says, "For as the body without works is dead, so faith without works is dead also." If your faith doesn't produce obedience toward God and mercy toward others, then your faith is a dead faith. You say you love God but do you obey and trust Him? You believe the gospel message but do you share it with others? You go to church but do you serve there and make sacrifices for its growth? Jesus gave His blood, what are you willing to give? You say you want to grow up spiritually but do you spend time alone with God and daily meditate in His Word? Are you bearing good fruit in your life? Are you faithful to do what He tells you to do? Think about it.

-19-

"LIFE AND DEATH"

James is writing a letter to fellow believers and he talks to them about their conduct in various situations. It is his hope and desire that what he says will help these people grow up spiritually and mature in the things of God. He has told them to face their trials with a working faith and their temptations with godly action. He stresses the need to be doers of the Word and to treat everybody the same. He confronts those who say that faith without works is all that is required and drives home the truth that true faith is only alive when it is expressed by doing good works. False teachers were making their way into the local church and many were taking upon themselves the task of becoming teachers without being called by God to do so. James insinuated in the first chapter that people were saying they were being tempted by God while others said it was acceptable to show partiality between the rich and the poor. These were false teachings that are misleading and untrue and James pulls no punches as he deals with this problem bluntly and openly.

James knows that prudence is one of the basic requirements to be a teacher of the Word of God so he says in James 3:1, "My brethren, let not many of you become teachers, knowing that we shall receive a stricter judgment." He is saying one shouldn't rush to become a teacher because they bear the heavy responsibility to teach correctly, to teach the Word of

God the way it's supposed to be taught. There are many false teachers in the world who lead people astray. They teach what another false teacher taught them without studying the Bible for themselves and finding out what the Word says about it. Teachers will receive a stricter judgment than non-teachers for they will be held accountable for what they teach. 1 Peter 4:11 (NLT) says, "Do you have the gift of speaking? Then speak as though God himself were speaking through you." If you're a teacher called by God, you invest yourself in learning the truths of God's Word. You learn the scriptures, you live it out, and then you teach it.

Those who stand behind a pulpit are not the only ones who teach the Word of God. All believers have the responsibility to tell others about the saving grace of Jesus Christ (2 Cor. 5:18). At some point in your life, you will be inspired by God to reach out to others and tell them what He did for you and is willing to do for them. James is saying when you do this, be sure you've heard from God and what you say lines up with the holy scriptures. Always use wisdom and good judgment when you speak. The Message Bible says, "Don't be in any rush to become a teacher, my friends. Teaching is highly responsible work. Teachers are held to the strictest standards." God hears every word you're saying and He examines very closely the lives of those who teach others for He holds them up to a higher standard. For this reason it is required that they control the words that come out of their mouth. James says, "For we all stumble in many things. If anyone does not stumble in word, he is a perfect man, able also to bridle the whole body" (vs. 2).

Let's face it, people talk all the time. So much do people talk that a fifty-page book would be needed to record all the words a person speaks in a single day. That's a lot of words. The problem is that people talk without thinking about the significance of what they're saying. They're making sound waves not realizing the impact their words have on their own life and the lives of other people. So powerful are words that Prov. 18:21 (BSB) says, "Life and death are in the power of the tongue." The quality of the life you'll live and the degree to which you'll grow up spiritually is based in part on the words that come out of your mouth. They have the power to bring life or death, the power to bless or curse, the power to heal or wound. The Message Bible says, "Words satisfy the mind as much as fruit does the stomach; good talk is as gratifying as a good harvest. Words kill, words give life; they're either poison or fruit - you choose" (vs. 20,21). James is saying a person who cannot control their tongue is not fit to teach anybody anything.

Everything God created was through the words He spoke. You were created in His image so there is also a creative force available to you that brings forth either life or death. That force is in the words you speak. Don't try to get God in agreement with your words, get your words in agreement with God. Prov. 18:21 asks the question, "Are you agreeing with life or are you agreeing with death?" Understand that words of encouragement bring life to a relationship while degrading words bring about its demise. People crave freedom of speech but wrong words spoken can cost you dearly. Giving your boss a piece of your mind could very well cost you your job. Husbands who say the wrong thing to their wives will probably be sleeping on the couch this evening. People cover up sarcasm by saying they're only joking around when in truth they meant every hurtful word they said. Prov. 26:18,19 (MSG) says, "People who shrug off deliberate deceptions, saying, 'I didn't mean it, I was only joking,' are worse than careless campers who walk away from smoldering campfires."

The war plan of the enemy is to gain control of your tongue. If he can do that, he can destroy your life and the lives of those closest to you. He knows that an uncontrolled tongue can start a flame that has the ability to grow and destroy everything in its path. Words are containers and bad words are filled with hate, unbelief, sarcasm, and all kinds of negativity. They're like a venomous snake full of deadly poison. Prov. 12:18 says, "Reckless words pierce like a sword, but the tongue of the wise brings healing." So often do people speak without thinking or caring about the consequences of what they're saying. The harsh words they speak bring emotional trauma and heartache that can last a lifetime. These people are audacious, thoughtless, and foolhardy. They think of nobody but themselves. Little do they realize the future that awaits them. Matt. 5:22 (MSG) says, "Carelessly call a brother 'idiot!' and you just might find yourself hauled into court. Thoughtlessly yell 'stupid!' at a sister and you are on the brink of hellfire. The simple moral fact is that words kill."

Prov. 6:2 says, "You are snared by the words of your mouth." Your tongue can corrupt your entire person and Jesus said wrong words can send you to hell. Words are powerful so watch what you say for your life will go in the direction of the words you speak. Yes, your tongue controls your destiny. If you don't learn to control your words, your words will control you. It's true, the words you speak have an impact on your life. If you use hurtful words to tear another person down, those same words will come around and tear you down. If you're giving out poison, that same poison will effect your life. Prov. 12:13 says, "A man's harmful speech will harm him." If you say words that destroy, you also will be burned by the fiery words that come out of your mouth. The Message Bible says, "The gossip of bad people gets them in trouble; the conversation of good people keeps them out of it." Never let your guard down for the enemy is forever seeking to destroy your life. He's very persistent in what he does and is more active than most believers.

The devil is a liar and the father of lies (John 8:44). He has no interest in the truth. His only interest is getting you to use your tongue to fan the flame of the evil work he is doing. He knows if he can get you to speak in haste that you'll soon regret what you said but then it will be too late. The damage is done for your words gave life to a negative situation. Why would the devil personally attack someone if he can use you and the words you speak to do it for him? That's his plan, to use you like a puppet on a string. More times than not, his most powerful and destructive weapon used against the body of Christ is the tongue of a born again believer. Churches have been destroyed and flocks of sheep have been scattered because of the uncontrolled use of a believer's perverted tongue. This is not a new problem for it's been around since the dawn of the Christian church. James was aware of this and he addresses the power of the tongue head on here in his letter, the first book written in the New Testament. What he has to say will shock most people.

In the very first chapter James said to be "swift to hear, slow to speak" (vs. 19) and in vs. 26 he says if anyone "does not bridle his tongue but deceives his own heart, this one's religion is useless." James isn't finished. Here in the third chapter he sets the bar on the seriousness of your words. He begins by saying that not many should become teachers for they will receive a stricter judgment. This exhortation is to those who claim to be speaking on God's behalf or explaining something He said. James is saying they better get their words right because God is listening to every word they're saying. Jesus said in Matt. 12:36, "But I say to you that for every idle word men may speak, they will give account of it in the day of judgment." Idle words in Greek are "careless or inactive or unprofitable words." The Message Bible says, "Every one of these careless words is going to come back to haunt you. There will be a time of reckoning. Words are powerful, take them seriously. Words can be your salvation. Words can also be your damnation" (vs. 36,37).

James is giving this exhortation because teachers are the very people the enemy is after the most. Teachers have a great influence over other people and for this reason Jesus says in Matt. 18:6, "And whoever causes one of these little ones who believe in Me to sin, it would be better for him if a millstone were hung around his neck, and he were drowned in the depth of the sea." This is a warning about leading the spiritually young down the wrong path. God cares about what you tell other people, especially when you say you're speaking on His behalf. Many of these false teachers are teaching for the wrong reason. They desire positions of influence because of self-centered ambition and not to be a blessing to those they're teaching. It should not come as a shock to you that the majority of the devil's work takes place inside the church. This is why James is saying to be careful who you allow to become teachers. Not everyone's motive is as pure as it should be and it is for this reason that those who teach will be judged more strictly.

James is talking to born again, blood bought Christians who have given their tongues over to the control of the devil. He knows this is a common occurrence and says in vs. 2 (MSG), "We get it wrong nearly every time we open our mouths. If you could find someone whose speech was perfectly true, you'd have a perfect person, in perfect control of life." The person who can control his words is a perfect man. If he can control his mouth, he can control his entire body. He won't overeat nor will he lust and pursue sensual desires. In Greek the word "perfect" means 'complete in integrity and virtue; not lacking any moral quality.' In other words, if you can't control your tongue, you'll never grow up spiritually. People who talk all the time often stumble with their words and this prevents spiritual maturity from happening. The tongue is a fire and it sets ablaze everything else that pertains to your life. Therefore, if you can stop sinning with your words, you can stop sinning in other areas of your life as well. It's what determines the direction your life will go.

The bottom line is that your tongue controls your destiny. If you can control the direction of your tongue, you can control the direction of your life. James 3:3 says, "Indeed, we put bits in horses' mouths that they may obey us, and we turn their whole body." Just as you can control the direction of a horse with a bit and bridle, so can you control the direction of your life with your tongue. The words you speak determines the direction your life will take, the direction of your life determines your destiny. The person whose words are filled with anger, bitterness, and criticism will live a hard life whereas a person whose speech is characterized by love, joy, and peace will live a good life. The direction of their tongue is setting the direction of their life just like the bit in the mouth of a horse determines the direction the horse will go. A person's tongue only weighs two ounces yet it has the power and ability to do great things, either good or bad.

"Look also at ships: although they are so large and are driven by fierce winds, they are turned by a very small rudder wherever the pilot desires" (vs. 4). The rudder on a ship is a small thing but it can do great damage. In 1989 the pilot of the Exxon Valdez was careless with the rudder and the huge ship ran aground in Prince William Sound, Alaska. Eleven million gallons of crude oil spilled out of that ship and destroyed over a thousand miles of beautiful coastline and the animals that dwelt there. James is saying you run the same risk in your life if you don't understand the power of the tongue. How many lives have been devastated because somebody did not have control of their tongue? "Even so the tongue is a little member and boasts great things. See how great a forest a little fire kindles!" (vs. 5). Notice there is an exclamation point after this verse. James is trying to get your attention. He's saying, "Wake up! These verses are for you!" This is one of the most brutal passages in all of scripture and James is forcing you to come to grips with the fact that what you say matters.

Every person has to deal with the evil nature of the tongue. You've been hurt by what people have said to you and they've been hurt by what you've said to them. "And the tongue is a fire, a world of iniquity. The tongue is so set among our members that it defiles the whole body, and sets on fire the course of nature; and it is set on fire by hell" (vs. 6). The tongue is a world of iniquity, a raging fire that is out of control. Out of one's mouth come lying, gossip, slander, vulgarity, destructiveness, and blasphemy. The word "hell" used here is not referring to the fiery pit of Hades. It's the Greek word "Gehenna" which is a small valley south of Jerusalem where some of the godless kings of Judah sacrificed their children by fire to the god Moloch (Jer. 7:31). Later the valley became the dumping ground for the sewage and refuge of the city. It was a place crawling with worms and maggots. Fires burned continually to destroy the garbage and a terrible and putrid smoke rose continually. It was a place deemed to be cursed and came to symbolize the destruction of the wicked.

Is. 66:24 (MSG) says, "And then they'll go out and look at what happened to those who rebelled against Me. Corpses! Maggots endlessly eating away at them, an endless supply of fuel for fires. Everyone who sees what's happened and smells the stench retches." It is from this dreadful place that the evil words people speak come from. As detestable as all this is, James wants you to take this personal. He's not talking about your neighbor here, he's talking about you. He's saying your tongue is a fire that contains all the wickedness that is in the evil world system. This is not an opinion, it is a statement of fact. Your tongue is evil and is set on fire by hell itself. The Message Bible says, "By our speech we can ruin the world, turn harmony to chaos, throw mud on a reputation, send the whole world up in smoke right from the pit of hell." Not only do bad words hurt other people, the NCV says "the tongue spreads its evil through the whole body." Be hateful with your tongue and you will become hateful in your behavior.

Words are containers. They can contain life or they can contain death. They can bring encouragement and healing or they can bring destruction. Ps. 64:3,4 says, "They sharpen their tongues like swords and aim their bitter words like arrows. They shoot from ambush at the innocent, attacking suddenly and fearlessly." This is what James is talking about when he says "the tongue is a fire, a world of iniquity." Never should a believer cause this much destruction and pain. Paul said in Eph. 4:29, "Let no corrupt communication proceed out of your mouth, but what is good for necessary edification, that it may impart grace to the hearers." The Message Bible says, "Watch the way you talk. Let nothing foul or dirty come out of your mouth. Say only what helps, each word a gift." Always be mindful of the impact your words have on the people you're talking to. Don't allow the enemy to use your words like arrows to hurt them or tear them down. Yes, negative thoughts may come to you about these people but that doesn't mean you have to speak them out of your mouth.

Your whole life can be corrupted by the words you speak for the tongue sets on fire the entire course of life. The Greek word used here refers to the "wheel of life." Everything that pertains to your life, your relationships, your business and ministry, your dreams and goals, can all be turned into a pile of ash with an uncontrolled tongue. This is not a small matter. It's very serious and James wants you to get a clear image of the damage an evil tongue can do. Christians everywhere are deceiving themselves because they won't admit the problems they're going through were caused because they set some things on fire with their tongue. It's always the devil or some other person's fault, never their own. This is why they're deceived and the devil laughs at the calamity they're causing. He likes it when Christians are in denial because they're the ones doing the most damage. Come to grips with what James is saying here. If everything in your life is on fire, it might be that you said something you shouldn't have said.

More times than not, the person to blame for the mess you're in is the person you see in the mirror. You need to realize that it takes little or no effort to inflame the natural evil nature of the tongue. The French theologian John Calvin once said, "The tongue is an instrument for catching, encouraging, and increasing the fires of hell." He is saying there are words you can say that will produce death in you instead of life. Is. 59:2,3 says, "But your iniquities have separated you from your God; And your sins have hidden His face from you, so that He will not hear. For your hands are defiled with blood, and your fingers with iniquity; Your lips have spoken lies, your tongue has muttered perversity." In other words, you did what you did because you said what you said. James goes on to say, "For every kind of beast and bird, of reptile and creature of the sea, is tamed and has been tamed by mankind. But no man can tame the tongue. It is an unruly evil, full of deadly poison" (James 3:18). People go to church and think they're so holy but yet they can't tame their tongue. Try as they may, it can't be done.

The Message Bible says, "This is scary! You can tame a tiger, but you can't tame a tongue - it's never been done. The tongue runs wild, a wanton killer." The ESV says the tongue "is a restless evil." It never rests, never takes a break. It's uncontrollable and full of deadly poison. From the tongue comes criticism, slander, gossip, lying, filthy language, contentious speech, and blasphemy. The purpose of a wayward tongue is to poison its listeners. James 3:9,10 says, "With it we bless our God and Father, and with it we curse men, who have been made in the similitude of God. Out of the same mouth proceed blessing and cursing. My brethren, these things ought not to be so." Once again James addresses these words to "My brethren." He's talking to born again believers here, Christians who say they love God yet curse their fellow man. He's pulling no punches as he confronts these people with their blatant hypocrisy. He's telling it how it is and it takes a lot of pride and self righteousness to ignore what he's saying. Hear what James is saying and see the need for transformation.

James next asks a couple of rhetorical questions that will point you to the solution of taming an evil tongue. He asks, "Does a spring send forth fresh water and bitter from the same opening? Can a fig tree, my brethren, bear olives, or a grapevine bear figs? Thus no spring can yield both salt water and fresh" (vs. 11,12). What is James saying here? He is challenging you to consider the source of where your words are coming from. You must accept the fact that what's coming out of your mouth first originates in your heart. Jesus talked about this in Luke 6:45, "A good man out of the good treasure of his heart brings forth good; and an evil man out of the evil treasure of his heart brings forth evil. For out of the abundance of the heart his mouth speaks." People who have a problem with their words have, in fact, a problem with their heart. Heart problems cause tongue problems. Don't try to tame your tongue because you can't do it. Allow God to change your heart and your tongue problem will correct itself.

Listen carefully to the words you're speaking because they'll tell you what's in your heart. Evil words reveal you have an evil heart, good words show you've got a good heart. You are known by others by what you say for words give people a window into your soul. For example, a person with a harsh tongue has an angry heart and a person with a negative tongue has a fearful heart. A person with an over reactive tongue has an unsettled heart while a person with a boasting tongue has an insecure heart. A person with a filthy tongue has an impure heart and a person with a critical tongue has a bitter heart. On the other hand, a person with an encouraging tongue has a happy heart, a person with a gentle tongue has a loving heart, and a person with a truthful tongue has an honest heart. Remember, words have the power to reveal who you are so learn to listen to the words you speak. Other people are listening so why don't you? You'll be surprised by what your words say about you.

Randall J. Brewer

-20-

"WHAT GOD SAYS"

You're a born again believer but still you have an evil tongue that you cannot tame. Daily you struggle with this problem. What can you do? Paul had a similar struggle and he wrote in Rom. 7:18 (NLT), "And I know that nothing good lives in me, that is, in my sinful nature. I want to do what is right, but I can't." This is exactly what James is saying about the tongue. Nothing good lives there and nobody can tame it. Paul cries out in vs. 24 (NLT), "Oh, what a miserable person I am! Who will free me from this life that is dominated by sin and death?" Without waiting a moment longer, the Holy Spirit answers Paul in the very next verse, "Thank God! The answer is in Jesus Christ our Lord" (vs. 25 NLT). God's answer to your tongue problem is to make Jesus Christ your Lord. He must be more than a Savior to you. He becomes Lord when you go through the transformation of allowing His life to take over yours. It's when His will gets done and not your own.

Rom. 8:2 (NLT) says, "And because you belong to Him, the power of the life-giving Spirit has freed you from the power of sin that leads to death." The Message Bible says, "The Spirit of life in Christ, like a strong wind, has magnificently cleared the air, freeing you from a fated lifetime of brutal tyranny at the hands of sin and death." Because you belong to Jesus, the Holy Spirit has freed you from the power of sin.

No longer are you in bondage to its deadly grasp. Now, if bad words come out of your mouth, it's because you chose to speak them out. Jesus has given you the power to crucify your flesh. The same power that raised Jesus from the dead lives inside of you. The choice is yours. Are you going to serve the evil nature of the tongue, or are you going to submit to the power of the Holy Spirit that's residing in you? Paul says in Rom. 8:6 (NLT), "Letting your sinful nature control your mind leads to death. But letting the Spirit control your mind leads to life and peace."

It all comes down to the choices you make. Are you going to choose life or are you going to choose death? Remember, life and death is in the power of the tongue. Words kill and words give life. Allowing the evil nature of the tongue to control what you say leads to death and destruction, letting the Holy Spirit control your words leads to life and peace. Paul sums it up in Rom. 8:12,13 (NLT), "Therefore, dear brothers and sisters, you have no obligation to do what your sinful nature urges you to do. For if you live by its dictates, you will die. But if through the power of the Spirit you put to death the deeds of your sinful nature, you will live." If Jesus lives in your heart, then the power of the Holy Spirit is in you. This means you no longer have any obligation to do what your sinful tongue tells you to do. However, a choice still has to be made. You must make the choice between life and death every time you open your mouth. Your future depends on it.

Words matter. So important are words that the entire universe was created by the words God spoke. Heb. 11:3 says, "By faith we understand that the worlds were framed by the word of God." Several times in the first chapter of Genesis it is written "Then God said" followed by "and it was so." Ps. 33:6 confirms this, "By the word of the Lord the heavens were made, and all the host of them by the breath of His mouth." Vs. 9 says, "For He spoke, and it was done; He commanded, and it stood fast." Words are powerful. God's words have power and because you are made in His image, your words have power as well. He created you as a speaking spirit with a free will. He made you to function like He does with the ability to freely choose what words you want to speak. He gave you the ability to create the world you want to live in. With faith-filled words your body can be healed and your needs can be met. Like a bit in a horse's mouth or the rudder on a ship, words that matter have the power to direct your life.

God has given you the freedom to believe and say whatever you choose. Because of that freedom, if you say and allow something, God will allow the same thing. Those who want to live a good life, those who want to grow up spiritually, need to learn to say the same things God says. Heb. 3:1 says Jesus is "the Apostle and High priest of our confession." The word "confession" literally means 'to speak the same thing.' You quoting scripture and saying the same thing God says gives Jesus something to work with in your life. With this understanding, the Word of God should have special meaning to you. So important is the Word that Ps. 138:2 says, "For You have magnified Your word above all Your name." God respects His Word more than anything else. Jesus said in Matt. 4:4, "Man shall not live by bread alone, but by every Word that proceeds out of the mouth of God." When you read the Word and confess what it says, God is able to make it come alive in your heart. This causes faith to come for "faith comes by hearing, and hearing by the Word of God" (Rom. 10:17).

2 Cor. 4:13 says, "But since we have the same spirit of faith, according to what is written, 'I believed and therefore I spoke.' we also believe and therefore speak." Speaking the Word is the only proof that you believe the Word. Faith is born in the heart but is expressed with the mouth. What you say gives expression to your faith. Rom. 10:10 says, "For with the heart man believes unto righteousness; and with the mouth confession is made unto salvation." It's the power of

declaration that makes faith work. It's the confession of the Word that renders the enemy silent. At the temptation in the wilderness Jesus confessed the Word and the devil departed from Him (Luke 4:13). Jer. 23:29 says, "'Is not My word like a fire?' says the Lord, 'And like a hammer that breaks the rock in pieces?'" At the burning bush God called Moses to go to Egypt. Moses was hesitant and God said to him, "Now therefore, go, and I will be with your mouth and teach you what you shall say" (Ex. 4:12). Go read your Bible and learn what God is teaching you to say.

God never speaks an idle word and neither should you. Negative and idle words can hold you in bondage and stop you from fulfilling your destiny. What you say matters. If you say and allow something, God will allow it also. He gave you a free will and He won't override your confession. He'll respond to the words that come out of your mouth. Consider Matt. 10:32,33. Jesus said, "Therefore whoever confesses Me before men, him I will also confess before My Father who is in heaven. But whoever denies Me before men, him I will also deny before My Father who is in heaven." Notice that what Jesus says to the Father is based on what you say. If you'll confess Him, He'll confess you. If you deny Him, He'll deny you. Matt. 12:37 says, "For by your words you will be justified, and by your words you will be condemned." It is a sobering thought to realize that your words have a greater influence in your life than the words of anybody else, including God. Be careful what you say because Luke 19:22 says, "Out of your own mouth I will judge you."

Is. 55:11 says, "So shall My word be that goes forth from My mouth; It shall not return to Me void, but it shall accomplish what I please, and it shall prosper in the thing for which I sent it." God does not speak merely for the purpose of communication. When He speaks, power is released and alters that which He is speaking to. No word of God is void of power or incapable of being fulfilled. Imagine having this much power at your fingertips. You need to understand the value and importance of words. Do you want to change the direction your life is going? If so, change your words. The Message Bible says, "So will the words that come out of My mouth not come back empty-handed. They'll do the work I sent them to do, they'll complete the assignment I gave them." God is saying that His words are effective, they produce results. Your words can do the same thing. The problem in the ungodly world is that people use words to express thoughts and feelings instead of using words that matter to change things.

Paul said in Eph. 5:1 (NLT), "Imitate God, therefore, in everything you do, because you are His dear children." Most church going people don't do this nor do they believe their words have the same power that God's words have. People would change the way they talk if they truly believed that everything they said would come to pass. What people don't realize is that in the unseen spiritual realm the devil is giving influence to the words they say. He puts negative thoughts and phrases into people's minds knowing they'll express them with words that give birth to confusion, defeat, and failure. People believe the words they say and this is why their lives are in the mess it's in. Stop being so loose with the words you speak but be like God and use words to create a better life for yourself and those closest to you. He speaks words that matter and so should you. Everything God has ever said has come to pass and you need to speak knowing the same thing will happen to you.

A conversation took place when God called Jeremiah into ministry. Jeremiah was young, fearful, and insecure when this happened and he needed some encouragement. Jer. 1:11,12 says, "Moreover the word of the Lord came to me, saying, 'Jeremiah, what do you see?' And I said, 'I see a branch of an almond tree.' Then the Lord said to me, 'You have seen well, for I am ready to perform My word.'" In Hebrew the root word for "almond tree" means 'watch' or 'wake.' God had Jeremiah look at an almond tree because it is one of the first trees to "wake up" and produce fruit after winter time. God is saying to be encouraged during hard times. Like an almond tree that awakens after the winter, God will keep His promises. He is watching over His Word that you speak out of your mouth making sure it is fulfilled. He is a faithful God and you can have the confidence that His Word will surely come to pass in your life. This is how God works. He uses His Word to accomplish His will in your life and throughout the world.

God is the almond branch over His Word. He is watching over it to perform it. This is interesting because when turned sideways the almond has the same shape as a human eye. An almond tree blooms and bears fruit quickly. Near the end of January or early February, from a dormant state, the almond tree receives a command from God to prepare for blossoming. The tree hears the command and begins to awaken from its slumber. Shortly thereafter it clothes itself in light pink blossoms that turn white before falling to the ground one to two weeks later. Bees then deliver pollen to the blossoms and the firstfruits soon begin to emerge and will hastily grow to full size in only eight weeks. This is symbolic of how fast God is willing to respond to His Word. The end is near and there is an acceleration on how fast God will move in your life. What God said, He will perform with His actions. All you have to do is speak His Word out of your mouth. When you say what God says, the manifestation of what you're saying will come to pass.

Prov. 13:2 (HCSB) says, "From the words of his mouth, a man will enjoy good things." The Good News Translation says, "Good people will be rewarded for what they say." When you say words that matter, you give life to what you're saying. Words are like seeds that grow and where you're at today is the result of what you've said in the past. The good news is when you say what God says, you are in fact prophesying over your own life that a bright future is ahead of you. Always say the right things because, like it or not, you will eat the fruit of your words. You can't say bad things and live a good life. Say things like "I will lend and not borrow" and "Whatever I touch prospers." Sow good seeds and watch them grow into what you're believing for. God is watching over His Word to perform it and He'll perform it for you when you say what He says. Pay attention to what you're saying for your future depends on it. What you'll do, where you'll go, and what you'll become in life is determined by the words you say. Choose wisely when you speak.

Words have the power to change things. Don't use words to describe your situation, use words to change your situation. Be on guard during tough times, when things aren't going the way you'd like them to. Talking about the problem won't change anything but talking about the answer will. Don't be bitter when the storms of life blow but use your words to make things better. It may not happen overnight but eventually you'll eat the fruit of what you say. That's a promise from God. Anybody can give up but champions never quit. Defeat is not an option for "in due season we will reap if we do not lose heart" (Gal. 6:9). People who want to grow up spiritually press on no matter what. The Message Bible says, "At the right time we will harvest a good crop if we don't give up, or quit." Victory is just around the corner so keep believing, keep hoping, and keep saying the right thing. Most of all, never give up. Heb. 10:35 says, "Therefore do not cast away your confidence which has great reward."

Faith is built on the foundation of knowing that God's Word always comes to pass. This is why you'll never grow up spiritually unless you learn to say what God says. This will not be hard to do once you realize that God honors His Word and watches over it to perform it. God will go to work in your life when He hears His Word coming out of your mouth. You speak the Word and He performs the Word. What could be better than that? All you have to do is believe that God will do what He says He will do, that He is alert and active and watching over His Word to make sure it comes to pass. Why does He do this? Because His Word is His bond. Heb. 6:13 says, "For when God made a promise to Abraham, because He could swear by no one greater, He swore by Himself." His Word is also the expression of His nature and the measure of His character. It's what makes God who He is for it gives substance and validity to His name. In other words, His name is only as good as His Word. Of course He'll perform His Word in your life, otherwise He wouldn't be God. All you have to do is speak it out and believe that what you say will come to pass.

You can change your life with the words you speak. If you want to live a long, good life, 1 Peter 3:10 tells you how, "He who would love life and see good days, let him refrain his tongue from evil, and his lips from speaking guile." This lines up with James 3:2 (NIV), "Anyone who is never at fault in what they say is perfect, able to keep their whole body in check." Your words give direction to your life just like a steering wheel gives direction to a car. If you don't like the direction your life is going, change what you say. Prov. 18:20 says, "A man's stomach shall be satisfied from the fruit of his mouth, and from the produce of his lips he shall be filled." The Amplified Bible says, "He will be satisfied with the consequence of his words." Words have consequences, and you're the one who chooses what they will be. With your words you're choosing life or death, blessing or cursing. The steering wheel of life is in your hands. You're making a choice every time you open your mouth.

You are royalty, you're the child of the King, so you need to act like it. A king in the kingdom of God speaks, he declares things. Any king who says nothing is no better off than a slave. Job 22:28 says, "You shall also declare a thing, and it will be established for you; So light will shine on your ways." The Message Bible says, "You'll decide what you want, and it will happen; your life will be bathed in light." Your future is shaped and determined by what you say. Five times David declared what he was going to do to Goliath before he met him in battle. If you want to grow up spiritually and live a good life, you've got to say something. Ps. 107:2 says, "Let the redeemed of the Lord say so." God doesn't give you what He says, He gives you what you say. God will meet you at the point of your declaration. The woman with the issue of blood said, "If only I may touch His clothes, I shall be made well" (Mark 5:28). She declared what was going to happen and it came to pass exactly as she said (vs. 34).

Jesus set the example of what you need to do in Mark 1:40-42, "Then a leper came to Him, imploring Him, kneeling down to Him and saying to Him, 'If you are willing, You can make me clean.' And Jesus, moved with compassion, put out His hand and touched him, and said to him, 'I am willing; be cleansed.' As soon as He had spoken, immediately the leprosy left him, and he was cleansed." Jesus said something and the leper got healed. It is now time for you to say something for "where the word of a king is, there is power" (Eccl. 8:4). Say something about your marriage. Say something about your ministry. Say something about your health. Say something about your finances. Call those things that be not as though they were (Rom. 4:17). Say what God says and watch Him perform His Word. Never forget the famous words of Mark 11:23, "For assuredly, I say to you, whoever says to this mountain, 'Be removed and be cast into the sea,' and does not doubt in his heart, but believes that those things he says will come to pass, he will have whatever he says."

Jesus is the King of kings. If you are born again, then you are one of the kings Jesus is King over. Your word has power and never should the storms of life overtake you. Micah 4:9 asks the question, "Now why do you cry aloud? Is there no king in your midst?" Stop seeing yourself as a victim and start seeing yourself for who you truly are. You are a king and your words have power. The word of a king is established (Ps. 119:89). It is supreme, it is law. It supersedes anything the devil or anyone else may say. The word of a king is all powerful.

When he speaks, the power is in the word he spoke. His word and the power to bring it to pass go together, they work hand-in-hand. You've been crowned with glory and honor (Ps. 8:5) so act like it and speak like it. Say what God says and have dominion over your kingdom. Ps. 8:2 (NLT) says, "You have taught children and infants to tell of Your strength, silencing Your enemies and all who oppose You." If a child can do it, so can you! You speak the Word and God will do the work. It's as simple as that.

Words are the master tool that gets things done. Most of the things Jesus did was with words and He said only what the Father told Him to say (John 12:49). He said what God said and you need to do the same. Every word in the Bible is for your benefit. Read it, believe it, speak it. Say what God tells you to say knowing that life and death are in the power of the tongue. You create your world with your words because what you say becomes your reality. Your words give you ownership of whatever you say. Jesus said you can have whatever you say if you don't doubt in your heart. Saying what God says allows you to believe the unbelievable and receive the impossible. Don't be limited by speaking your own words when saying what God says makes you unlimited in what you can have and become. Why choose the lesser when you can have the greater? It only makes sense to say words that allow you to do what others say can't be done. In your mouth is a miracle waiting to happen. God gives you the power and the resources to fulfill your destiny. That power is in your words and believing what you say.

God wants you to grow up spiritually because maturity is needed to handle the power words give you. Like a gun in the hands of a six year old, great damage can be done if you don't know how to use it right. You've got to grow up so you'll know where to point the gun and when to pull the trigger. Words are so important. They can start a forest fire or they can put it out. Speak in such a way that you'll be identified by the world as a Bible believing Christian. Do what Jesus did and only say what God says. That's the language of faith, speaking words that are filled with the power to change things for the better. The consistency of saying what you're supposed to say will give you the life you've always dreamed of. Understand that God never intended for the Bible to be read silently. It was written with the intention of being read out loud. Josh. 1:8 says, "This Book of the Law shall not depart from your mouth, but you shall meditate in it day and night, that you may observe to do according to all that is written in it." If you'll do that, you will always be saying what God said and that's where the power of faith comes from.

Prov. 3:6 says, "In all your ways acknowledge Him, and He shall direct your steps." Your paths begin with your mouth. Acknowledge God and He'll direct you to a Bible verse that He wants you to speak out loud. Point that verse at your problem and boldly say what God says about it. Say out loud, "My God shall supply all my need according to His riches in glory by Christ Jesus. Many are the afflictions of the righteous, but the Lord delivers him out of them all" (Phil. 4:19;Ps. 34:19). Train yourself not to speak too quickly but to wait on God until He tells you what to say. This is why James tells you to be swift to hear and slow to speak. Prov. 15:28 says, "The heart of the righteous studies how to answer, but the mouth of the wicked pours forth evil. Prov. 16:23,24 says, "The heart of the wise teaches his mouth, and adds learning to his lips. Pleasant words are like a honeycomb, sweetness to the soul and health to the bones." Wait on God for no word from Him is void of power. It will produce wherever it's sent.

Spiritual maturity is measured by how well you can control your tongue. A wise man studies how to answer and he only says what God says. Prov. 21:23 says, "Whoever guards his mouth and tongue keeps his soul from troubles." People who are depressed are always talking about how miserable they are. They're not guarding their mouths. They're creating their world with the words they're speaking. They're saying they're miserable and so they are. These people need to learn to say what God says. Prov. 16:1 says, "The preparation of the heart belong to man, but the answer of the tongue is from the Lord." It's the Word He gives you to speak that removes mountains. It's not your strength and ability, it's His strength and ability. Guard your mouth and be disciplined in what you say. If you haven't heard from God, say nothing at all. The most mature and powerful children of God are those who talk sparingly. They're swift to hear and slow to speak. When they do talk, it's the Word of God coming out of their mouth.

-21-

"WISDOM FROM ABOVE"

Long ago, when Adam first walked the earth, life was beautiful, life was grand. The entire world was Adam's to explore and dominate and he even had personal conversations with God in the cool of the evening. Life couldn't get any better, or could it? The day came when God said, "It is not good that man should be alone" (Gen. 2:18). He was saying that relationships are important and shortly thereafter He took a rib from Adam's side and made from it a wife for the man He had created. From that moment on, relationships became one of the most important things on earth. A common element in all relationships is that people communicate with one another. They talk and they listen, they give opinions and share information. People have opinions about everything and are forever ready to tell you what they think. Whenever a conversation is taking place, people are sharing their wisdom with one another. The question to be asked is where is this wisdom coming from? Is it an earthly wisdom or wisdom from above?

A good chef knows that when cooking a meal different spices and ingredients can be added that will enhance its flavor. In the same way, there is a special ingredient that when added to any relationship will make it feel like heaven on earth. All it takes is a little wisdom to spice up your life and any relationship you may be involved in. Wisdom is a valuable thing. Prov. 8:11 says, "For wisdom is better than rubies, and all the things one may desire cannot be compared with her." As people are sharing their wisdom with you, you've got to discern the source of that wisdom so you'll know if you should pay attention to what's being said or if you should turn away. Prov. 14:12 warns, "There is a way which seems right to a man, but it's end is the way of death." These people may be very sincere but they can also be seriously wrong. James knows that sincerity is not the foundation wisdom and godliness is built on. He proceeds to tell you things to look for that will reveal the source of what's being said.

James 3:13 (NLT) says, "If you are wise and understand God's ways, prove it by living an honorable life, doing good works with the humility that comes from wisdom." James is saying you can look at a person's life and determine if what they're saying is from above or below. The Message Bible says, "Live well, live wisely, live humbly. It's the way you live, not the way you talk, that counts." This goes back to what he said in James 1:22, "But be doers of the word, and not hearers only, deceiving yourselves." The first thing James wants you to understand is that godly wisdom is not based on how much you know, it's based on what you do with the knowledge you do have. Wisdom is a lifestyle. A truly wise person is not known by the degrees and diplomas hung on their wall but rather by the way they live their life. Yes, they may be very smart but if they're not a person of character and integrity then all that knowledge won't do them any good.

Solomon was a very smart man but confusion and disorder were the mark of his many fractured relationships. You show by good conduct that you are a person of wisdom, by doing good works with meekness and humility. The Greek word for "good" means 'beautiful' and 'well-pleasing.' James is saying that a wise person lives a beautiful life, a life marked by doing good deeds, a life well-pleasing to God. If a person is giving their opinion to you, and surely most people will, you need to look at their lifestyle and this will help you to easily decide if you should be listening to them or not. Are they speaking with humility or are they in pride? Are they arrogant and conceited and think their opinion is always right? If so, don't listen to what they're saying. Humility, on the other hand, does not have to defend its own opinion nor does it have to win every disagreement. People who are prideful think very highly of themselves but those who walk in humility know they don't have to prove anything to anybody.

James is very serious here and he uses tough love to pierce the hearts of those he is writing to. He says in vs. 14 (NLT), "But if you are bitterly jealous and there is selfish ambition in your heart, don't cover up the truth with boasting and lying." It's sad but true, many believers are living a life of hypocrisy. Acts 5:1-10 tells a story of hypocrisy in the early church. Desiring to make a good impression in front of others, Ananias and his wife Sapphira sold some land and claimed to give all the proceeds to the church. Through a word of knowledge, Peter knew the couple had withheld a portion of the money. He exposed the lie and this deception cost Ananias and Sapphira their physical lives. Hypocrisy in the church does exist. There are people who are always voicing their opinion as a means of covering up a sinful heart. They're talking and acting all spiritual but inside they're hostile, resentful, and full of self-centered ambition and envy. They deceive people by using divisive words to promote their own views.

The Message Bible says, "Mean-spirited ambition isn't wisdom. Boasting that you are wise isn't wisdom. Twisting the truth to make yourselves sound wise isn't wisdom." Pride loves to boast and nothing makes a person more proud than the wisdom they think they have. It's through pride that people are eager to display themselves more than the truth of

God's Word. Paul deals with this in Phil. 2:3, "Let nothing be done through selfish ambition or conceit, but in lowliness of mind let each esteem others better than himself." The result of bitter jealousy and selfish ambition is rivalry, discord, and division in the church. Listen closely to what you hear for it's a sign that reveals the origin of what's being said. The heart is the problem but gets revealed by what people say. The tongue always reveals the source of wisdom for out of the abundance of the heart the mouth speaks (Matt. 12:34). The Message Bible says, "It's your heart, not the dictionary, that gives meaning to your words."

James uses some pretty strong language in vs. 15 when he says, "This wisdom does not descend from above, but is earthly, sensual, demonic." He detects the work of demons when people give voice to their opinions in an effort to cover up their sins of pride, jealousy, and selfishness. He already said in vs. 6 that the tongue "is set on fire by hell." Earthly wisdom is the wisdom of the world. It's based on what the world thinks and not what God thinks. It is sensual, unspiritual, and void of anything to do with God. The word "demonic" means 'that which proceeds from an evil spirit.' James is saying people who cover up their sins with false wisdom can be used by the devil to do great damage to those who listen to them. Just because a person says they're a Christian doesn't mean what they're saying is wisdom from above. Be very careful who you listen to. Do what Jesus said and "be wise as serpents and gentle as doves" (Matt. 10:16). He said that because the disciples were being sent out "like sheep among wolves."

You also are being sent out like sheep among wolves. The problem is some of these wolves are your fellow brothers and sisters in the Lord. The thing to learn about wolves is they are intentional about the harm they inflict upon sheep. What they do, they do on purpose. To avoid being a victim to this heresy, Jesus says you must combine the wisdom of the serpent with the harmlessness of the dove. The word "wise" is the Greek word "pronimos" which means 'prudent, careful, cunning, discerning, thoughtful, intelligent, sensible.' These words perfectly depict the behavior and actions of snakes. Jesus is saying you need to be discerning and careful when people are talking to you. A serpent is wise, with keen eyesight and is quick to learn. With the serpent's eye you'll have quick insight into the truths of God's Word. Prov. 14:18 says, "But the prudent are crowned with knowledge." With the eye of the serpent you'll be divinely illuminated and will be able to tell the difference between what's true and what's false.

A dove, on the other hand, is innocent, meek, and gentle. Jesus says you must be both wise and innocent. You must have the wisdom of the serpent so others won't hurt you and the innocence of the dove so you won't hurt others. The dove is the emblem of meekness and 1 Peter 3:4 (MSG) says, "Cultivate inner beauty, the gentle, gracious kind that God delights in." A dove is innocent and pure. It breathes the purest air and eats the purest grain. Solomon called his beloved "my dove, my perfect one" (Song of Solomon 5:2). The dove is a chaste, pure creature and you should be also. Paul told Timothy to "keep yourself pure" (1 Tim. 5:22) and he said in 2 Cor. 7:1, "Let us cleanse ourselves from all filthiness of the flesh and spirit, perfecting holiness in the fear of God." A dove does not deceive nor does it harm anybody. It is a harmless creature and has nothing with which to offend. It has no horns or claws to fight with and uses its wings to defend itself by flying away. Like a dove, turn the other cheek and walk away when trouble brews.

James is telling you what to look for when somebody is talking to you. If you detect pride, bitterness, jealousy, envy, divisiveness, and selfish ambition, then what you're hearing is not wisdom from above. What you're hearing is earthly wisdom that is influenced by the demonic realm. Paul makes it clear what you're supposed to do. He says in 2 Tim. 3:1-5 (MSG), "Don't be naive. There are difficult times ahead. As the end approaches, people are going to be self-absorbed, money-hungry, self-promoting, stuck-up, profane, contemptuous of parents, crude, coarse, dog-eat-dog, unbending, slanderers, impulsively wild, savage, cynical, treacherous, ruthless, bloated windbags, addicted to lust, and allergic to God. They'll make a show of religion but behind the scenes they're animals. Stay clear of these people." People who make a show of religion go to church regularly. Some of them may be sitting on the pew right next to you. Be careful among strangers at church for "even Satan disguises himself as an angel of light" (2 Cor. 11:14 NLT).

Perhaps God is telling you to go to a new church. If so, move slowly and be wise as a serpent. Serpents have a way of blending into the environment when they move into a new territory. They don't announce their presence but lay low and stay quiet. They are nearly invisible for their skin is camouflaged that allows it to blend into the landscape. You could walk right by a snake and not even know it. Not being seen allows the serpent to identify places of shelter and where to find the easiest prey. It takes time for the serpent to settle in but once this is done it can go ahead and do what snakes are supposed to do. If a new door of opportunity is being opened for you, it is a wise thing to move slowly and carefully. Take the time to gather all the facts needed to do the job right. Lay low, stay quiet, and blend into the environment. Moving too fast may cause you to make poor decisions you'll greatly regret farther down the road. Moving slowly may take more time but in the end it will produce more stable and lasting results.

Wherever you go, whatever new opportunity comes your way, always take the time to discern the wisdom that is in the people you're associated with. A snake knows when to remain still and be quiet and it knows when to strike and take action. Timing is everything, it's the key to fulfilling any assignment God has given you. For the serpent, this knowledge is the key to its survival. If its prey passes before him and the snake waits too long to strike, he'll miss the opportunity put before him and he'll go hungry. There is a time to act, a time to lay aside all fears and emotions and seize the moment. Don't allow these God-given opportunities to pass you by. If you hesitate too long it may be too late. Stay in prayer and allow the Holy Spirit to lead you and direct your steps. He'll tell you when to lay low and when to strike. He is 'the Spirit of truth" and you can trust He'll give you the guidance you need. Thankfully, He uses James to reveal to you those things you should be looking for when dealing with other people.

James 3:16 says, "For where envy and self-seeking exist, confusion and every evil thing will be there." The NLT says, "For wherever there is jealousy and selfish ambition, there you will find disorder and evil of every kind." If what people tell you is divisive and doesn't make for peace, it's time to end that conversation then and there. If you don't, there will be "disorder, unrest, rebellion, and every evil thing and morally degrading practice" (AMP). The Greek word for "envy" is "zelos" and is where the word "zealot" comes from. It means to have a fierce desire to promote one's own ideas and convictions to the exclusion of everyone else. It refers to a person who is so obsessed with his own opinions that he won't consider the views of other people. He is lopsided in his thinking and militant in his perspective, an extremist in the worst possible way. It's people like this who cause strife that leads to division in relationships. Their minds are so clouded by their own opinions that they have no tolerance for anyone who sees things differently than they do.

The result of all this is confusion and every evil work. An atmosphere of disorder and anarchy sets in and begins to destroy relationships where people end up getting hurt. The word "evil" describes something that is terribly bad or exceedingly vile. It's where the word "foul" comes from. James is saying that envy and strife lead to a foul-smelling relationship, one that people walk away from. In Greek,

James 3:16 can be translated, "For where there is a fierce desire to promote one's own ideas and convictions to the exclusion of everyone else's, it produces divisions so great that people end up taking sides and forming differing parties with conflicting agendas. This is a terrible event because it creates great unrest among people who should be united. Ultimately, the whole situation becomes a stinking mess!" The devil knows that envy and self-seeking can destroy those special relationships that God intended to be a blessing in your life. The enemy doesn't care who he divides as long as division is made.

Thankfully, there is some good news. There is wisdom from above and James gives clear evidence of what godly wisdom looks like. James 3:17 says, "But the wisdom that is from above is first pure, then peaceable, gentle, willing to yield, full of mercy and good fruits, without partiality and without hypocrisy." True wisdom always comes from above. It is not the attainment of man but the gift of God. Prov. 2:6 says, "For the Lord gives wisdom; From His mouth come knowledge and understanding." Ancient Jewish writers have described wisdom as "the breath of the power of God, and a pure influence flowing from the glory of the Almighty." The top priority of wisdom is that it must be pure, it must be undefiled by sin. God is holy and pure and so is the wisdom that comes from Him. There is no pride, jealousy, or selfish ambition is wisdom that comes from above. It is sweeter than honey to the taste. The Message Bible says, "Real wisdom, God's wisdom, begins with a holy life and is characterized by getting along with others."

Man's wisdom leads to rivalry and war (James 4:1) but wisdom from above leads to peace. It desires peace, promotes peace, seeks peace. True wisdom brings people closer to one another and to God. Gossip and slander does not lead to peace but instead promotes division. From such talk turn away. Don't say things that tear other people down and don't listen to those who do. The church can never function as a family with this kind of negative talk taking place. But if the church is pure and devoted to God, then peace will be there and the will of God will be fulfilled. James says that wisdom from above is also gentle. So important is this that Jesus said in Matt. 5:5 (NASB), "Blessed are the gentle, for they shall inherit the earth." To be gentle means to be "kind-hearted, sweet-spirited, self-controlled" (AMP). In this ego driven world, a world where everybody thinks they're always right, gentleness is hard to come by. People will literally fight with you if you don't agree with what they say.

The word "gentle" comes from the Greek word that describes a wild horse that has been tamed. A tame horse is no less strong than a wild horse. The difference is its strength is under control and ready to be used by its master. Those who are gentle are the strongest and wisest people on the planet. They don't over react and are not driven by their emotions. It's those who are weak that are arrogant, rude, argumentative, and mean. There are many benefits that come from having strength under control. Prov. 15:1 (NIV) says, "A gentle answer turns away wrath, but a harsh word stirs up anger." What people don't realize is that their brains are programmed to mimic the behavior patterns of those they're communicating with. If somebody yells at you, you'll yell back at them. If somebody is depressed, you'll join them and get depressed also. Knowing this, use your words to control the situation you're in. Gentleness diffuses conflict, it's the remedy for uncontrolled anger.

Eccl. 10:4 (NLT) says, "If your boss is angry with you, don't quit! A quiet, gentle spirit can overcome even great mistakes." If somebody raises their voice to you, you lower your voice to them. That is strength under control. A soft, gentle answer will turn away their wrath. They'll mimic the tone of your voice and will refrain from their outburst of anger. Conflicts are resolved and relationships are saved when you do this. Paul said in 1 Cor. 4:13 (NLT), "We respond gently when evil things are said about us." That's the gentleness of wisdom from above. Titus 2:8 (LB) says, "Your conversation should be so sensible that anyone who wants to argue will be ashamed because there won't be anything to criticize in anything you say." Gentleness is very persuasive. Prov. 25:15 (MSG) says, "Gentle speech breaks down rigid defenses." The New Century Version says, "A gentle word can get through to the hard-headed." The CEV says, "Patience and gentle talk can convince a ruler and overcome any problem."

The more wise you are, the more pleasant you will be. And the more pleasant you are, the more persuasive you will become. Prov. 16:21 (TEV) says, "A wise, mature person is known for understanding. The more pleasant his words, the more persuasive he is." If you want to convince somebody of something, you must be pleasant and gentle in the way you present your views. Remember, who you are is the type of people you will attract. If you are a godly person, godly people will be attracted to you. Likewise, gentleness attracts gentleness. 1 Tim. 6:11 (GWT) says, "As a man of God, pursue what God approves of: godliness, faith, love, endurance, and gentleness." These are the marks of a godly person, one who has grown up spiritually. You're Christlike and you want Jesus to live His life through you. You trust God in every area of your life. You're loving and unselfish. You don't give up, you always press on, and you have strength that is under control.

The best way to improve any relationship is to speak in a gentle voice. Ruth said to Boaz, "You are very kind to me. You have made me feel better by speaking gently to me" (Ruth 2:13 TEV). When someone disagrees with you, you can be tender with them without surrendering to their point of view. Rom. 14:1 (MSG) says, "Welcome with open arms fellow believers who don't see things the way you do. And don't jump all over them every time they do or say something you don't agree with - even when it seems that they are strong on opinions but weak in the faith department. Remember, they have their own history to deal with. Treat them gently." You don't have to devastate those you disagree with. It's not worth it to win an argument at the price of losing a relationship. If you respect other people, they will respect you. Be gentle with them. Be understanding, not demanding. Be like Jesus who said, "Take My yoke upon you and learn from Me, for I am gentle and humble in heart, and you will find rest for your souls" (Mark 11:29 NIV).

James also says that wisdom from above is willing to yield. The ESV says it is "open to reason." It means to be teachable and willing to listen. If you think you're right all the time then you are probably not operating in godly wisdom. Get rid of the pride that says you're always right and nobody can ever change your mind. Be open to reason. Check the scriptures and consider that what the other person is saying may be true. Next, James says the wisdom from above is full of mercy and good fruits. Mercy is compassion that leads to action. The NCV says it is "always ready to help those who are troubled and to do good for others." A person's actions can reveal if the words they speak is wisdom from above. If a person is loving and considerate and always looking to help meet another person's needs, then what they say in humility originated in the throne room of God. All you have to do is listen to what you hear and watch what you see for this is what tells you where the wisdom is coming from.

The wisdom from above is also without partiality. It is constant and unwavering, "not hot one day and cold the next, not two-faced" (MSG). Wisdom from God does not create division and discord. It has no hidden motives. It doesn't speak for the purpose of getting something from someone else. It is very sincere and without hypocrisy. It doesn't compliment a person to their face and then talk bad about them behind their back. Wisdom from above does not wear a mask for it is straight forward and genuine. James closes out this portion of scripture by saying, "Now the fruit of righteousness is sown in peace by those who make peace" (vs. 18). James says one of the primary traits of those who have godly wisdom is they are peacemakers. They "do the hard work of getting along with each other, treating each other with dignity and honor" (MSG). In the midst of a conflict, those with wisdom from above bring peace and reconciliation into the situation. Find a person sowing peace and you'll find wisdom from above.

-22-

"THE WAR WITHIN"

In the world today, everywhere you look, there is conflict. There is social unrest and disorder in the home, at church, at work, and certainly among all the nations of the world. Sad to say, peace is almost non-existent. Arguments and disagreements abound everywhere and relationships are spiraling out of control. Why is this happening? Because the world is full of sinners and selfish people. So bad is it that one is tempted to cry out, "Can't we all just get along?" The Jewish philosopher Philo of Alexandria once wrote, "Consider the continual war which prevails among men even in times of peace. Observe the unspeakable raging storm in men's souls that is excited by the violent rush of the affairs of life." James asks a couple of rhetorical questions in hopes of getting to the root of the problem. Get ready for he shines a spotlight deep down into your innermost being.
He asks, "Where do wars and fights come from among you? Do they not come from your desires for pleasure that war in your members?" (James 4:1).

It cannot be denied that James is talking to Christians in this passage of scripture because he says these wars and fights are happening "among you." He is saying that many Christians are known more for their fighting and hypocrisy than they are for loving others as Christ loved the church. It is a sad commentary that the Bible records many conflicts among the members of the early church. Members of the Corinthian church were suing each other in court (1 Cor. 6:6), the Galatian believers were "biting and devouring" one another (Gal. 5:15), and there were two women in the church at Philippi who could not get along (Phil. 4:2). All believers belong to the same family, the family of God, so why are so many Christians at war with one another? James answers that question by saying there is another war going on. The Message Bible says, "Where do you think all these appalling wars and quarrels come from? Do you think they just happen? Think again. They come about because you want your own way, and fight for it deep inside yourselves."

James is pointing his finger at every born again believer. He is saying, "The problem is you. The conflict you are now in is because of your own passions that are at war within you." In other words, Christians are at war with themselves. The war in the heart, the war within, is what causes conflicts and division in the church and the rest of the world. Is. 53:6 (MSG) says, "We're all like sheep who've wandered off and gotten lost. We've all done our own thing, gone our own way." The root of all sin is selfishness. Eve ate the forbidden fruit because she wanted to become wise like God. Achan selfishly took some of the forbidden treasure from the ruins of Jericho and caused Israel to be defeated in battle. Titus 3:3 says, "For we ourselves were also once foolish, disobedient, serving various lusts and pleasures, living in malice and envy, hateful and hating one another." In the parable of the sower it was the cares, riches, and pleasures of this life that choked the good seed and made it unproductive (Luke 8:14).

James is firing on all cylinders as he says the cause of all conflict is distorted desires in the hearts of people. If you want something different than someone else, sparks are going to fly. Wives want the toilet seat down and husbands want the toilet seat up. Men want to watch sports and women want to sit down and talk. Friction arises when one person doesn't get their way and it's the natural tendency to blame the other person for the conflict that follows. Adam blamed Eve and Eve blamed the serpent. The quarrel isn't your fault, it's the other person's fault. There is no way what's happening is because of you. Not a chance! No way! If you're sure of that, you are in direct conflict with the Word of God. God is saying the quarreling and fighting that is happening is coming from inside of you. It really is your fault. If you disagree with that, you can take it up with Him. The NLT says these quarrels and fights "come from the evil desires at war within you."

There is a mentality in the world today where people think life is all about their own personal needs and desires. There is something in you called "self" and it demands to be pleased. They say you only live once so do whatever it takes to make yourself happy even if it hurts someone else. It's this attitude that James says is the root of all conflict in the world. The Greek word for "evil desires" is "hedone" which is defined as 'the desire to please self.' Seeking pleasure and sensual self-indulgence becomes the highest purpose in life to those who don't crucify their flesh and make Jesus the Lord of their life. The compulsive desire to please self is alive and well and it is at war within you. Selfish desires always lead to war. If there is war on the inside, there will be war with others on the outside. It's because of hedonism, the desire to please self, that there is fighting, quarreling, arguing, slander, backbiting, and despicable evil in the church.

The book of James is unique in that its purpose is to rattle your cage and wake you up to the fact that there is a sin nature you must deal with. His message is so clear and so strong. Whenever you are in a conflict, it's because evil desires and selfish passions are at war within you. Paul dealt with the same thing. He wrote in Rom. 7:23 (MSG), "I truly delight in God's commands, but it's pretty obvious that not all of me joins in that delight. Parts of me covertly rebel, and just when I least expect it, they take charge." He also wrote in Gal. 5:17 (NLT), "The sinful nature wants to do evil, which is just the opposite of what the Spirit wants." Paul knew the war within steals, kills, and destroys. It causes fights and arguments in the church which lead to division. Why do you think cities have a different believing church on almost every street corner? It's because they're full of people set in their own ways and are unwilling to change even when the Bible contradicts what they believe.

Selfish desires are dangerous things. They cause division and lead to wrong actions. James says these cravings are a desire for pleasure, a yearning to feel good. In and of themselves, these desires are not bad. 1 Tim. 6:17 says God "gives us richly all things to enjoy." The problem comes when these pleasures come at the expense of someone else, when you use and manipulate people to get that which you're craving for, when people become stepping stones to get you where you want to go. James identified the source of all conflicts and now he reveals the consequence of the self-focused sin nature. James 4:2 (ESV) says, "You desire and do not have, so you murder. You covet and cannot obtain, so you fight and quarrel." When people are striving for the same things, things such as power, wealth, and prestige, they'll go to war with one another and trample under foot anybody who gets in their way. They'll do anything, including murder, to eliminate a rival so they can get what they're craving for.

The last of the Ten Commandments is "Thou shall not covet" (Ex. 20:17). The word "covet" portrays the false need of wanting more and more and more of something. It carries the idea of overreaching for more than you need. It depicts control. You can want something so much that the thing you desire can gain control of you. James is saying if you break this command to not covet, you are capable of breaking the other nine. Indeed, he is trying to rock your world and startle you with his words. The Message Bible says, "You lust for what you don't have and are willing to kill to get it. You want what isn't yours and will risk violence to get your hands on it." People don't appreciate what they do have because they're consumed with getting what they don't have. They're greedy for more and more and covet those things other people have that they don't. No longer do they love people and use things, now they love things and use people. They don't see people as being God's children but rather as a means to an end, a means to getting what they selfishly want.

Pride is when all you do is think about yourself and Prov. 13:10 (NLT) says, "Pride leads to conflict." When life is centered around you, there will be strife and contention. James is saying that conflict is a symptom of a deeper sin, the sin of pride. There is something in your heart that is not right, something unsettled. When you hurt people to get what you want, there is something internally messed up, something wrong that needs to be dealt with. James then makes a startling statement, "Yet you do not have because you do not ask" (vs. 2). What is James saying here? He's saying that not only is your relationship with people damaged, your relationship with God is altered as well. He's saying you'd rather argue with people than talk to God about it. You're in a state of mind where you don't talk to God anymore. Your communication with Him is broken. Not praying is the greatest proof that pride has taken over your life. You think you've got life figured out and don't need God anymore. Why pray to a God you don't need?

Do not be misled by what James is saying here. He is not saying you can ask God to fulfill your selfish desires and He'll do it. What people don't understand is that there is a void in their life that only God can fill. Problems come when people use selfish desires to fill that void. They don't have fulfillment, peace, or happiness because they're looking for it in all the wrong places. They're not asking God for what they need and for what He wants them to have. Instead, they're asking for what they themselves selfishly crave and desire.

What they need can never be filled with a selfish sin nature. Never! Instead of turning to God as the giver of every good and perfect gift (James 1:17), they're fighting to satisfy what they think they need. Instead of crucifying their flesh and looking to God, they struggle to get what their selfish desires are demanding. The war within is taking place and strong envy and resentment toward others is causing them to lose the war. Nobody wins in a conflict. Fights and quarrels damage everybody, nobody more than yourself.

Then there are those who try to manipulate God, people who use prayer to try to get from Him something they desire more than Him. James 4:3 (ESV) says, "You ask and do not receive, because you ask wrongly, to spend it on your passions." These people are not seeking God's face, they're seeking His hand. They're praying Godless prayers, seeking things more than Him. The Message Bible says, "You're spoiled children, each wanting your own way." How many prayers are motivated by one's desire to please themselves? "God, I want this! I want that!" When you pray with selfish desires, you pray with the same motives that you fight and quarrel with. God rejects selfish motives and greedy prayers. James says if you pray with selfishness as a motive, you should not expect to receive anything from the Lord. He is not a genie in a bottle waiting to grant your every wish. That's not who He is! If selfishness is your only motive for praying to God, what type of God would He be if He answered those prayers?

A selfish person can never have a good prayer life. Instead of seeking God's will, they instead tell Him what they want Him to do. What's more, they'll get angry at Him if they don't get what they want. In turn, this same anger will be taken out on other people. Churches have been divided because people have taken their frustration with God out on fellow believers. James is being very direct as he talks about the poison of wrong motives and selfish desires. He knows if your sin nature is not dealt with, it will draw you into the death trap of having a love affair with the world. He can't sit idly by as those under his care travel down the broad and twisted road that leads to destruction. Righteous anger now rises up in the heart of James as he says in vs. 4, "Adulterers and adulteresses! Do you not know that friendship with the world is enmity with God? Whoever therefore wants to be a friend of the world makes himself an enemy of God." No longer does James address these people as "My brethren." They've declared war on God and James doesn't like it. Neither does God.

The Amplified Bible says, "You are like unfaithful wives having illicit love affairs with the world and breaking your marriage vow to God. Do you not know that being the world's friend is being God's enemy?" The world system is filled with sin and its god is the devil himself. James is saying you know that, don't you? There is a war going on between right and wrong, good and bad. It's between the righteousness of God and the sinfulness of the world. Every believer must choose which side of the war they're on and 1 John 2:15,17 (NLT) shows the results of which side you pledge your allegiance to, "Do not love this world nor the things it offers you, for when you love the world, you do not have the love of the Father in you. And this world is fading away, along with everything that people crave. But anyone who does what pleases God will live forever." A choice must be made. You can stand with God, or you can stand with the world. Choose wisely knowing that whichever side you choose, the other side becomes your enemy.

Whoever is a friend of the world cannot be the friend of God. When people go after things more than God, they're committing adultery with Him. God said in Jer. 3:20, "Surely as a faithless wife leaves her husband, so have you been faithless to me, O house of Israel." The root of every conflict is spiritual adultery. Conflict with people begins with a conflict with God. James is not saying they're cheating on their spouses, he's saying they're cheating on God. Hosea 9:1

says, "Do not rejoice, O Israel, with joy like other peoples, for you have played the harlot against your God." Even Jesus spoke of a sinful, wicked, and adulterous generation (Matt. 16:4; Mark 8:38). Selfish desires rise up when a person is not satisfied with God and all He has done for them. This in turn leads to conflict with other people because cheaters always covet what other people have. The world lives for the here and now and so do many believers. Their lives are driven by envy and their selfish ambition drives them to get what they want at any cost.

The Message Bible says, "You're cheating on God. If all you want is your own way, flirting with the world every chance you get, you end up enemies of God and His way." James doesn't say if you love the world that God becomes your enemy, he's saying that you become God's enemy. Rom. 8:7,8 (MSG) says, "Focusing on the self is the opposite of focusing on God. Anyone completely absorbed in self ignores God, ends up thinking more about self than God. That person ignores who God is and what He is doing. And God isn't pleased at being ignored." People who are double-minded are spiritual harlots. Their hearts are divided between God and their love for the things of the world. Paul said in 2 Tim. 4:10 (NLT), "Demas has deserted me because he loves the things of this life." If a person dedicates his life to material things, he cannot dedicate his life to God. Jesus said in Matt. 6:24 (MSG), "You can't worship two gods at once. Loving one god, you'll end up hating the other. Adoration of one feeds contempt for the other."

Jesus said, "He who is not with Me is against Me" (Matt. 12:30). You can't be married to Christ (Rom. 7:4) and yet love the world. In a marriage ceremony the bride and groom both vow to forsake all others and be devoted exclusively to their spouse. The same thing happens when you get born again. You must forsake the world and its sensual pleasures if you are to remain committed to God. Still, people pray and ask God for things that will allow them to commit adultery with the world. That's the same despicable thing as a wife asking her husband for money to hire a male prostitute. Doing this dissolves the spiritual marriage between you and God. Ps. 73:27 says, "For indeed, those who are far from You shall perish; You have destroyed all those who desert You for harlotry." The Message Bible says, "Deserters, they'll never be heard from again." Deserters are those who seek in the world that which can only be found in God. The pleasures of the world come and go but the blessings of God last forever.

Evangelist Billy Sunday once said, "You might as well talk about a heavenly devil as talk about a worldly Christian." You cannot enjoy the ways of the world without being entangled with the cares and pleasures of it. Avoid at all costs covetous friendships with the world for a person caught up in this world is not ready for the next one. Col. 3:5 calls covetousness "idolatry" but here it is called adultery. It is treason to put the world above God. It is diabolically wrong to do this for treason is the highest crime of a civil nature of which a person can be found guilty. The world was not made to be your master, it was made to be your servant. You fulfill your destiny by using the things of the world to bring glory to God and to bless your fellow man. You can use the world or it can use you. The choice is yours. Take heed to the words of 2 Cor. 6:17, "Come out from among them and be separate, says the Lord. Do not touch what is unclean, and I will receive you." This was not a suggestion, it was a command so do it now!

James asks in vs. 5, "Or do you think that the Scripture says in vain, 'The Spirit who dwells in us yearns jealously'?" Scripture does not hide the fact that God is a jealous God. He said, "I the Lord your God am a jealous God" (Ex. 20:5). He said in Zech. 8:2, "I am jealous for Zion with great jealousy." James is saying that God jealously yearns for the full devotion of your heart. The word "jealous" in Greek has in it the idea of burning heat. He is saying that God loves people with such a burning passion that He cannot bear any other love within the hearts of His people. God is a jealous lover and He is not passive. He aggressively and actively pursues a relationship with all His people. The Greek translation of James 4:5 says, "The Spirit who has come to settle down, make His home, and permanently dwell in us is moved by an all-consuming, ever-growing, passionate desire to possess us - and He is envious and filled with malice toward anything or anyone who tries to take His place in our lives."

God is a jealous God and He will not tolerate divided allegiance. Christians are indwelt with God's Spirit who yearns for the undivided loyalty and love of God's people. Just as the world is the enemy of the Father, so the flesh is the enemy of the Holy Spirit. James is saying, "You are grieving the Holy Spirit who has come to dwell within you, who yearn with a jealous envy to possess your entire nature for Himself." Living for the flesh grieves the Holy Spirit. A part of your heart is given to God, but not all of it. This causes God to have the same pain a spouse would feel if their loved one was not faithful to them. There is no greater pain than the loss of affection that at one time had been whole and complete. God has a jealous love for those who are His. A godly jealousy is defined as "a consuming single-minded pursuit of a good end." It's used to describe God's holy zeal for the honor of His name and the good of His people who are bound to Him in a marriage-like covenant.

When you covet and embrace the ways of the world, God's jealousy is stirred up. He continually longs to keep you near to Him. He urgently corrects, rebukes, and guides you into a closer relationship with Him. He is a jealous God and He wants all of you, not a part of you. He is filled with a burning desire for you to be holy, righteous, and truly good. James is asking, "Do you think it's in vain that Scripture says God has a divine jealousy for you?" No, it is not in vain. The first of the Ten Commandments says, "You shall have no other gods before Me" (Ex. 20:3). God then says in vs. 5 (NLT), "You must not bow down to them or worship them for I, the Lord your God, am a jealous God who will not tolerate your affection for other gods." Don't make gods and idols out of lust, greed, envy, and the sensual pleasures the sinful world is offering you. God requires that you be passionately loyal to Him at all times and at all costs. He loves you with a jealous love and He won't tolerate spiritual adultery.

Be extremely aware that the sin nature inside of you is being drawn by fleshly desires to become friends with and secretly in love with the world and its evil ways. James is giving you an opportunity to not let this happen. He is telling you to wake up and take notice of your current lifestyle. No, there is nothing wrong with having the finer things in life. God wants you to have a good job, a nice house, a new car, and beautiful clothes. All these things are part of God's will for you to live an abundant life on the earth. They are not wrong unless they consume all your thoughts and actions. Even good things, when taken to the extreme, become adulterous in the eyes of the Lord. All God wants is for your relationship with Him to be the top priority in your life. You are His top priority and He yearns jealously to be yours. This can happen when you become aware of how much He loves you. His love is pure, unfickled, and forever established. All He wants is for you to love Him the same way. He is a jealous God and will not tolerate any rival to that love.

Randall J. Brewer

-23-

"EMBRACE THE GRACE"

God is a jealous God. He is jealous when He sees the affections of His people set on anything other than Himself. He loves you with an everlasting love (Jer. 31:3) and Augustine once said "God gives what He demands." He demands that your love and loyalty be given to Him instead of to the evil world system. He wants to be your first and only love and He'll even help you do it. James 4:6 (AMP) says, "But He gives us more and more grace, the power of the Holy Spirit, to meet this evil tendency and all others fully. That is why He says, God sets Himself against the proud and haughty, but gives grace continually to the lowly, those who are humble enough to receive it." Here is God's answer. He is offering you more of His grace and this will save you from the destruction of having a love affair with the world. Grace is God treating you as if you were Jesus Himself. His grace is more than adequate to meet the requirements of His jealousy. It's the grace of God that allows you to be in the world but not of the world (John 15:19).

Take comfort knowing that God has provided a way to save you from the snare of the enemy and the clutches of the world. God demands absolute fidelity and total allegiance and with that demand He gives the grace that makes it happen. He gives a greater grace, a grace that is strong and more remarkable in magnitude and effectiveness. Ps. 107:9 says, "For He satisfies the longing soul, and fills the hungry soul with goodness." It is only through His grace that you can say no to the magnetic pull of worldly pleasures. Titus 2:11,12 (NLT) says, "For the grace of God has been revealed, bringing salvation to all people. And we are instructed to turn from godless living and sinful pleasures. We should live in this evil world with wisdom, righteousness, and devotion to God." Grace does not give you the license to do as you please, it's the power that allows you to do what pleases God. It's given so that you can obey His commands and it's what insures that you'll persevere all the days of your life.

Eph. 2:4,5 (NLT) says, "But God is so rich in mercy, and He loved us so much, that even though we were dead because of or sins, He gave us life when He raised Christ from the dead. It is only by God's grace that you have been saved!" Grace is not to be demanded but received. It is the gift of God which allows you to overcome the struggle with pride and the temptation to live life according to worldly wisdom. Col. 1:21,22 (MSG) says, "Christ brought you over to God's side and put your lives together, whole and holy in His presence. You don't walk away from a gift like that!" Grace changes everything. It changes your relationship with God and it changes how you deal with others. It's grace that breaks the bondage the world has you in. It truly is an amazing grace. James then tells what must happen in order for this grace to be poured out into your life. Yes, it is an unending grace but getting it is conditional. "Therefore He says, 'God resists the proud, but gives grace to the humble'" (vs. 6).

The only way to be a benefactor of God's greater grace is to maintain a humble attitude. It is in the act of being humble that you will find all the grace you need. God said in Is. 57:15, "I dwell in the high and holy place, with him who has a contrite and humble spirit, to revive the spirit of the humble, and to revive the heart of the contrite ones." The Message

Bible says, "And what I do is put new spirit in them, get them up and on their feet again." God has chosen to put His temple, His dwelling place, in the hearts of the humble. It is through humility where one is made capable of receiving the fullness of God. He gives grace to the humble because the humble give Him all the glory. John the Baptist said, "He must increase, but I must decrease" (John 3:30). That's humility. Frances Quarles, the English poet, adds, "The best way to see divine light is to put out thine own candle." This is not a suggestion but a command. You must humble yourself! You must decrease! You must be made low so that you can be made high.

Charles Spurgeon once said, "Humble hearts lie in the valleys where streams of grace are flowing, and hence they drink of them." Humility is not thinking less of yourself, it's thinking of yourself less. Phil. 2:3 says, "Instead, be humble and give more honor to others than to yourself." In other words, you and what you want is not always on your mind. Focusing on yourself all the time is a sure recipe for conflict. It creates all kinds of strife which results in division and separation. It is the nature of sin to think about yourself, talk about yourself, and focus on yourself. Your "self" is always crying out for attention. It pathetically says, "What about me?" Biblical humility is to crucify your "self." It's not thinking low of yourself, it's not thinking of yourself at all. Humility is an emptying of yourself so that you have no more "self" left in you. The biggest spiritual battle you will ever fight is with your "self" nature. "Self" is your enemy and it is the enemy of humility. "Self" must be eliminated so that Jesus Christ can take its place.

Andrew Murray says, "Humility is perfect quietness of heart. It is to expect nothing, to wonder at nothing that is done to me, to feel nothing done against me. It is to be at rest when nobody praises me, and when I am blamed and despised. It is to have a blessed home in the Lord, where I can go in and shut the door, and kneel to my Father in secret, and am at peace in a deep sea of calmness, when all around and above is trouble." The conflict you allow yourself to be in is because you are concerned about your "self." How can you have strife if you feel nothing done against you? If your "self" is crucified, there would be nothing to have conflict. Remove "self" and there will be peace. Tyndale's Bible Dictionary uses Jesus Christ as the prime example for its definition of the word "humility." Referring to Phil. 2:7,8 it says, "As Son of God, Jesus took no thought of Himself but lived a life of obedience and trust in God the Father. A self-emptying by which He humbled Himself and took on the form of a servant."

Sin abounds when pride and selfishness prevail. Thankfully, Paul wrote in Rom. 5:20, "But where sin abounded, grace did much more abound." God's grace is measureless and inexhaustible. The word "abound" comes from a Greek word which means 'to overflow' like a river overflowing its banks and flooding everything around it. The grace of God is lavish and bountiful and goes above and beyond anything sin dares to accomplish. The answer to every conflict is more and more grace. It can soften the hardest heart and it allows forgiveness to happen. Grace can totally and radically change you and any situation you may find yourself in. Trust God for He "is able to make all grace abound toward you" (2 Cor. 9:8). Don't allow this grace to pass you by. God wants to give it to you but He needs humility to do it. He needs you to admit you can't do this on your own and that you need His help. He said to Paul in 2 Cor. 12:9, "My grace is sufficient for you, for My strength is made perfect in weakness."

What should you do? Embrace the grace! Grab it and hold onto it. Heb. 4:16 says, "Let us therefore come boldly to the throne of grace, that we may obtain mercy, and find grace to help in time of need." In New Testament times, freedom of speech was restricted and people who violated the rules were punished. It just wasn't acceptable to speak boldly and candidly. God does not feel that way. When you go to the

Lord, He wants to hear exactly what you have to say. You don't have to concern yourself that you're being too blunt and forthright when you bear your heart to Him. Even if you're wrong, God is not bothered when you are honest about your feelings and concerns with Him. He may correct you but it pleases Him when you speak freely from your heart. He is willing to give you what you need but you've got to receive it by faith. The word "obtain" means 'to lay hold of it, take it and make it your own.' Reach out and forcibly lay hold of the mercy and help God is offering you.

Not only will you obtain His mercy, you'll also find grace to help in time of need. The word "find" expresses the idea of a discovery that is made by an intense search and investigation. Jesus said in Matt. 7:7, "Ask, and it will be given to you; seek, and you will find; knock, and it will be opened to you." The Message Bible says, "Be direct. Ask for what you need." Be persistent like the woman who knocked on the judge's door and never gave up (Luke 18:1-8). If you'll do that, if you'll embrace the grace, God promises that you will receive exactly what you need from Him. You'll find help in time of need. The word "help" is a military term meaning God will go to battle for you and fight until you are delivered and set free. He is the greatest Warrior in all the universe. He is the Lion of Judah and He is on your side. Jesus is seated at the right hand of the Father where He ever lives to make intercession for anyone who comes to Him by faith (Heb. 7:25). The Message Bible says He is "always on the job to speak up for them."

James wants all his readers to swim triumphantly in the river of grace. He wants them to repent and turn away from all their ungodly behavior. Then, like a military commander, he issues a series of commands that call for immediate action. He begins by saying, "Therefore submit to God" (vs. 7). Humility always manifests itself in submission. Jesus said, "Not My will but Thine be done" (Luke 22:42). To grow up spiritually you must say the same thing. The command to submit is a basic requirement which must precede obedience to the subsequent commands. It's a military term that means "get into your proper rank." The Greek word "hypotasso" means literally 'to place under in an orderly fashion.' It implies that the one who is subordinate is ready and willing to obey their superior's commands. Webster's Dictionary says submission is "a yielding of one's will to the will or appointment of a superior without murmuring. Entire and cheerful submission to the will of God is a Christian duty of prime excellence."

James commands his readers to make a conscious choice to submit their imperfect will to God's perfect will. This you must do daily. Submitting to God must be done sincerely, freely, and faithfully. Ps. 119:60 says, "I made haste, and did not delay to keep Your commandments." When the heart submits to God in sincerity, the work of grace begins. To be a partaker of God's grace, you must get rid of pride and arrogance and daily choose to surrender your will to His. Let God be God in your life. Put Him on the throne of your life and give Him full control. Command those wrong attitudes to "be pulled up by the roots and be planted in the sea" (Luke 17:6). This is a deliberate action for there is no accidental deliverance from these attitudes. With gritted teeth you must wrap both hands around the problem and rip it out of your soul. So they don't come back, Jesus said these attitudes must be planted in the sea where the salt water will kill its roots. Never again will that problem be able to grow and produce life. Once in the sea, it's dead forever.

Your willingness to yield to God is a reflection of genuine humility. James is commanding you to give your full allegiance to God and God alone. There should be no doubt in your mind whose side you're on. Lam. 3:28,29 says, "Let him sit alone and keep silent, because God has laid it on him; Let him put his mouth in the dust - there may be hope." The Message Bible says, "When life is heavy and hard to take, go off by yourself. Enter the silence. Bow in prayer. Don't ask questions: Wait for hope to appear." A person is not saved until they bow before the supreme majesty of God. They can say they believe in Jesus but if they're not submitted to Him, if they follow their own desires and passions, they are only pretenders, a wolf in sheep's clothing. Remember, you're not in charge. God is! You are His creation and you must come under His authority. Rom. 12:1 says to "present your bodies a living sacrifice." You are here to serve God and submission to Him will always be manifested by prompt obedience.

James then says, "Resist the devil and he will flee from you." Are you doing that? Do you stand firm against pride, jealousy, and selfish ambition? Are you fiercely opposed to what the devil is doing? Are you determined to resist him, to stand against him, to defy his operation in your life? The word "devil" is not the name of your adversary but is a description of how he operates. The word means to "repetitiously throw something, striking again and again until the object being struck has finally been completely penetrated." The devil doesn't assault your mind once but many times over. He keeps on striking until he wears down the resistance of the person being assaulted. Weak-kneed believers then lower their guard thus allowing the devil to penetrate their mind with evil thoughts and attitudes. If that person will listen to those lies, the devil can begin to control and manipulate him. A mental stronghold has been built and will remain there until that person wakes up and begins to resist the devil, the enemy of their soul.

Just as there is a real God, there is also a real devil and you must be aggressively determined to stand against him. You must be firm, unyielding, and steadfast. Dig your heels into the ground and brace yourself for a fight. Cowardice never wins against the devil, only courage. Take your stand on the Word of God and watch the devil flee from you. John 1:4,5 (NLT) says, "The Word gave life to everything that was created, and His life brought light to everyone. The light shines in the darkness, and the darkness can never extinguish it." James is telling you to take a stand against the devil. Set yourself against him and his deceitful schemes. Eph. 6:11 says, "Put on the whole armor of God, that you may be able to stand against the wiles of the devil." This is a face to face confrontation just like when David confronted Goliath. Just remember, before you can stand against the devil, you must first submit and bow before God. When you fear the Lord, you'll be able to stand against your adversary in the strength provided by your submission to God.

There is a sequence of events that take place in standing firm against the devil. First you submit to God, then you resist the devil. Webster's Dictionary says that "resist" means, "Literally, to stand against, to withstand; hence, to act in opposition, or to oppose. A dam or mound resists a current of water passively, by standing unmoved and interrupting its progress. An army resists the progress of an enemy actively, by encountering and defeating it." One of the greatest promises in all the Bible is that when you resist the devil, he will flee from you. The word "flee" depicts a lawbreaker who flees in terror from a nation where he broke the law. The Greek word "pheugo" means 'to flee away; to take flight in order to seek safety.' It's where the word "fugitive" comes from, defined as one who escapes from something or someone. He runs away from danger toward a place of security because he doesn't want to face the consequences of the wrong he did. The devil flees because he knows if you resist him, it won't be long until you begin to rule and dominate him.

Humility, manifested by submission, is not weakness but in fact is your strength to live the supernatural Christian life. You've submitted to God. You've resisted the devil. James 4:8 (AMP) tells you what to do next, "Come close to God and He will come close to you. Recognize that you are sinners, get your soiled hands clean; realize that you have been disloyal, wavering individuals with divided interests, and purify your hearts of your spiritual adultery." The command to draw near to God is given because ungodly behavior and friendship with the world puts distance between you and God. At the same time, you cannot be close to God if you're angry and bitter toward someone else. The number of conflicts in your life are in direct proportion to the time you spend with God. The more you draw closer to God, the less conflicts you will have. Is. 26:3 (MSG) says, "People with their minds set on You, You keep completely whole, steady on their feet, because they keep at it and don't quit."

In order to submit to God there must be a wholehearted return to God, personal cleansing, open repentance, and humility. The Message Bible says, "Quit dabbling in sin. Purify your inner life. Quit playing the field." Sin is departing from God, grace is returning. David draws near to God in Ps. 63:1, "O God, You are my God; Early will I seek You; My soul thirsts for You; My flesh longs for You in a dry and thirsty land where there is no water." He then asks God to draw near to him in Ps. 64:18, "Draw near to my soul, and redeem it; Deliver me because of my enemies." David was a man after God's own heart. He had fellowship with Him and spent time alone in His presence. You also need to be in close contact with the King of kings and Lord of lords. Ps. 145:18 says, "The Lord is near to all who call upon Him, to all who call upon Him in truth." Draw near to God. Abide in the Word, in worship, and in your works of service to Him. Ps. 73:28 says, "But it is good for me to draw near to God; I have put my trust in the Lord God, that I may declare all Your works."

James knows that light and darkness don't mix so after telling his readers to draw near to God he says, "Cleanse your hands, you sinners; and purify your hearts, you double-minded." Once again, James does not address these people as his brethren. He calls them sinners and double-minded because he wants to pierce the heart and conscience of those he's writing to. The word "sinner" describes a person who is devoted to sin and lives in continual opposition to the will of God. Christians everywhere need to examine their lives and deal with the problem of sin. Ps. 24:3,4 says, "Who may ascend into the hill of the Lord? Or who may stand in His holy place? He who has clean hands and a pure heart." The Greek word for "cleanse" is "katharos" and it means 'pure, clean, without stain or spot.' Is. 1:16 says, "Wash yourselves, make yourselves clean; Put away the evil of your doings from before My eyes. Cease to do evil." The closer one draws near to God, the more sensitive he is to sin."

You can't live like God and the world at the same time. A person who is going to be used by God has to be clean both on the outside and the inside. Cleansing your hands speaks of your outward actions and purifying your heart speaks of the inner attitude and motives leading to sinful actions. People say they're sorry for what they do wrong and then go out and do the same thing over and over again. When this happens, clearly they weren't sorry they sinned in the first place. Those who are truly repentant will confess their sins and forsake them. Prov. 28:13 says, "He who covers his sins will not prosper, but whoever confesses and forsakes them will have mercy." The Message Bible says, "You can't whitewash your sins and get by with it; you find mercy by admitting and leaving them." The Greek word for "purify" is "hagnizo" and is defined as 'a freedom from defilements and impurities, a withdrawal from the profane, a removal of that which disqualifies one for acceptable worship, resulting in a condition of purity and chastity.'

Martin Luther once said, "A cup for show only has to be cleansed on the outside." James, on the other hand, is speaking of a purity that affects not only a person's conduct but also their inner motives. You must be pure inside and out. 1 John 3:3 says, "And everyone who has this hope in Him purifies himself, just as He is pure." Sin is a problem that must be taken seriously and what James is saying cannot be overlooked. He says in vs. 9, "Lament and mourn and weep! Let your laughter be turned to mourning and your joy to gloom." The truth be told, there is not enough sorrow for sin among born again believers. There should be more godly grief in the body of Christ. The Amplified Bible says, "As you draw near to God, be deeply penitent and grieve, even weep over your disloyalty. Let your laughter be turned to grief and your mirth to dejection and heartfelt shame for your sins." Sin kills your fellowship with God and James tells of a grief so deep and profound that it simply cannot be contained or concealed.

James is giving an urgent demand for open and thorough repentance. The Message Bible says, "Hit bottom, and cry your eyes out. The fun and games are over. Get serious, really serious." The intensity of these words are startling. They're intended to shake those believers who are double-minded. The NLT says, "Let there be tears for what you have done." Never make light of when you sin. Lament. Be miserable and experience distress and a sense of brokenness. Ps. 38:6 says, "I am troubled, I am bowed down greatly; I go mourning all the day long." Mourn. This is grief and sorrow caused by profound loss, often associated with death or great tragedy. Weep. These are not silent tears but refers to loud and audible weeping. Sin should bring such deep, inner agony that it causes one to lament with sobbing. Jacob wept and prayed (Hos. 12:4) and the children of Israel wept and offered sacrifices (Judges 2:4,5). Ps. 6:6 says, "I am weary with my groaning; All night I make my bed swim; I drench my couch with my tears."

Now that James has your attention, he says in vs. 10, "Humble yourselves in the sight of the Lord, and He will lift you up." The word "humble" means 'to make low, to bow down, to have a genuine realization of complete unworthiness and lostness because of sin.' In one of the Lord's parables, a tax collector beat his chest in sorrow and said, "O God, be merciful to me, for I am a sinner" (Luke 18:13). Jesus went on to say this was a man with true humility. He also said in Matt. 18:4, "Therefore whoever humbles himself as this little child is the greatest in the kingdom of heaven." As a child is lowly, you shall willingly become by spiritual process what the child is by nature. Only an empty vessel can God fill with His grace. The flesh is not able to humble the flesh. Inside of you is the Spirit of God and He provides the grace that enables you to obey this command. Phil. 2:13 (NLT) says, "For God is working in you, giving you the desire and the power to do what pleases Him." This power is the grace of God and this is why you must embrace the grace.

-24-

"FATHER KNOWS BEST"

James is writing to a group of believers who say they possess faith when in reality their faith does not possess them. He is saying that real faith never stands alone and, when God comes into your life, you're going to think and act differently than you did before. More than once James has dealt with issues of separation and division among the people. The fleshly nature of being self-centered causes offense, conflict, strife, and separation. The key to success of any organization is unity among its members. This is especially true with the local church. Eph. 4:2,3 (NLT) says, "Always be humble and gentle. Be patient with each other, making allowance for each other's faults because of your love. Make every effort to keep yourselves united in the Spirit, binding yourselves together with peace." Unity and humility go together. Humility is the opposite of self and is the key that unlocks true happiness. One of the greatest causes of unhappiness is conflict with other people. Pride causes conflict but humility takes it away.

Daily humble yourselves before God. Understand that God will not force you to crucify your flesh. You must start the process on your own. You must empty yourself of your self. If you'll do that, God will step in and provide the grace and power for you to walk in biblical humility. 1 Peter 5:5 says,

"Yes, all of you be submissive to one another, and be clothed with humility." To end all conflict you must put off self and put on humility (Col. 3:12). You must replace self with Christ. You've got to replace the bad with something good. If you don't, the bad will return and will be more destructive than it was before. The self-indulgent nature of the flesh reveals itself in conflict, quarreling, jealousy, outbursts of anger, and selfish ambition causing division among people and the feeling that everyone is wrong except you. Phil. 2:3 says, "Let nothing be done through selfish ambition or conceit." These two things always bring conflict. Selfish ambition says, "It's all about me" and vain conceit says, "I'm always right." Is it any wonder that God resists the proud but gives grace to the humble?

Grace is the ability to forgive when you don't feel like doing so, the capability to resolve conflicts, the power to compromise and get along. Paul wrote in Phil. 2:2 (NLT), "Then make me truly happy by agreeing wholeheartedly with each other, loving one another, and working together with one mind and purpose." Paul is saying that happiness comes from being in harmony with other people. Humility leads to harmony and harmony leads to happiness. Every relationship needs these four types of harmony if peace and happiness are to abound. Mental harmony comes from having the same mind, emotional harmony emerges when people share the same love, spiritual harmony is the result of being united in spirit, and directional harmony flows when everybody is intent on one purpose. If you're not humble, harmony will vanish and all your relationships will fall apart. To be humble you've got to learn the lost art of paying attention to other people. Phil. 2:4 says, "Don't be interested only in your own life, but be interested in what concerns others too."

Everywhere you go it seems like everybody has attention deficit disorder. People just don't pay attention anymore.

Modern technology has trained people to no longer pay attention to other people and what's going on around them. People pay more attention to their smart phone than they do to people. They're always texting or playing video games. Social media feeds your pride and distracts you from seeing those around you. People are just too wrapped up in themselves to notice other people. Thankfully, Jesus was not that way. He paid attention to sinners and tax collectors and those society rejected. He spoke to the woman at the well in Samaria and touched lepers and was friends with prostitutes. He paid attention to these people knowing this is one of the greatest forms of love there is. Your attention is time and time is your life. Paying attention goes beyond listening. When you pay attention to somebody, you're giving them a portion of your life. You're telling the other person they're important and what they're saying matters to you.

James continues his narrative of telling people how to get along with one another. "Do not speak evil of one another, brethren. He who speaks evil of a brother and judges his brother, speaks evil of the law and judges the law. But if you judge the law, you are not a doer of the law but a judge. There is one Lawgiver, who is able to save and to destroy. Who are you to judge another?" (James 4:11,12). James goes back to calling his readers "brethren" but still he forcefully asks, "Who do you think you are to slander another person?" People think so highly of themselves that they think they can say bad things about other people. That's pride and it leads to slander. Webster's Dictionary defines "slander" as 'a false charge or misrepresentation which damages a person by lessening them in the eyes or the opinions of another person.' The local church is too casual when it comes to slander. They pass it off as innocent gossip not realizing the damage it's doing. The truth be told, there is no such thing as innocent gossip.

Gossip is a sin that grieves the Holy Spirit. Eph. 4:29,30 says, "Let no corrupt communication proceed out of your mouth, but what is good for necessary edification, that it may impart grace to the hearers. And do not grieve the Holy Spirit of God." In Greek the word "corrupt" refers to something that stinks or to something that is rotting, such as meat that is full of maggots. Gossip is communication that is dead, decaying, and it stinks. It is offensive to the Spirit of God and it grieves Him. The Message Bible says, "Watch the way you talk. Let nothing foul or dirty come out of your mouth. Say only what helps, each word a gift. Don't grieve God. Don't break His heart." The Greek word for "gossip" means 'to whisper.' This means that gossip almost always takes place in secret. A person's fleshly nature thrives on gossip and slander proven by the number of gossip magazines that are sold. People love gossip and are drawn to it. Prov. 18:8 (ESV) says, "The words of a whisperer are like delicious morsels; they go down into the inner parts of the body."

In the Bible, the wicked are characterized by slander and gossip. Ps. 50:19,20 says, "You give your mouth to evil, and your tongue frames deceit. You sit and speak against your brother; You slander your own mother's son." Without a doubt, slander is one of the most damaging sins that exists in the church today. Prov. 6:19 defines slander as "a false witness who speaks lies, and one who sows discord among brethren." More times than not, gossip is usually based on hearsay and is usually inaccurate. What it does do is create suspicion that eventually divide people. Gossip is like a deadly poison. It kills relationships and it destroys trust. Slander grows like a virus because Christians accept it in their daily conversations with other believers. They drink their coffee and eat their donuts before church all the while they're talking bad about another believer. They even act spiritual by asking for prayer for this wayward individual. This is all a cover-up for gossip and slander and God hates it.

Slander comes from a prideful heart and a tongue that is uncontrolled. Nothing destroys a Christian's life more than his own tongue. The sin of gossip causes more problems in the church than any other. Prov. 16:28,29 (NLT) says, "A trouble-maker plants seeds of strife; gossip separates the best of friends. Violent people mislead their companions, leading them down a harmful path." Jesus spoke about slander in Matt. 15:18,19 (ESV), "But what comes out of the mouth proceeds from the heart, and this defiles a person. For out of the heart come evil thoughts, murder, adultery, sexual immorality, theft, false witness, slander." Slander, speaking bad about another person, is listed right alongside murder and adultery. That's how bad it is. Jesus sees murder and slander as the same thing. God hates it and so should you. The problem is people don't hate it enough. They give approval to the bad things people say by their silence. They don't address the sin when it occurs. By saying nothing, the sin of slander grows like cancer and does great harm to the local church.

James asks, "Who are you to judge another? Who do you think you are?" There is one Lawgiver and when you judge another believer you're taking God's place. This is a terrible sin. The law says to love your fellow brethren but gossip tries to remove the grace that protects them. God has found these people innocent through the blood of Jesus Christ and through gossip you're saying they're guilty and that Jesus died in vain. Don't slander a person who is the apple of God's eye. When you judge another person, you're viewing your own opinion as being better and higher than God's. It causes you to reject God's law of love. You're taking God off the throne and making yourself judge in His place. Who do you think you are to judge someone who belongs to God, someone who Jesus gave His life for? Why are you taking the place of God and sitting in judgment over another person? When you judge someone you're not loving them and you're not loving God.

What should you do? Every listener has the ability to walk away from a bad conversation. You have a choice to stay and listen to harmful gossip or you can walk away and refuse to listen to what's being said. Without a listener, the gossiper's voice is silenced. Prov. 26:20 says, "Where there is no wood, the fire goes out; And where there is no talebearer, strife ceases." Refrain from gossip and walk away from those who do. If you can't say something publicly, don't say it at all. Prov. 11:13 says, "A talebearer reveals secrets, but he who is of a faithful spirit conceals a matter." Also, learn to help those who are caught in the snare of sin. Gal. 6:1 says, "Brethren, if a man is overtaken in any trespass, you who are spiritual restore such a one in a spirit of gentleness, considering yourself lest you also be tempted." The word "restore" means 'to set a bone that has been broken.' There is no judgment here. What people need is a solution to their problem, not a confirmation of their failure.

The book of James is written with hard hitting conviction. It is very confrontational as James tries to drain from your life the poison of pride, arrogance, and presumption. James has already said that pride is the reason for not receiving the things you ask for from God. It's also the reason you sit in judgment and slander other people. Pride is the root of all this. In fact, pride is the root of all sin. To top it off, the craziest sin of all is to think you can actually plan and direct your own life. Let's face it, people live in a busy world. They're involved in and committed to a lot of different things. All these activities are a world all their own and they demand more and more of your time. There are people who plan their lives and think God will somehow step in and support their plan. To think that you're in charge of what happens to you is the most arrogant and presumptuous thing pride would have you do. Those who think this way are living as if God doesn't even exist, making them Christian atheists.

There are people who put plans together without ever consulting God. They don't ask for divine direction because they're afraid of what He's going to say. They think it's better to ask for forgiveness than permission. They don't ask because they're afraid He might say "no." Some people foolishly think they have a better plan than God has. There are Christians who pridefully think they can control their own lives without acknowledging God and submitting to Him. They're doing the same thing unbelievers do. They say they're following God but ignore Him in all their plans and decisions. Because of attitudes like this, it should come as no surprise that the number one requested song at all funerals is Frank Sinatra's "I Did It My Way." The primary thing people want to be remembered for is that they set their own direction, they made their own plans, they choose their own course. They lived life their own way and for that they were very proud.

James is now ready to warn his readers about planning their lives without God in it. He knows this is one reason the world can't tell who's a Christian and who isn't. Believers are making the same choices and doing the same things as everybody else. They seek God's help when they're sick or if there's a conflict in their relationships but rarely, if ever, do they seek His sovereignty in the every day affairs of life. James uses business dealings as his illustration of the need to ask God what His will is for the situation you find yourself in. James 4:13,14 says, "Come now, you who say, 'Today or tomorrow we will go to such and such a city, spend a year there, buy and sell, and make a profit'; whereas you do not know what will happen tomorrow. For what is your life? It is even a vapor that appears for a little time and then vanishes away." James begins this portion of scripture by saying "Come now." He's trying to get your attention. He's saying, "Wake up! Listen to me!"

James is not against you being in business and making a profitable income. It's not unscriptural to make plans. God wants you to plan things out. You should plan, you should have goals. The issue James deals with is in the process of planning your life and scheduling daily activities, do you consider what God's will is in the matter? Is it God's agenda or your own? The truth be told, these are some carefully made plans. They give a time frame: "today or tomorrow." They give a location: "such and such a city." These plans include the length of time this business deal will take: "spend a year there." The person who made these plans even tells the activity he'll be doing: "buy and sell, make a profit." In and of itself, there is nothing wrong with these plans. In fact, these are very good business plans. The problem is what's not mentioned. There is no mention of God and His will in these plans.

Making plans for the future without seeking God is arrogance. There are people who make business plans as if they're in control, as if they know what's going to happen in the days ahead. This gives them a feeling of superiority, boasting of what they've accomplished without making reference to God. There are those who say, "My power and the might of my hand have gained me this wealth" (Deut. 8:17). This is pride for they're taking the glory for something that God has accomplished. This is a dangerous thing to do because Prov. 16:18 says, "Pride goes before destruction, and a haughty spirit before a fall." People need to realize how fragile life is. They're here today, gone tomorrow, forgotten two days later. Every person on the planet lives one event away from eternity. There are hurricanes, earthquakes, automobile accidents, heart attacks, and war. People think life goes on forever when the truth is nobody is guaranteed tomorrow. Prov. 27:1 says, "Do not boast about tomorrow, for you do not know what a day may bring forth."

Life is too short for God not to be in the center of everything you do. Your life is only a vapor and you can't live in total disregard of God's sovereignty and His purpose. You don't know what tomorrow holds but in arrogance people still make their own plans. And since Jesus is their Lord, or so they say, they're going to ask Him to help them do what they want to do. They think God exists to fulfill their will and not for them to fulfill His. That is total arrogance and unadulterated presumption. You have to remember how brief and unpredictable life is. Your life goes by quicker than the blink of an eye. What's so deceiving about death is that people know they're one day going to die, they just don't think it will be today. Surely tomorrow will come, or so they think. This is how sinners live their lives and, sad to say, many so-called Christians. In the parable of the rich fool (Luke 12:16-21) a man made plans for his life without first seeking God to which the Lord responded, "You fool! You will die this very night."

Only God knows what's best for your life and only He knows what your future looks like. Ps. 139:16 (MSG) says, "The days of my life all prepared before I'd even lived one day." The NLT says, "You saw me before I was born. Every day of my life was recorded in Your book. Every moment was laid out before a single day had passed." God knows when you'll take your last breath. It would be wise to consult Him on what He would have you do between now and then. James says in vs. 15, "Instead you ought to say, 'If the Lord wills, we shall live and do this or that.'" The words "Lord willing" should be the theme of your life. Follow the example of Jesus who said in the Garden of Gethsemane, "Not My will, but Yours, be done" (Luke 22:42). You need to say that every day. Jesus taught His disciples how to pray to the Father. He told them to say, "Your kingdom come. Your will be done on earth as it is in heaven" (Matt. 6:10). Jesus is saying that the Father knows best. He knows what's best for your life and you need to submit to His will.

Prov. 16:9 says, "A man's heart plans his way, but the Lord directs his steps." Make plans with your heart and not your mind for plans made with the heart will always be centered on the will of God. Plan your life with God's will in mind. Live your life as if He is in charge. Col. 3:17 (MSG) says, "Let every detail in your lives - words, actions, whatever - be done in the name of the Master, Jesus, thanking God the Father every step of the way." Father knows best and this is His will for your life. Whatever it is you do, God's will is for you to do it as a representative of the Lord Jesus Christ. Do everything in His name, for His glory. If Jesus is the Lord of your life, this is what you do. Take time out of your busy schedule and ask God what His will is. Ask Him, "Lord, what do You want me to do?" Make Him the architect of your life. Allow Him to draw up the blueprint of how He wants your life to be lived. You then follow those plans. Build your life on the foundation of His Word and His plan for your existence.

Ps. 31:3 says, "For You are my rock and my fortress; Therefore, for Your name's sake, lead me and guide me." How do you find God's will? It first starts with you knowing Him personally. John 1:12 says, "But as many as received Him, to them He gave the right to become children of God, even to those who believe in His name." Paul said in 1 Tim. 2:4 that God "desires all men to be saved and to come to the knowledge of the truth." God wants you to grow up spiritually so you can live differently from the rest of the world, that your morals and standards would not be based on what your social peers are doing (1 Thess. 4:3,4). Next, you need to have a thankful attitude, an attitude of appreciation (1 Thess. 5:18). Don't be demanding, don't insist on your own way, don't complain, and don't be envious if another person has more than you. This change of attitude will change everything in your life. You'll be able to study the scriptures and learn what the will of God is. Eph. 5:17 says, "Therefore do not be unwise, but understand what the will of the Lord is."

Making plans without seeking God first is a sign of arrogance and overconfidence. James 4:16 says, "But now you boast in your arrogance. All such boasting is evil." It's evil because if you're calling the shots, it makes God insignificant in your life. It turns you into a practicing atheist. The Amplified Bible says, "You boast falsely in your presumption and your self conceit." People like this think they're so gifted and special that they don't need anybody else. They claim to be a self-made man or a self-made woman. To say such things is as disrespectful to God as you can possibly get. In 1875 English poet William Ernest Henley wrote a poem about a man who knows that God exists but doesn't seem to care. The poem is called "Invictus" and in it the author wrote, "I am the master of my fate. I am the captain of my soul." Really? Isn't Jesus supposed to be the master of your fate and the captain of your soul? He said in John 15:5 (NLT), "For apart from Me you can do nothing."

Don't be like those people who mentally acknowledge there is a God but live their lives as if there's not. James is crying out and telling you to never forget God. If God's not God, then who's playing God in your life? He then says in vs. 17, "Therefore, to him who knows to do good and does not do it, to him it is sin." People know what they should be doing but they procrastinate. They keep putting things off until tomorrow not realizing that tomorrow may never get here. Wisdom is not just what you know, it's what you show. It's what you do that counts. Knowing to do something good and not doing it is sin. Never put off until tomorrow what you should be doing today. Do it now! Prov. 3:27,28 (CEV) says, "Do all you can for everyone who deserves your help. Don't tell your neighbor to come back tomorrow, if you can help today." James has already told you to draw near to God and not to be double-minded. Daily submit your will to His will. Father knows best so submit all your thoughts, plans, and desires to Him.

God clearly has a plan for your life. People know they're supposed to do something with their life but they're not doing it. They're not doing what they know they ought to do. The result is they miss God's best for their lives and James calls this sin. The problem is most believers think sin is something they do, not something they don't do. When accused of wrong doing they say, "But I didn't do anything." They're absolutely correct. They didn't do anything and this is called the sin of omission. They didn't do what God intended for them to do, they did what they wanted to do. A perfect example of this is the story of Jonah. God wanted him to go to Nineveh but Jonah didn't want to go. He took drastic measures to not go and eventually God created a catastrophic incident to get him there. You don't want God to do something similar in your life. Get God's plan and do it with all your heart and soul and strength. James is saying you know what to do, now go do it. Live every day as if it might be your last. For some of you, it may very well be.

-25-

"WEEP AND HOWL"

A wealthy business owner once said the order of priorities in his life was God, family, business. He went on to say this order reverses Monday through Friday. He gave God the weekends but during the week his top priority was making money. Indeed, there is no stronger master in the world system than money. It can enslave the best of people, those who willingly bow and succumb to its fame, riches, and power. 1 Tim. 6:10 (NLT) says, "For the love of money is the root of all kinds of evil. And some people, craving money, have wandered from the true faith and pierced themselves with many sorrows." The Message Bible says, "Lust for money brings trouble and nothing but trouble." To love God is to deny self, to love money is to serve self. James is now going to speak to those who trust in their riches more than they do God. He's speaking to those rich people who abuse their wealth wanting them to know that without Jesus Christ, without being rich in faith, they have nothing. Get ready for James uses some of the strongest language in the New Testament.

James begins by saying, "Come now, you rich..." (James 5:1). He is trying to get your attention because he's going to give a warning every person on this planet needs to hear and take seriously. Don't make the mistake of thinking these words are for somebody else. God, through James, is speaking directly to you. This is a message everybody needs to hear no matter how much finances you have or don't have. Somewhere in this world there is somebody worse off than you and this makes you rich in their eyes. James wants you to evaluate your attitude about wealth and how you use the resources God had graciously given you. The reason this message is so important is because your use of money reveals where your heart is. What believers do with money will indicate the level of their commitment to Christ. Matt. 6:21 says, "For where your treasure is, there your heart will be also." Money takes on the character of those who have it. It can be good or evil, a blessing or a curse.

"Come now, you rich, weep and howl for your miseries that are coming upon you" (vs. 1). James is not messing around and he definitely comes out swinging. He doesn't waste time or words trying to be polite. He knows eternity is at stake and he doesn't have time to waste trying to be warm and friendly. What James says is troubling because it's a message about materialism. It's a message about the wrongful use and abuse of wealth. He sees what's taking place and feels the injustice of what's happening. His heart is breaking and he passionately preaches a very strong message about the barbarism and corruption of misused finances and wealth. James is shouting a war cry. He's warning people that with wealth comes great responsibility. "To whom much is given, from him much will be required" (Luke 12:48). You are going to be judged according to the manner in which you use your wealth. A day of reckoning is coming and James is desperately seeking to awaken you to this impending reality.

The Amplified Bible says, "Come quickly now, you rich who lack true faith and hoard and misuse your resources, weep and howl over the miseries, the woes, the judgments that are coming upon you." The word "howl" means 'to wail; to shriek.' It depicts the frantic terror of those on whom the judgment of God has come. Is. 13:6 says, "Wail, for the day of the Lord is at hand! It will come as destruction from the Almighty." People need to realize that death strips every person of all their material riches. On the day of judgment, their gold and silver is going to be worthless when they stand before God where they'll give an account for the way they lived their lives. Is. 65:14 says, "But you shall cry for sorrow of heart, and wail for grief of spirit." Don't be appalled by the straight forward method by which James is speaking. Don't react to his language but try to understand why James is speaking in such a manner. He uses firm words in an effort to soften your heart toward God and your fellow man. He wants you to know you can't ignore God's will when it comes to your wealth.

God is not opposed to wealth and He doesn't care how much you have. What He does care about is how you get it and how you use it. God wants you to be successful so your success will allow you to help establish His kingdom on earth. Abraham, Job, David, and Solomon were all very wealthy and God used them to bless the whole world. God's only requirement is that you serve Him and not money. Matt. 6:24 (NLT) says, "No one can serve two masters. For you will hate one and love the other; you will be devoted to one and despise the other. You cannot serve both God and money." A statement in the Wall Street Journal said, "Money is an article which may be used as a universal passport to everywhere except heaven, and as a universal provider of everything but happiness." Christians have heard that all their lives but still they think more money is the path to more happiness. This is why they buy lottery tickets all the time instead of sowing that money into the kingdom of God. This is the same mindset of the people James is writing to.

James knows there are people whose desire for wealth supersedes their trust in God. They find security in how much money they have and for that reason they will never be satisfied because no amount of money will ever be enough. This is how greed sets in. Jesus said in Luke 12:15 (NLT),

"Beware! Guard against every kind of greed. Life is not measured by how much you own." He then said in vs. 21 (NLT), "Yes, a person is a fool to store up earthly wealth but not have a rich relationship with God." The parable of the rich fool (Luke 12:16-20) tells of a man who was rich according to the standards of the world but wasn't rich in faith. He wasn't content with what he had so he made plans to build bigger barns so he could store more of his crops. He thought bigger barns meant he would live a longer life, that his wealth was a safeguard for the future. God said he was a fool to think this way. He said to the man, "You fool! This night your soul will be required of you." Mark 8:36 asks, "For what will it profit a man if he gains the whole world, and loses his own soul."

There is nothing wrong with having nice things, there is something wrong if you can't be content without them. Eccl. 6:9 (GNT) says, "It is better to be satisfied with what you have than to be always wanting something else." It was the lack of contentment that caused the downfall of Adam and Eve. They were created by God to be content in their knowledge of Him and the world He provided. Satan then came along and tempted them with the chance to become more than they were created to be. He said they could become as wise as God. Discontentment set in, they ate the forbidden fruit, and the rest is history. Yes, there are people who are never content no matter how much they have so they spend their life pursuing more and more worldly goods and financial wealth. They overwork and are always tired and fatigued. They sacrifice their health in the pursuit of money. Leo Tolstoy told a story of a rich man who offered a peasant all the land he could walk through in a single day. The poor man took off and ran so hard that by the end of the day he died of exhaustion.

People are so deceived. They think they don't make enough money when the truth is they're greedy and want too much.

Eccl. 5:10 (GNT) says, "If you love money, you will never be satisfied; if you long to be rich, you will never get all you want. It is useless." Solomon wrote this, the richest man who ever lived. The Living Bible says, "It's foolish to think wealth brings happiness." The people James was writing to were not content with what they had and were told they would experience a world of misery. James then says, "Your riches are corrupted, and your garments are moth-eaten. Your gold and silver are corroded, and their corrosion will be a witness against you and will eat your flesh like fire. You have heaped up treasure in the last days" (vs. 2,3). Hoarded treasures are a deficit. Prov. 11:24 (MSG) says, "The world of the stingy gets smaller and smaller." The word "hoard" means 'to hide away, conceal, to keep back.' Because it is not being used, what is hoarded is really lost. Hoarded money is of no value and hoarded lives are useless as well.

James saw people who were hoarding and flaunting their wealth and it grieved him greatly. Accumulating wealth was the primary goal of their lives. They adopted the mentality of wanting more and more and more. They wanted wealth for the sake of having it, not to do something good with it. God gives you the power to get wealth for the purpose of putting it into circulation, for the purpose of using it for His purposes. These people James is writing to accumulated wealth for wealth's sake. In Biblical times most wealth was used to accumulate food, clothes, and jewelry made of gold and silver. James says their food will rot, their garments will be moth-eaten, their gold and silver will corrode. This is what happens when you hoard up wealth and material possessions. Clothes you wear regularly don't get eaten by moths. It's the clothes you hoard up and never use that get moth-eaten. Likewise, food that gets rotten is food that sits in the back of the refrigerator for three months and never gets eaten.

James says their corroded wealth will eat their flesh like fire. The love of money has consumed them and they are being eaten alive. Abraham was a rich man but he maintained his faith and character. When his nephew Lot became rich it ruined his character and eventually ruined his family. Ps. 62:10 says, "If riches increase, do not set your heart on them." If you do, destruction and misery will come. A few short years after James wrote this letter Jerusalem fell to the Romans and all their accumulated wealth was taken out of their greedy hands. God doesn't want you to hoard your money but He does expect you to save your money. Prov. 21:20 tells how a wise man saves for the future but the foolish man spends whatever he gets. There is a difference between hoarding and saving. You hoard and heap up treasure so you can have it all for yourself, you save for the purpose of helping someone else at a later time. Don't hoard your money, use your money. Be a good steward with the things God gives you.

Holding nothing back, James vehemently opposes the ungodly rich who hoard up their wealth for the purpose of keeping it all for themselves. He now confronts them with another heartless atrocity that is taking place. "Indeed the wages of the laborers who mowed your fields, which you kept back by fraud, cry out; and the cries of the reapers have reached the ears of the Lord of Sabaoth" (James 5:4). Instead of being generous to the poor, these wealthy landowners were exploiting their workers and cheating them out of their wages. The wage of the day laborer was small and he continually lived on the verge of starvation. It was impossible for him to save anything and if he was not paid his family would not eat. These ungodly people were getting rich off the backs of those who worked in their fields. James is saying that God sees the injustice that is happening. It cries out to Him. The NLT says, "The cries of those who harvest your fields have reached the ears of the Lord of Heaven's Armies."

At this time in history, the majority of the people were living at the poverty level and there were two types of poor people. They were the day laborers (Matt. 20:1-16) who would work on a day-to-day basis or they were lame, lepers, or orphans and widows who couldn't work at all. It is taught in every part of the Bible that God is concerned for the rights of the poor and those who do righteous labor. Mal. 3:5 says the judgment of God is "against those who exploit wage earners and widows and the fatherless." To help the poor, God instituted various laws to ensure that the poor people were taken care of. First of all, God says the laborers shall get paid immediately for the work they did. Deut. 24:14 (NLT) says, "You must pay them their wages each day before sunset because they are poor and are counting on it." James says when the poor aren't paid their wages cry out. One is reminded of when Cain killed his brother Abel. God said to him, "What have you done? The voice of your brother's blood cries out to Me from the ground" (Gen. 4:10).

Another law that was set up was that people would be released from all debt every seven years. Deut. 15:1 (NLT) says, "At the end of every seventh year you must cancel the debts of everyone who owes you money." Vs. 4 says "There should be no poor among you." This law would stop the society from being a place where the rich got richer and the poor got poorer. Laws were also set up to help orphans and widows who couldn't take care of themselves (Deut. 14:28,29). God even set up interest free loans. Ex. 22:25 (NLT) says, "If you lend money to any of My people who are in need, do not charge interest as a money lender would." The rich were also told to leave excess food in the fields. "When you harvest the crops of your land, do not harvest the grain along the edges of your fields, and do not pick up what the harvesters drop. It is the same with your grape crop - do not strip every last bunch of grapes from the vines, and do not pick up the grapes that fall to the ground. Leave them for the poor and the foreigner living among you. I am the Lord your God" (Lev. 19:9,10 NLT).

To top it all off, there was the wonderful Year of Jubilee (Lev. 25:8-27) where the unfathomed mercies of God would be gloriously manifested. Every fifty years all prisoners and captives were set free, all slaves were released, all debts were forgiven, and all property was returned to the original owner. It was a time of liberty, restitution, and jubilation. Yes, God cares about the poor and He takes it personal when wrong is done to them. Jesus said in Matt. 25:40, "Assuredly, I say to you, inasmuch as you did it to one of the least of these My brethren, you did it to Me." Is it any wonder that James is so adamant as he tells of the judgment to come on the ungodly rich who are taking advantage of the godly poor? Amos 5:11 (NLT) tells what happens when the rich abuse the poor, "You trample the poor, stealing their grain through taxes and unfair rent. Therefore, though you build beautiful stone houses, you will never live in them. Though you plant lush vineyards, you will never drink wine from them."

James is not finished. He points his finger at those responsible for this atrocious behavior and says, "You have lived on the earth in pleasure and luxury; you have fattened your hearts as in a day of slaughter. You have condemned, you have murdered the just; he does not resist you" (James 5:5,6). Luxury through self-indulgence, with no regard for others, is a horrendous sin that destroys the inner character of all who succumb to this treacherous lifestyle. These people stole money from the laborers and used it all on themselves for their own personal comfort and satisfaction. James says eventually their wealth will rot, decay, and be of no value. If it's gained dishonestly, in time it will all go to waste. Abused wealth will be judged in eternity along with their own pitiful souls. God said in Amos 8:4,7, "Hear this, you who swallow up the needy, and make the poor of the land fail. Surely I will never forget any of their works. Shall the land not tremble for this, and everyone mourn who dwells in it?"

Money is powerful and people often abuse their wealth to cause great injustice. They threaten to leave a loved one out of their will if they don't do what is being demanded of them. Manipulation is used to control people and get them to do some undesirable task. They use their affluence for evil influence and the poor are powerless to stop them. They have condemned the innocent and murdered the just who stand there and take it. Greedy self-indulgence destroyed their moral fibre and caused them to ignore the call to help those less fortunate. Prov. 21:13 says, "Whoever shuts his ears to the cry of the poor will also cry himself and not be heard." God will not listen to those who don't listen to the cries of people around them. They have chosen the path they're on and the final destination where it leads. Jesus said in Luke 6:24,25, "But woe to you who are rich, for you have received your consolation. Woe to you who are full, for you shall hunger. Woe to you who laugh now, for you shall mourn and weep."

Those who have sought luxury at the expense of the poor are like men who have fattened themselves for the day of judgment. Selfishness always leads to destruction of the soul and the end of their pleasure is grief, misery, and judgment. Like a pig that's about to become bacon, James is saying they're fattening themselves up for the day of slaughter. He's saying, "You've fattened your hearts to become bacon." The heart is the center of who you are. It contains your thoughts, emotions, and desires. These people have fed their inner desires, fattening themselves up for the day of judgment. Luke 16:19-31 tells the story of a rich man who abused his wealth and a poor beggar named Lazarus. This beggar was covered with sores and desired to eat the crumbs that fell from the rich man's table. They both died and Lazarus went to paradise while the rich man went to hell. He saw Abraham and cried out, "Father Abraham, have pity on me and send Lazarus to dip the tip of his finger in water and cool my tongue, because I am in agony in this fire."

The question to be asked is should a Christian be rich? If so, what is God expecting you to do with your money? First of all, you need to understand that it is God's will for all believers to "prosper in all things and be in health, just as your soul prospers" (3 John 2). God has no problem with believers who acquire wealth in an honest way. Prov. 13:11 says, "Wealth gained by dishonesty will be diminished, but he who gathers by labor will increase." The NLT says, "Wealth from get-rich-quick schemes quickly disappear; wealth from hard work grows over time." This is why you should never gamble or buy lottery tickets. Instead, you need to make money the old fashioned way. Prov. 14:23 says, "In all labor there is profit." The Bible teaches the value of hard work. God instituted work. When He created the heavens and the earth He worked six days and then He rested. He created Adam and immediately put him to work (Gen. 2:15). Prov. 12:27 (GNB) says, "If you are lazy, you will never get what you are after, but if you work hard, you will get a fortune."

No matter how much you have, you need to be content and learn to live within your means. The richest person is not the one who has the most, it's the one who is content with the least. Paul said in Phil. 4:12, "I have learned the secret of being content, whether living in plenty or in want." The Message Bible says, "I've learned by now to be quite content whatever my circumstances. I'm just as happy with little as with much, with much as with little. I've found the recipe for being happy whether full or hungry, hands full or hands empty." By nature, people are not content for they're never satisfied with what they have. They don't realize that God said He would supply all their needs (Phil. 4:19). He didn't say He'd supply all their greeds. Be careful what you wish for. Prov. 23:4 (NLT) says, "Don't wear yourself out trying to get rich. Be wise enough to know when to quit." 1 Tim. 6:9 (NLT) says, "People who long to be rich fall into temptation and are trapped by many foolish and harmful desires that plunge them into ruin and destruction."

Paul is saying contentment is a secret you must learn. First of all, you need to stop comparing yourself to others. 2 Cor. 10:12 (NIV) says, "We do not dare to classify or compare ourselves with some who commend themselves. When they measure themselves by themselves and compare themselves with themselves, they are not wise." Learn to rejoice in other people's prosperity and success without getting jealous or envious because they have something you don't have. That's contentment. Desire is not evil but uncontrolled desire is. It's a sin that becomes a lust that leads to covetousness. Next, you need to enjoy and be thankful for what you do have. People buy big expensive houses but they're never home to enjoy it because they're out working day and night to pay for it. Eccl. 5:19 (MSG) says, "Yes, we should make the most of what God gives, both the bounty and the capacity to enjoy it, accepting what's given and delighting in the work. It's God's gift!" The GNT says, "If God gives a man wealth and prosperity, he should be grateful and enjoy what he has. It is a gift from God."

Life is not about things so never be possessed by your possessions. Never judge your self worth by your net worth. Realize that the greatest blessings in life are not material things. Life is about relationships. It's about love for God and love for other people. Focus on what will last forever. Do not lay up for yourself treasures on earth but lay up for yourself treasures in heaven (Matt. 6:19,20). Give your attention to permanent values. Build your life on eternal priorities. Nothing you see will last forever. It will all wear out and decay. Every possession is temporary so never build your life on possessing possessions. 2 Cor. 4:18 says, "We fix our attention, not on the things that are seen, but on things that are unseen. What can be seen lasts only for a time; but what cannot be seen lasts forever." Become like David who said in Ps. 17:15 (LB), "But as for me, my contentment is not in wealth but in seeing You and knowing all is well between us. And when I awake in heaven, I will be fully satisfied, for I will see You face to face."

God will give you the power to get wealth (Deut. 8:18) so that, like Abraham, you'll be blessed to be a blessing (Gen. 12:2). It honors God when you share your blessings with others. When God touches your life, you just automatically want to be generous with your time, your talents, and your treasure. Generosity is a lifestyle in which you share all you have and all that you are as a demonstration of God's love and as a response to His grace. Jesus said in Acts 20:35, "It is more blessed to give than to receive." Indeed it is. Prov. 11:24, 25 says, "It is possible to give away and become richer. It's also possible to hold on too tightly and lose everything. Yes, the generous man shall be rich. By watering others, he waters himself." God owns everything (Ps. 24:1) and you're His asset manager. He expects you to use what He has given you. He expects you to step out and be active in managing all that belongs to Him. 1 Tim. 6:18 (NLT) says, "Tell them to use their money to do good. They should be rich in good works and generous to those in need, always ready to share with others."

Stewardship is the active and responsible management of God's creation for God's purposes. God has given you a mission and He expects you to fulfill it. In the parable of the talents (Matt. 25:14-30) one servant buried the one talent given to him and did nothing with it. This man was lazy and what he did was wicked and evil (vs. 26). This unprofitable servant committed the sin of passivity, the sin of inactivity. Adam was also passive while the serpent tempted his wife Eve. He didn't use the power and dominion God had given him. God's grace covers failure but it cannot make up for passivity. You must do your part. It's not a sin to try and fail, it is a sin to fail to try. The bottom line is God expects you to do something. You must trust God and step out of the boat. If you don't, you'll be like that wicked and lazy servant to whom the master said, "And cast the unprofitable servant into the outer darkness. There will be weeping and gnashing of teeth" (vs. 30). The Message Bible says, "And get rid of this 'play-it-safe' who won't go out on a limb. Throw him out into utter darkness."

Two other servants were also given talents according to their own ability (vs. 15) and they went out and doubled what the master had given them. They knew the master expected them to use what they'd been given and that God measures success by faith and faithfulness. 1 Cor. 4:2 says, "Moreover, it is required in stewards that one be found faithful." The Message Bible says the requirements of a good steward are "reliability and accurate knowledge." These two servants possessed both these qualities and were greatly rewarded for their faithful works of service. God looks for and delights in rewarding good stewardship. He rewards with affirmation and words of encouragement. He said to them, "Well done, good and faithful servant" (vs. 21). He also rewards with promotion. "You were faithful over a few things, I will make you ruler over many things" (vs. 21). He even rewards with celebration. "Enter into the joy of your Lord" (vs. 21). This parable reveals that while it's your faith that determines where you'll spend eternity, it's your faithfulness that determines how you'll spend eternity.

Randall J. Brewer

-26-

"THE RIGHT TIME"

God knows what your oppressors have done and James has just told of the horrible outcome of their lives. But what about you? What are you supposed to do when you are mistreated by those in the world system, when you find yourself in the midst of unjust suffering? James is going to tell you what to do. "Therefore be patient, brethren, until the coming of the Lord" (James 5:7). Like most people, this is probably not the answer you wanted to hear. Still, it's the most important thing you can possibly do. Get rid of any thoughts of vengeance and retaliation. Just settle down and be patient. The truth be told, everybody knows they need patience. In fact, they need it so much they wish God would hurry up and give it to them. They've heard that patience is a virtue yet today's culture encourages and rewards impatience. When people want something, they want it now. The sooner the better. That's why the world and all its new inventions are doing everything they can to assure that people won't have to wait longer than the bare minimum.

Patience is the ability to delay gratification and everybody needs it. Why? Because people simply don't like to wait on anything, not even if it's a few short minutes. It's because of this that their lives are in such a mess. The inability to wait is the cause of all debt. People don't want to wait until they can afford something so they buy it on credit and go in debt. People get sexual diseases because they don't wait for marriage to satisfy their physical desires. Married couples get divorced because they don't want to take the time to work out their differences. The fact remains, people just don't like to wait. They're always in a hurry but God is not. Eccl. 3:11 (NCV) says, "God does everything just right and on time, but people can never completely understand what He is doing." More times than not, God has to get you to be patient and slow down before He can give the solution to your problem. Contrary to what some people think, being patient is not a hard thing to do. James says you can do it if you'll start focusing on the coming of the Lord.

What you set your mind on determines how you'll live your life. Indeed, where the mind goes, the body will follow. If you set your mind on money like the ungodly rich did, you're going to live for money. If you set your mind on the coming of the Lord, you'll live for Jesus and His glorious return. Col. 3:2 says, "Set your mind on things above, not on things on the earth." When you set your mind on the coming of the Lord, you can be patient knowing your trying circumstances are only temporary. Paul said in 2 Cor. 4:17,18 (NLT), "For our present troubles are small and won't last very long. Yet they produce for us a glory that vastly outweighs them and will last forever. So we don't look at the troubles we can see now; rather we fix our gaze on things that cannot be seen. For the things we see now will soon be gone, but the things we cannot see will last forever." You can have peace in the storm if you'll let God deal with those who are mistreating you and set your mind over the horizon and focus on the coming of the Lord.

The term "be patient" means 'to be even tempered while enduring trying circumstances.' It's a state of emotional calm in the face of misfortune. James continues in this verse and gives an example of this type of patience. "See how the farmer waits for the precious fruit of the earth, waiting patiently for it until it receives the early and latter rain" (vs. 7). In the land of Canaan, there were two seasons of the year when the rain fell in abundance. In the fall came the early rain that softened the ground after the blistering heat of summer. This rain broke up the hard soil and prepared it for planting. The farmer then worked real hard planting seeds and then waited patiently for the rains of late spring. This latter rain ripened the grain and prepared it for harvest. The term "waited patiently" is the Greek word "eckdechomai" and means 'to look with anticipation' or 'to wait expectantly.' To live the life of a farmer is to live a life of patience in the midst of uncontrollable circumstances. Patience is the settled reality that you are not in control.

A farmer has no control over the weather. He knows too much rain can cause the crop to rot, too much sun can burn it up, and an early frost can destroy the whole thing. A farmer also has no control over whether or not people will buy their crops. All the farmer can do is trust God and wait patiently for Him to send exactly what is needed at the right time. While you're waiting on God, like the farmer you also have to remember that there is a natural delay between planting and harvesting. Eccl. 3:1,2 says there is a time for everything, and a season for every activity under heaven. There's a time to plant and a time to harvest, a time to scatter and a time to gather. You don't plant and harvest in the same season. During the waiting season you trust God and wait expectantly without murmuring and complaining. Heb. 6:11,12 says, "And we desire that each one of you show the same diligence to the full assurance of hope until the end, that you do not become sluggish, but imitate those who through faith and patience inherit the promises."

If your prayers aren't getting answered as quickly as you'd like, remember that not only are there natural delays, there are spiritual delays as well. There's an unseen battle going on in the spiritual realm and you're caught in the middle of it. Eph. 6:12 (TEV) says, "We are not struggling and fighting against human beings but against evil spiritual forces in the heavenly realm - the rulers, authorities, and powers of darkness." Dan. 10:11-13 tells of such a battle. The good news is that the manifestation finally came. The same thing happened to Abraham. Heb. 6:15 says, "After waiting patiently, Abraham received what was promised." Take comfort knowing a delay is not a denial. There's a difference between "no" and "not yet." Some delays are by design. They teach you to trust God and to grow up and mature in your character. While you're waiting, realize that God is preparing you for the blessing to come. He has big plans for your life and He has to prepare you for what's ahead. Rom. 8:23-25 (MSG) says, "Waiting does not diminish us. We are enlarged in the waiting. The longer we wait, the larger we become, and the more joyful our expectancy."

Don't feel isolated in your waiting. Everybody waits. Noah waited a hundred and twenty years before the rain came and flooded the earth. Abraham waited many years for his promised son to be born. Joseph waited fourteen years in prison for the dream God gave him to be fulfilled. Hannah waited years for the baby she prayed God would give her. All these people waited for the promise God gave them to be fulfilled and Heb. 11:2 (ICB) says, "People who lived in the past became famous because of their faith." Even God waits. After Adam and Eve sinned, God waited four thousand years before He sent Jesus the Messiah to the earth. Clearly, God is not in a hurry. He does, however, keep His promises. God said in Hab. 2:3 (CEV), "At the time I have decided, My words will come true. You can trust what I say about the future. It may take a long time, but keep on waiting - it will happen." God has the power and the ability to fulfill all seven thousand promises that are in the Bible and He'll fulfill them at the right time. What should you do? Keep on waiting.

What happens between the early and latter rain? The seeds germinate and begin to grow. It's during the waiting phase of life where most spiritual growth takes place. There are things God wants to teach you before He answers your prayers, for He is more interested in your character than He is your comfort. Keep a journal of your spiritual progress while you're waiting on God to answer your prayers. Deut. 11:2 (TEV) says, "Remember what you have learned about the Lord through your experiences with Him." A journal is not a diary. A diary is a record of things you do, a journal is a list of things you've learned. Many times, it's the small lessons that lead to big success. Ps. 119:33-35 (MSG) says, "God, teach me insight so I can do what You tell me - my whole life one long, obedient response. Guide me down the road of Your commandments; I love traveling this freeway." The way to the promised is through the wilderness of waiting on God. Don't get frustrated but open your heart and mind to the things God wants to teach you.

As the seeds are nurtured and continue to grow, the farmer is keeping busy preparing for the coming harvest. He's acting as if the harvest is a manifested reality and this is called faith. Jesus said in Mark 11:24 (NIV), "I tell you, whatever you ask for in prayer, believe that you have received it, and it will be yours." Waiting is not passivity. Waiting is the time to develop spiritual growth and maturity, to develop habits and skills that will benefit your life in the days ahead. Phil. 4:9 (NLT) says, "Keep on putting into practice all you learned from me and heard from me and saw me doing." When you're expectantly waiting in faith, you take action. Don't be like most people who sit around and wonder, worry, and whine. No, when you've planted your time, talents, and treasure you prepare and act like the prayer is already answered. Don't put your life on hold. Don't be lazy, don't be idle, don't be passive. God can't steer a parked car. Do something! Keep praying, keep sowing, keep believing and never let fear grip your heart. Ps. 56:3 (CEV) says, "Even when I am afraid, I keep on trusting You."

The example of the farmer is an illustration about patience and how you must stand strong in the midst of unjust suffering. James then says in vs. 8, "You also be patient. Establish your hearts, for the coming of the Lord is at hand." Trust God and don't take matters into your own hand. Let Him bring justice to those who have wronged you. He has not forsaken you and you can trust Him at all times. Never allow the way people are treating you to pull you down to their level. If things get tough and a little out of hand, make sure you don't take it out on people around you. James 5:9 says, "Do not grumble against one another, brethren, lest you be condemned. Behold, the Judge is standing at the door." The people who are hurting you are not the only ones the Lord is watching. He's also watching you and He's standing at your door. As you endure unjust suffering, be careful not to cause unjust suffering to other people. If your stress level causes you to take your frustration out on your loved ones, James says you'll be in the same boat as the ungodly rich who are going to be judged.

In response to unjust suffering, James next says to consider the heroes of faith from times past. James 5:10 says, "My brethren, take the prophets, who spoke in the name of the Lord, as an example of suffering and patience." The word "take" means literally 'to hold before your mind.' The job of the prophets was to speak on God's behalf to His people. The prophets were trying to change the hearts of these people and with it the direction of their lives. They continued to preach and plead to those they were sent to but the people were hardened, stubborn, and rebellious. They were stiff-necked, hardhearted, and unchangeable but still the prophets remained loyal to the call on their lives. The Bible tells of their patience and the brave endurance through which they suffered unjust persecution. James is calling you to do the same. The Greek word for "patience" used in this verse is "makiothumia" and means 'long heat.' It refers to a person who remains steadfast under affliction without succumbing, a person who takes a long time to get heated in the midst of unchangeable people.

Jesus encouraged the disciples to boldly face persecution like the prophets of old (Matt. 5:11,12). Jeremiah suffered greatly under the hands of pagan kings and his own people as he faithfully delivered God's message of sin and repentance. He preached his entire life and there is no record that anybody turned to God based on what he said. How about Daniel? He was taken from his home as a young boy and served in Babylon faithfully to the Lord. He suffered adversity there and was even thrown into a den of lions at a very old age for not compromising his faith. Consider Hosea whose marriage to a harlot and all its hardships was an example of God's love toward His people. Isaiah was sawed in two and Amos faced lies and continual scorn as did Ezekiel. Heb. 11:36,37 says these faithful servants were scourged, stoned, imprisoned, and slain with the sword. They wandered about in sheepskins and goatskins, being destitute, afflicted, and tormented. Hold all of this in your mind as an example of what God calls you to do when you suffer unjustly.

Vs. 11 then says, "Indeed we count them blessed who endure." The word "endurance" means 'to hyper-stand; to be steadfast.' Strong's Concordance says, "It speaks of a man who is not swerved from his deliberate purpose and his loyalty to faith and piety by even the greatest trials and sufferings." Jesus endured the cross. He stood fast, He held His ground, He didn't let the enemy win. When people frustrate you, don't give up on them. Be the unwavering person you were before the trial. Respond to them with grace and kindness even if they refuse to change and when they're being difficult. James has already told you not to grumble at these people. A lack of patience causes you to raise your voice in uncontrolled anger. It means you've given up the possibility that they may one day change. The devil only wins if you quit. To win the battle of life, all you have to do is remain steadfast. Hold on to the examples of the prophets of old. Allow them to remind you that the blessings of God comes to those who remain steadfast in the midst of unjust suffering.

There is no better example of this than Job. Vs. 11 (NLT) says, "We give great honor to those who endure under suffering. For instance, you know about Job, a man of great endurance. You can see how the Lord was kind to him at the end, for the Lord is full of tenderness and mercy." Job was a righteous man who loved God with all his heart and soul yet he suffered greatly and lost everything he had. He went from being the envy of every person in the land to being the pity of every person who heard of his ordeal. The hardest thing for Job is he didn't understand why all these tragic things were happening. Everybody has unexplained problems and this is when patience and endurance is needed most. Job didn't deserve the trials he suffered but he had the inward fortitude necessary to withstand hardship and stress. This is what it means to remain steadfast. Draw a line in the sand and say you're not moving until Jesus comes. Be steadfast in the faith and in what God has called you to do. You can do this if you'll remember that God is full of tenderness and mercy.

James is saying you need to have patience and trust God when your circumstances are uncontrollable, when people are unchangeable, and when your problems are unexplainable. Stop wondering when your deliverance will come. Trust God and live one day at a time. Jesus said in Acts 1:7 (MSG), "You don't get to know the time. Timing is the Father's business." In a round about way, Jesus is saying the timing of things in your life is none of your business. It's God's business and that should bring comfort to your soul. He knows the right time when things should happen. Eccl. 3:1 (TEV) says, "Everything that happens in the world happens at the time God chooses." God is always at work behind the scenes and He is never in a hurry. He lives and operates in a timeless realm. 2 Peter 3:8 says, "With the Lord, a day is like a thousand years, and a thousand years are like a day." The good news is that God can do in a second what people can't do in a hundred years. Is. 60:22 (TEV) says, "I am the Lord, so when the right time comes, I will make it all happen quickly."

Hab. 2:3 says, "The vision will happen at the time I have appointed. It moves steadily toward its goal and it will not be proven false. If it seems slow or delayed, just wait for it. It will certainly happen. It will not be late." The Message Bible says, "If it seems slow in coming, wait. It's on its way. It will come right on time." That's good news, isn't it? God's timing will not always be convenient for you but trust that He knows what He's doing. Jesus said in Mark 5:36 (NLT), "Don't be afraid. Just trust Me." Pray the words of Ps. 31:14,15 (NIV), "I trust in You, Lord. You are my God and my times are in Your hands." You trust God with everything else, why not trust Him with your time? Ps. 69:13 (CEV) says, "I pray to You, Lord, so when the time is right, please answer me and help me with Your wonderful love." If you'll pray that prayer, you'll be confirming to God that He knows the right time to make things happen in your life. You're trusting God and that is what faith is all about.

Most people don't mind waiting if they can gripe about it. Don't do that. Instead, be patient and humble. Trust God who said in Is. 49:8 (NCU), "At the right time I will answer your prayers." Stop looking at and comparing yourself to other people. Look instead at what God has planned for your life. Stress comes when you don't know what God promised to do. Daily read your Bible for in its pages are over six thousand promises God made personally to you. The good news is that He's a promise-keeping God. 1 Peter 5:6 (MSG) says, "God's strong hand is on you; He'll promote you at the right time." If you'll study and obey the Word of God, you'll bear fruit and live a productive life. Your life will be meaningful and significant and you'll fulfill your destiny. No good thing will God withhold from you if you'll walk uprightly (Ps. 84:11). Don't give up, look up! Be determined, be diligent. Keep on keeping on. Be steadfast and have endurance. Gal. 6:9 says, "We must never get tired of doing what is right and good, for at the right time we will reap a harvest of blessing if we don't give up, or quit." Stressed or blessed? The choice is yours.

The purpose of the book of James is to help believers mature in the things of God which, in turn, leads to spiritual growth. He closes out this portion of his letter to once again talk about something he has written about since chapter one. He just told his readers not to grumble and this gives James one more opportunity to give another exhortation about the sinful use of the tongue. If you can grasp it, what James says can radically and permanently transform your life. James 5:12 says, "But above all, my brethren, do not swear, either by heaven or by earth or with any other oath. But let your 'Yes' be 'Yes,' and your 'No,' 'No,' lest you fall into judgment." What is James saying here? He's exhorting you to tell the truth, the whole truth, and nothing but the truth, so help you God. He is not saying that all oaths are forbidden by God. Marriage vows are an oath couples make to one another. Those in the military take an oath to defend their country at all costs. James is, however, forbidding the use of superficial oaths that enable a person to say they're telling the truth when they're not.

The Message Bible says, "Just say yes or no. Just say what is true." The key to always telling the truth is to live in such a godly way that you'll have no reason to lie. People who don't tell the truth are those who carry the burden of some secret sin. They try to cover up some wrong they did by lying about it and not telling the truth. This is so destructive because one lie always leads to more lies. The devil is the father of lies (John 8:44) and he uses this diabolical sin to destroy lives. Lying damages your life, the lives of your loved ones, and the church you attend. James is exhorting you to live a radical Christian life and let your "yes" be yes and your "no" be no. He just said to be patient in the midst of unjust suffering, set your sights on the return of the Lord, don't grumble, and consider the suffering of the prophets of old. He then says in vs. 12, "But above all..." Above all what? Because the sin of the tongue can be so destructive, James is saying, above all, do not fall into the swearing of some trivial and ridiculous oath. Be committed to speaking the truth, the whole truth, and nothing but the truth, so help you God.

The word "swear" is defined as "the attempt to strengthen something you say by adding some type of oath to it." Swearing on a stack of Bibles is a senseless oath people take in an effort to convince somebody they're telling the truth when, in truth, they're probably not. Not only do people lie, they swear an oath that they're telling the truth. This is the type of swearing James is talking about. Stop being two-faced. Stop telling one person one thing and another person something else. Let your "yes" be yes and let your "no" be no. People foolishly think they're allowed to lie if their fingers are crossed behind their back. How absurd is that? Don't play that game because Heb. 4:13 says, "All things are naked and open to the eyes of Him to whom we must give account." You can fool others but you can't fool God. Your sin will find you out. It always does. James said in vs. 9 to not grumble against one another so you won't be judged. He's saying the same thing here. Being saved doesn't mean you won't experience judgment by the consequences of habitual sin in your life.

Gal. 6:7,8 says, "Do not be deceived, God is not mocked; for whatever a man sows, that he will also reap. For he who sows to his flesh will of the flesh reap corruption." The word "mocked" is the Greek word "mukterizo" and literally means 'to suffer from nose-bleeding.' It means to 'turn up one's nose' and is a picture of ridicule, contempt, and scorn. Mocking God is scornfully thinking you can do wrong and get away with it. It's not going to happen. The Message Bible says, "No one makes a fool of God." Sooner or later, payday will come because actions always have consequences. Time may pass before the crop ripens but the harvest is inevitable. Jobs get lost and divorces happen as the result of habitual sin that is not confessed and forsaken. This doesn't mean you're not saved but there is a judgment that affects the every day activities of your life. Instead of lying like the devil, commit yourself to living in wholeness of integrity. Live like Jesus who said, "I am the way, the truth, and the life" (John 14:6). Jesus exists as the truth and you need to walk in that truth every day of your life, so help you God.

-27-

"POWER OF PRAYER"

As a Christian, your lifestyle must be centered around meeting God daily, to experience His presence in every situation you find yourself in. There must be constant interaction between you and the great God of the universe. You must draw near to Him, cling to Him, and meet with Him daily in prayer. It's through this prayerful communion that the Christian life is defined, where you live life to the fullest, and become all He designed you to be. Prayer is the doorway into the presence of God. It's the avenue through which needs are met, answers come, and lives get changed. It's through prayer that you'll lay hold of God's power that will bring you victory in the midst of diverse circumstances. The disciples saw Jesus perform many powerful miracles and preach countless sermons and they knew prayer is what made all this happen. Luke 11:1 says, "And it came to pass, as He was praying in a certain place, when He ceased, that one of the disciples said to Him, 'Lord, teach us to pray, as John also taught his disciples.'"

Of all the things the disciples could have asked for, they asked to be taught how to pray. They didn't ask how to do miracles or how to preach. No, they asked to be told how to pray. By observing Jesus they knew how powerful prayer is. It changes things, it moves the hand of God. They knew that the power that flowed out of Jesus was connected to the close intimacy He had with the Father through prayer. The disciples wanted this same power to flow through them and you should want the same thing. Luke 18:1 says, "Then He spoke a parable to them, that men always ought to pray and not lose heart." The Message Bible says you should "pray consistently and never quit." Prayer brings God's kingdom to the earth and it is a powerful force in the life of a believer. The question is, are you praying? Is prayer at the heart of your walk with God? James closes out his letter by telling you about the priority of prayer in your life. He wants you to know that you've got to be in constant interaction with God, day in and day out.

James 5:13 says, "Is anyone among you suffering? Let him pray. Is anyone cheerful? Let him sing psalms." James uses the extremes of life's circumstances to get his point across. No matter what you're going through, whether good or bad, you need to be in constant communication with God. He tells you to pray in difficult times and to praise Him in good times. Wherever you may be in the spectrum of life, you need to continually be interacting with God. Prayer is universal for God has wired into the subconscious of every person to be people of prayer. Evert culture throughout history had a system of appealing to some higher form of deity. Every human being has inside of them a natural inclination to reach up and address a higher source of power for help in time of stress and need. Not everybody prays to the same person, but everybody prays. Every religion, every culture, and every race of people does it. Eccl. 3:11 (NLT) says, "God has planted eternity in the human heart." Everybody knows there's more to life than what they see around them.

Somewhere in the expanse of the great universe there is a Supreme Being and people are wired to seek Him out and talk to Him. Everybody prays at some point in their life. Still, very few people believe prayer works even though they do it all the time. They think prayer is boring and fruitless but they still do it as a ritual and not as an activity that has impact. Even among Christians, the smallest meeting in the local church is the prayer meeting. This happens because people subconsciously pull away from things they believe doesn't work. They tried it once, they didn't get the results they wanted, so they avoid it at all costs. They're discouraged not realizing they're missing out on what could have been the greatest meeting of their lives. Why? Because God designed prayer to get results every time you pray. Jesus promised in John 14:13,14, "And whatever you ask in My name, that I will do, that the Father may be glorified in the Son. If you ask anything in My name, I will do it." How many people pray as if this were true? Based on the condition of their lives, probably not many.

The mature believer knows and understands the power of prayer. Instead of complaining about their problems, they talk to God about them. They don't grumble, they're not envious or critical of those not going through the same struggle, and they never blame God for their difficulties. They don't ask, "Where is God my Maker, Who gives songs in the night?" (Job 35:10). Instead, they're like Paul and Silas who in jail at midnight prayed and sang praises to God (Acts 16:25). Singing at the midnight hour of your life is an expression of faith in God and deep spiritual maturity. James is describing the life of a person who's always talking to God, in good times and bad. Whether you're happy or in distress, you are always to be in communication with God. Prayer keeps you spiritually active. You're not being passive but instead you're continually focusing on God and not your struggles. Not only did James teach about prayer, he lived a life of prayer. Tradition says he was a man of such devotion that long praying made his knees as hard as camel knees.

If life's dilemmas seem a bit overwhelming, if you've reached a point where you feel there's nothing you can do, take comfort knowing you can always pray. Jesus said in Matt. 16:19, "And I will give you the keys of the kingdom of heaven, and whatever you bind on earth will be bound in heaven, and whatever you loose on earth will be loosed in heaven." Keys give you control over something. If you have keys to a car, you have control over that car. James is saying that prayer gives you access to heaven and control over what happens on the earth, especially in your own personal life. This is a powerful promise you need to tap into. Keys represent authority, access, ownership, control, power, freedom, and permission. God is giving you permission to determine what happens on earth and how heaven will affect what happens in your life. That is the power of prayer. People think prayer is begging God to give them something when in reality it's used to give God something. Through faith, prayer is giving God permission to operate on the earth.

Prayer is not an option. You are commanded by God to pray (Eph. 6:18; Luke 21:36). To get results in prayer, you must make sure the right key is going into the right lock. If you have the right key, you'll get the right results. People's frustrations with prayer are caused by their misconception about prayer and what it is. They don't understand the authority they themselves have. The truth is, what happens on earth depends on you. In the beginning, God gave man dominion over the earth (Gen. 1:26). According to the plan of God, the earth is under the complete control and management of man. All legal authority on earth belongs to humans and for this reason God took Himself out of direct interference of what happens on the planet. Since dominion belongs to man, God will not interfere on earth without the cooperation of a human. This is why prayer is so important and necessary. It's an earthly license for heavenly interference. Man has the authority, God has the power. When you give God permission to move, He'll move. This is why you must pray without ceasing. When you stop praying, God stops interfering.

An example of this is found in 2 Chron. 7:14 where God said, "If My people who are called by My name will humble themselves, and pray and seek My face, and turn from their wicked ways, then I will hear from heaven, and will forgive their sin and heal their land." Notice that God did not move until the people prayed. Why? Because God is a Spirit and only a human can have dominion on earth. God could not destroy Sodom and Gomorrah without Abraham's permission (Gen. 18). He said in Ex. 3:8, "I have come down to deliver My people from Egypt." He then said to Moses in vs. 10, "You go." God needed a human to give Him access to the affairs of man. Everything Moses said, God did. Jesus said what you bind and loose on earth will be bound and loosed in heaven. In other words, heaven depends on humans to determine what it can do on earth. This is why the life of Jesus was so powerful. He came to earth legally as a human and exercised the dominion and authority God gave man in the beginning. Jesus could only do what He did on earth not because He was the Son of God, but because He was the Son of Man (John 5:27).

1 Cor. 6:13 says, "Now the body is not for sexual immortality but for the Lord, and the Lord for the body." God designed the human body so He could come on the earth legally. Your body was made specifically to house God's Spirit (1 Cor. 6:19). Wherever you go, God will be there legally. Jesus said to pray, "Your kingdom come. Your will be done on earth as it is in heaven" (Matt. 6:10). Why do you have to pray for this? Because His kingdom cannot come to earth without man's permission. You have to legally give God permission to bring His governing authority to earth and impact your family, your community, and your country. Give God permission to do His will and He'll have access to do it. Prayer is powerful only when you understand the power you have with God. You've been given dominion on the earth. This is God's mission statement for your life. The word "dominion" means 'to govern, to rule, to control, to manage, and to lead.' All humans are accountable to God to manage the earth. God says it is your responsibility for whatever happens here.

Prayer is powerful and effective because God responds to it. It's in prayer where His thoughts and your thoughts come together. Prayer gives you the opportunity to put on the mind of Christ (1 Cor. 2:16). When His thoughts become your thoughts, you'll respond to life's trials in a way that reflects the faith and hope you have in Him. If you don't pray, if you don't communicate with God, you'll never become the person He created you to be. It's in His presence where spiritual growth takes place. Understand that God wants to do more than fix your problems. He wants you to walk with Him and be with Him in the midst of it all. David said, "Yea, though I walk through the valley of the shadow of death, I will fear no evil; For You are with me" (Ps. 23:4). David was still in the valley but he knew God was with him. That's what prayer does. It binds you together with God in every circumstance of life. Whether you're in the valley or on the mountaintop, you must be in constant fellowship with God. That's prayer.

Are you meeting God in the midst of your trial? Do you sense His presence as you walk through the valley? Your relationship with God is more important to Him than the situation you're currently in. He wants you to seek His face and not His hand because He wants to change your heart more than your circumstance. The purpose of prayer is to align your heart with God's heart, to get your will in agreement with His. It's in your closeness to Him that you'll find the answer to your problems. James continues his exhortation to pray in every situation by dealing with praying for the sick. James 5:14,15 says, "Is anyone among you sick? Let him call for the elders of the church, and let them pray over him, anointing him with oil in the name of the Lord. And the prayer of faith will save the sick, and the Lord will raise him up. And if he has committed sins, he will be forgiven." The Message Bible says, "Believing-prayer will heal you, and Jesus will put you on your feet. And if you've sinned, you'll be forgiven - healed inside and out."

James is continuing to show you the critical role of prayer in a person's life. If you're suffering, pray. If you're sick, have the elders come and pray also. Deut. 32:30 says one can put a thousand to flight and two can put ten thousand to flight. Think about it. You can do ten times as much with someone agreeing with you as you can by yourself. James is talking about unity in prayer. Jesus spoke on this in Matt. 18:19, "Again, I say to you that if two of you agree on earth concerning anything that they ask, it will be done by My Father in heaven." The reason for this heightened power is explained in the following verse, "For where two or three are gathered together in My Name, I am there in the midst of them" (vs. 20). Getting in the presence of God is what prayer is all about. It's what produces the answer to your prayers. With Jesus in your presence, you can pray in agreement with Him based on what's written in the Bible. While on the earth, Jesus was always praying and consulting with the Heavenly Father. You need to follow His example and find God's will before coming into agreement on a matter.

1 John 5:14,15 says, "Now this is the confidence we have in Him, that if we ask anything according to His will, He hears us. And if we know that He hears us, whatever we ask , we know that we have the petitions that we have asked of Him." The Message Bible says, "And how bold and free we then become in His presence, freely asking according to His will, sure that He is listening, we know that what we've asked for is as good as ours." Notice that it is the sick person's responsibility to call the elders. By doing this, they're demonstration their belief in the power of prayer. In the local church the elders are required to be mature, stable, faithful prayer warriors. They pray in faith believing God can do exceedingly, abundantly above all they can think or imagine (Eph. 3:20). They pray with the confidence that the Lord is able to raise them up. They anoint them with oil in the name of the Lord. This is symbolic of what's happening inside of you. Faith starts in the heart and being anointed with oil is a picture of the Holy Spirit immersing you in His presence and power which is what you need if you're sick.

In Biblical times, olive oil was thought to be useful in treating different wounds and ailments. Luke 10:34 tells how the good Samaritan poured oil and wine on the wounded man who had been beaten by thieves. Wine was an antiseptic that killed off possible infections that would try to set in and oil would soothe and aid in the healing process. Spiritually speaking, oil was symbolic in setting people apart for service to the Lord. David was called by God to be king over Israel and the prophet Samuel anointed him with oil. It is also symbolic of the Holy Spirit and His presence coming upon a person. This is what is needed most. You need the Holy Spirit to anoint you, engulf you, and overwhelm you. This anointing is done in the name of the Lord. This means what you do is to be in full accordance with His character and nature and according to His perfect will. James says the prayer of faith will save the sick. It's the prayer of faith that releases the power of God into your life. It shows you have confidence in the authority of Jesus over everything the enemy brings against you. It's believing there is no obstacle too big to stop the will of God from being fulfilled in your life.

A mature faith trusts God completely. It causes you to trust His will, His timing, His purpose, and His plan. God is sovereign and when you pray you need to trust Him in complete faith as you wait on Him to move in your life. James says, "And if he has committed sins, he will be forgiven." The construction of this verse does not indicate that when someone is sick it is always because of sin in their life. It does, however, indicate it is possible that sickness is associated with sin. Sin can be defined as "rebellion against the known will of God." Murder is not sin, it's the result of sin. Sin is declaring independence from heaven and the influence of God. Sin blocks access to the kingdom of God. Ps. 66:18 says, "If I regard iniquity in my heart, the Lord will not hear me." For sure, the presence of sin can open the door that allows the enemy to put sickness on your body (1 Cor.

11:30). The best medicine you can ever take is to get right with God. In Mark 2:5-11 the man's sins were forgiven before he was healed. Check up on yourself and confess your sins to Him. Have your conscience cleared and your guilt removed.

To be totally well, you need to deal with all areas of your life. Mental, physical, spiritual. Ps. 139:23,24 says, "Search me, O God, and know my heart; Try me, and know my anxieties; And see if there is any wicked way in me, and lead me in the way everlasting." The point James is making is that if sin is involved in your sickness, the prayer of faith and your confession of sin will bring healing and forgiveness. James 5:16 says, "Confess your trespasses to one another, and pray for one another, that you may be healed." Don't just confide in anybody. Choose carefully a mature, righteous person who will keep what you say confidential between you and them. James is saying you need to have an accountability partner, somebody you can be open and honest with. The person preferably should be older than you, somebody who is stable in the faith. Also, never is sin to be confessed beyond the circle of that sin's influence. Private sin requires private confession and public sin requires public confession. Never hang your sins out for all to see for doing so may do more harm than the original sin.

James next makes one of the most powerful statements in all the Bible. He says, "The effective, fervent prayer of a righteous man avails much" (vs. 16). The fact that prayer can be effective should have you running to your prayer closet as fast as you can go. How amazing is it that your words can bring God on the scene at any given moment? The Message Bible says, "The prayer of a person living right with God is something powerful to be reckoned with." Little is the call to a righteous lifestyle preached in the local church today. Many pastors shy away from confronting the presence of habitual sin in the lives of born again believers. What's more, there is a distorted message about the grace of God going around the world that minimizes the necessity to obey God. The grace of God is being magnified in a way that is non-biblical because it's being taught that your obedience doesn't matter because Jesus obeyed for you. In this wave of false teaching there is a complete absence of the exhortation to righteousness and the need to forsake sin. Beware of these false teachings because grace is no substitute for obedience.

It is no small thing to miss the mark of God's call to righteousness. He longs for you to be in His presence and sin stops that from happening. Is. 59:2 says, "But your iniquities have separated you from your God; And your sins have hidden His face from you, so that He will not hear." Do the prayers of sinners get answered? Are these people righteous? Are they praying in faith or desperation? John 9:31 says, "Now we know that God does not hear sinners; but if anyone is a worshiper of God and does His will, He hears him." This is known for sure, God does answer the prayer of all those who cry out to Him for mercy, forgiveness, and salvation. True and perfect righteousness is not possible for man to attain on his own. The standard is simply too high. It is only by asking Jesus into your heart that you become righteous. 2 Cor. 5:21 says, "For He made Him who knew no sin to be sin for us, that we might become the righteousness of God in Him." Jesus told the woman caught in adultery, "Go, and sin no more" (John 8:11). He's saying the same thing to you today.

James gives an example of the power of prayer in the life of a righteous man. James 5:17,18 says, "Elijah was a man with a nature like ours, and he prayed earnestly that it would not rain; and it did not rain on the land for three years and six months. And he prayed again, and the heaven gave rain, and the earth produced its fruit." The Jews loved Elijah and in their eyes he was superhuman. James, however, says he was a man just like everybody else and had the same nature you have. He was a weak and broken man and prone to discouragement. What Elijah did have was a real, continual relationship with the living God. He was in tune with God even when he struggled with depression and fear. Because of his connection with God, many supernatural and miraculous things were done through him. God wants this same type of relationship with you and it all begins by getting in and staying in His holy presence. Pray to him in every circumstance, in good times and bad. Align your heart with His heart and your will with His will. Then step back and watch what happens.

Prayers that are effective are prayers that get results. It's when you partner with God to change the world by releasing His resources into the earthly realm. He wants things to happen and He needs you to do it. The destiny of every believer is to release the power of God on the earth through prayer. James says Elijah prayed earnestly. Most people don't do this. Instead they lazily say religious words and their hearts are not in their prayers. No, earnest prayer comes from a heart that is engaged with God. It's persistent, it doesn't quit, it never gives up when the will of God is known. Seven times Elijah prayed until the manifestation of rain came (1 Kings 18). He refused to be denied the answer to his prayer. Paul said to pray "with all perseverance" (Eph. 6:18). Stay engaged with God and never give up because persistence is the essence of earnestness. Jesus said in Matt. 7:7 (AMP), "Ask and keep on asking and it will be given to you; seek and keep on seeking and you will find; knock and keep on knocking and the door will be opened to you."

James has a pastor's heart and he closes out his letter with an exhortation for all believers to take care of one another. "Brethren, if anyone among you wanders from the truth, and someone turns him back, let him know that he who turns a sinner from the error of his way will save a soul from death and cover a multitude of sins" (James 5;19,20). James is sending his readers on a rescue operation. He's telling the people to rescue those who have wandered from the truth. Backsliding is dangerous both to the individual and to the church. A wandering offender can influence others and lead them astray as well. One bad apple can spoil the whole bunch. Eccl. 9:18 says, "One sinner destroys much good." This is why elders of the church must step in and help the person who has wandered away from the truth. Heb. 2:1 says, "Therefore we must give the more earnest heed to the things we have heard, lest we drift away." James is talking about Christians here and the result of wandering from the truth is sin and possible death.

These wandering believers need to be turned back onto the right path. The Greek word for "wander" means "planets" and refers to the seemingly wandering of the planets in the sky. The word implies a "gradually straying off course" and it leads toward their own destruction and maybe even death. Take this exhortation seriously. If you are saved, if you are spiritual and godly, then this is your responsibility. Paul said in Gal. 6:1 (NLT), "Dear brothers and sisters, if another believer is overcome by some sin, you who are godly should gently and humbly help that person back onto the right path. And be careful not to fall into the same temptation yourself." When other believers fall into the world of sin, you've got to stand up for Christ at all costs. You've got to be strong when they are weak because, if you're not, you could easily be pulled down with them. Go to that person in love for "love shall cover a multitude of sins" (1 Peter 4:8). Love not only helps the offender to face his sin, it also gives him the assurance that, once forgiven, their sins are remembered no more (Heb. 10:17).

-28-

"MARK OF MATURITY"

The church is in trouble. The ways of the world are creeping in and it's gotten so bad that Christians think they can live like everybody else. They think they can pick and choose what to believe, and what not to believe, as long as it conforms to the way they want to live. It's gotten to the point where you can't tell who's saved and who isn't. There are believers who have drifted away from their first love (Rev. 2:4) and their passion and zeal for living a godly life is no longer there. It's for this reason that believers need to take their Christianity seriously and grow up. If they don't, then somebody needs to tell them what Jesus said in Matt. 7:21-23, "Not everyone who says to Me, 'Lord, Lord' shall enter the kingdom of heaven, but he who does the will of My Father in heaven. Many will say to me in that day, 'Lord, Lord, have we not prophesied in Your name, cast out demons in Your name, and done many wonders in Your name?' And then I will declare to them, 'I never knew you; depart from Me, you who practice lawlessness!'" The Message Bible says, "You don't impress Me one bit. You're out of here."

Jesus is saying you can't live in the light on Sunday and in darkness the rest of the week. If you do, you'll be lukewarm and God said in Rev. 3:16, "So then, because you are lukewarm, and neither cold nor hot, I will spew you out of

My mouth." The Message Bible quotes God as saying, "You make Me want to vomit." People need to get saved and then they need to spiritually grow up. Not only does Jesus bring salvation, He also brings change to your life. The apostle John was changed from being one of the "Sons of Thunder" (Mark 3:17) to being the beloved apostle of love. A radical change came over him because of the close fellowship he had with Jesus. This is why spiritual growth begins with a close, personal relationship with God. John wrote, "Truly our fellowship is with the Father and with His Son Jesus Christ" (1 John 1:3). John knew that God is a God of light, a God of love, and a God of life. To engage in fellowship with God, you must walk in light and not darkness. A change has to take place inside of you that carries over and changes the way you act and the way you speak.

1 John 1:5 says, "God is light and in Him is no darkness at all." This means He is infinite in His glory, absolute in His truth, unconditional in His holiness. The mark of maturity is to respond to the truth that God is light. It's when you allow that light to bring about a positive change in your life. Whenever truth is revealed to you in the Bible, a response is always required. It is demanded by God that you order your steps accordingly to what is revealed to you. You must be doers of the Word and not hearers only (James 1:22). Vs. 6 says, "If we say that we have fellowship with Him, and walk in darkness, we lie and do not practice the truth." So often people's actions don't line up with what they say. They talk the talk but don't walk the walk. They're deceiving themselves into thinking they're okay with God because they say the right things. Examine yourself and make sure this isn't happening to you. Lam. 3:40 says, "Let us search out and examine our ways, and turn back to God." The Message Bible says, "Let's take a good look at the way we're living and reorder our lives under God."

Many believers, if not most of them, struggle with the temptation to be pulled back into the world's system of thinking and doing things. How can they not be tempted? Headlines daily declare that evil abounds everywhere. There's not a place you can go where you won't be surrounded by people living sinful lives. Their influence is knocking at your door trying to pull you into their evil lifestyle. Sometimes it doesn't seem fair that God is pulling you out of this world but still you have to live and function in this evil place. Consider what Paul said in Rom. 7:15, "For what I am doing, I do not understand. For what I will to do, that I do not practice; but what I hate, that I do." The NLT says, "I don't really understand myself, for I want to do what is right, but I don't do it. Instead, I do what I hate." The truth be told, change is not easy. If it were, everybody would do it. Satan is the accuser of the brethren (Rev. 12:10) and he's relentless in his war with the children of God. He don't change and the world don't change. Even so, change is to be a part of your daily walk with God. Changing for the better is the mark of maturity.

Yes, change is difficult but it's totally possible. You can do it because God has given you all the power you need to live differently from the rest of the world. 2 Cor. 5:17 says, "Therefore, if anyone is in Christ, he is a new creation; old things have passed away; behold, all things have become new." God has supernaturally changed you on the inside and this is what allows you to change and be different on the outside. It's been said that dead fish float downstream but it takes a live one to swim against the current. You're not the same person you were before you got saved. You're a new creation in Christ Jesus. Stop saying you're an old sinner saved by grace. That's not who you are. You're a born again child of the living God. You're forgiven and not condemned. You're an heir of God, the temple of the Holy Spirit, and you're seated in heavenly places. Eph. 2:4,5 (NLT) says, "But God is so rich in mercy, and He loved us so much, that even though we were dead because of our sins, He gave us life when He raised Christ from the dead." Paul is saying you don't have to go with the flow of the world and float downstream any longer.

Gal. 5:16,17 says, "Walk in the Spirit, and you shall not fulfill the lust of the flesh. For the flesh lusts against the Spirit, and the Spirit against the flesh; and these are contrary to one another, so that you do not do the things that you wish." You're not supposed to live the way you used to live because you're not who you used to be. That old life is worthless and leads to bondage and destruction. 2 Cor. 6:14 (MSG) says, "Don't become partners with those who reject God." Vs. 17,18 (NLT) says, "Therefore, come out from among unbelievers, and separate yourselves from them, says the Lord. Don't touch their filthy things, and I will welcome you. And I will be your Father, and you will be My sons and daughters, says the Lord Almighty." Turn away from the darkness of the world and walk in the power of God's light. Live freely, animated and motivated by God's Spirit. If you'll do that, you won't feed the compulsions of sin and selfishness. Jesus said in Matt. 5:14, "You are the light of the world. A city that is set on a hill cannot be hidden." You're here to be light, "bringing out the God-colors in the world" (MSG).

People get lost in the dark. This is why Paul said in Eph. 4:17,18 (MSG), "And so I insist - and God backs me up on this - that there be no going along with the crowd, the empty-headed, mindless crowd. They've refused for so long to deal with God that they've lost touch not only with God but with reality itself. They can't think straight anymore." Not only has their understanding been darkened, their hearts have become calloused and hardened as well. They've stopped caring about what God wants and they've lost interest in doing things God's way. Vs. 18 says they've become "past feeling." They're rough, cold, and insensitive. They've not moved when something bad happens to somebody else because all they care about is themselves. Vs. 19 (NLT) says, "They have no sense of shame. They live for lustful pleasure and eagerly practice every kind of impurity." Stay away from these people because, if you don't, you may become like them and suffer the same consequences they do. Col. 3:6 (NLT) says, "Because of these sins, the anger of God is coming." The Message Bible says, "God is about to explode in anger."

The problem with sin is that it's so common that people think it's no big deal, that it'a just a normal part of life. There are those who claim to be Christians but still sin habitually not realizing that sin hurts you in a bad way. It imprisons you in fear, jealousy, hatred, and guilt. It separates the best of friends and destroys relationships. It leads to violence, addictions, abuse, and ultimately death. Sin is lawlessness (1 John 3:4). It's when you willingly do something God told you not to do. It's a violation of His will, a willful rejection of His commands. This is outright rebellion, a lifestyle many Christians choose to live. These are the people who have not grown up spiritually. They need to either be a Christian or not be one because believers who sin habitually are an embarrassment to the kingdom of God. A person's lifestyle should correspond to the faith they're proclaiming. The apostle John wrote, "Whoever abides in Him does not sin. Whoever sins has neither seen Him nor known Him" (1 John 3:6). No one who fellowships with Jesus keeps on sinning and living the lifestyle Jesus died to set you free from.

What should you do? Rom. 12:9 says, "Abhor what is evil. Cling to what is good." The Message Bible says, "Run for dear life from evil; hold on for dear life to good." Stop doing the things you used to do. Col. 3:5 (NLT) says, "So put to death the sinful, earthly things lurking within you." Vs. 8 (NLT) says, "But now is the time to get rid of anger, rage, malicious behavior, slander, and dirty language." It's time for you to change. Don't go back to your old way of living. Eph. 4:22 says, "The old man grows corrupt according to the deceitful lusts." In other words, the old man is lying to you. He's saying it's okay to sin when in reality it isn't. You need to put off the old man and put on the new man. Out with the old, in with the new. Change what you put into your minds. Be careful what movies you watch and what music you listen to. Most are filled with the sins of the world and are ready to affect your life in a negative way. Garbage in, garbage out. Eph. 4:23 says, "And be renewed in the spirit of your mind." The NLT says, "Instead, let the Spirit renew your thoughts and attitudes."

Col. 3:1,2 says, "If then you were raised with Christ, seek those things which are above, where Christ is, sitting at the right hand of God. Set your mind on things above, not on things on the earth." It's important to know that you have to put off the old before you put on the new. You don't buy a new coat and put it on over the old one. No, you take off the old coat first and then you put on the new one. People struggle because they're trying to do both. They try to put one foot in heaven and one on the earth. You can't do that. You can't live in two worlds at the same time. You can't please God while still trying to please your flesh. Rom. 12:2 (NLT) says, "Don't copy the behavior and customs of this world, but let God transform you into a new person by changing the way you think. Then you will learn to know God's will for you, which is good and pleasing and perfect." Be proactive about the things you put in your mind. Meditate on things that are true, honorable, right, pure, lovely, and admirable. Think about things that are excellent and worthy of praise (Phil. 4:8).

Ps. 119:9-11 says, "How can a young man cleanse his way? By taking heed according to Your word. With my whole heart I have sought You; Oh, let me not wander from Your commandments! Your word I have hidden in my heart, that I might not sin against You." That's a good thing, in a good place, for a good purpose. God's Word in your heart gives you the capacity to have a renewed mind. It will cause you to think differently and to see the world as it truly is. It also causes you to think and talk about God every moment of every day "for out of the abundance of the heart the mouth speaks" (Luke 6:45). What you love, you talk about. That's an inescapable truth. Mal. 3:16 (TLB) says, "Then those who feared and loved the Lord spoke often of Him to each other. And He had a Book of Remembrance drawn up in which He recorded the names of those who feared Him and loved to think about Him." Think about that. There is a book in heaven where God records the names of those who think and speak about Him often. Is your name in that book?

The Christian life is a growing and progressive walk. You should always be changing and advancing forward in it. There are many, however, who have been saved but have not grown spiritually. The Bible says Jesus grew in wisdom and stature (Luke 2:52). Shouldn't you be growing also? 1 John 2:12-14 talks about the stages of the spiritual life and the need to go further and advance in maturity. Growing up is a process and John uses the stages of a physical life to show what the stages of spiritual development should look like. He begins by saying in vs. 12, "I write to you, little children..." The Greek word used here means 'newly born ones.' These are the baby Christians, those who have just recently been saved, people who are brand new in the faith. Much is known about little children. Newborn babes are ruled by their emotions, the same as new believers. They're easily frightened, easily excited, and easily distracted. A baby doesn't think, perceive, or reason well. They can't do things on their own and are totally dependent on others. They need someone to feed them, bathe them, and clothe them.

Most of all, newborns need love and security. A baby needs to know that someone cares and is present to take care of them. They need a family around them to help them grow. Newborn babes often trip and fall. Until they learn to walk they'll need someone to pick them up, dry their tears, and bandage their skinned knees. A baby is able to grow under normal circumstances. They need the correct environment, a place where they are taken care of. They can't be neglected and left to fend for themselves. A baby has to be able to breathe or else they will not grow. Breathing for the baby

Christian is prayer which makes contact with the Father. A growing baby must also eat properly. The Bible is spiritual food and 1 Peter 2:2,3 (NLT) says, "Like newborn babies, you must crave pure spiritual milk so that you will grow into a full experience of salvation. Cry out for this nourishment, now that you have had a taste of the Lord's kindness." The Message Bible says, "Drink deep of God's pure kindness. Then you'll grow up mature and whole in God."

"I write to you, little children, because your sins are forgiven you for His name's sake" (vs. 12). One of the most basic lessons a new believer must learn is that their sins are forgiven and they're a fully accepted and redeemed child of God. Forgiveness is central to everything in the Christian faith. Churches have communion to remind people that Jesus died on the cross and their sins are forgiven. These newborns need to be assured that falling down doesn't mean they'll never walk or they're not part of the family. Because of the shed blood of Jesus, they are justified and in right standing with God. Repentance (1 John 1:9) allows a person to override sin by receiving God's forgiveness so that the flow of His grace continues. When grace flows, growth follows. Why are they forgiven? For His name's sake. People don't deserve forgiveness but it happens because of who God is, because of His character. Ps. 25:11 says, "For Your name's sake, O Lord, pardon my iniquity, for it is great." As a new believer, you need to realize that God didn't save you because you're good, He saved you because He is good.

John writes again to the babes in Christ in vs. 13. "I write to you, little children, because you have known the Father." The Greek language reveals that John is not writing to the same newborn toddlers he addressed in the previous verse. Here the Greek word for "little Children" means 'immature ones.' This is referring to people who should have grown up but haven't. 1 Cor. 3:1 says, "But I, brothers, could not address you as spiritual people, but as people of the flesh, as infants in Christ." These people have been saved for many years but are still infantile in their lifestyle. John is saying that believers need to know who their Father is. They need to learn to walk with God through constant fellowship, consistent meditation on His Word, and by being aware of His presence in their life. It's impossible to develop intimacy in any relationship without spending time with the person you love. Immature believers go from the spiritual maternity ward straight to the spiritual retirement home with nothing to show for their lives. They never grew up in the Lord and their lives were wasted. They died of old age but spiritually they were immature babies.

John now moves on to the next level of spiritual growth. "I write to you, young men, because you have overcome the wicked one" (vs. 13). These young men are progressing toward maturity in the faith. They're no longer little children and are striving to grow in their walk with the Lord. They're the believers who take their bibs off and put on an apron. They are seeking to work with God and be used by Him in an effective manner. Ps. 92:12 says, "The righteous shall flourish like a palm tree, he shall grow like a cedar in Lebanon." The cedar is a cone-bearing tree that can grow up to a hundred and twenty feet tall. It was known in biblical times as the king of all trees and its wood was hewn into beams for the temple of God that was built in the Old Testament (Ezra 3:7). The word "cedar" means 'firm, strong' because the roots of the tree went as deep into the ground as the height of the tree was above ground. To grow spiritually you must be deeply rooted in God's truth and His way of life. You will only grow as tall as you are rooted deep.

God wants you to change, to mature, to grow up spiritually. He wants you to take the life you've been given and use it to the fullest extent, to use the resources He has entrusted to you. Those who are strong aren't afraid to attempt the impossibilities of life. They know that God has the power to do the impossible in them and through them. Weak believers are slaves to their trials but those who are strong are masters of their circumstances. These young men know what Jesus said in Matt. 16:18 (NLT), "I will build My church, and all the power of hell will not conquer it." They've grown up in the nurture and admonition of the Lord (Eph. 6:4) and are no longer being defeated by the evil one. The devil seems powerful to some but his fate is forever sealed. He is destined for the lake of fire but until then he will continue to make war against the saints of God. There are many battles yet to be fought and the young men are engaging in spiritual warfare daily. They walk in the light of Christ's victory and this is how they are able to overcome the darkness of the world, the flesh, and the devil.

How did these young men become so strong? John answers that question in vs. 14. "I have written to you, young men, because you are strong and the Word of God abides in you, and you have overcome the wicked one." The NLT says, "God's Word lives in your hearts, and you have won your battle with the evil one." The Word makes you strong. You mature and grow up spiritually by putting the Word inside of you and by doing what it says. You think about the Word and meditate on it. You use it to overcome the evil one, to break the power of sin in your life. Rom. 6:5 (MSG) says, "Our old way of life was nailed to the cross with Christ, a decisive end to that sin-miserable life - no longer at sin's every beck and call." Vs. 11 (MSG) says, "You are dead to sin and alive to God." There is a deepening in their prayer life and their understanding of the Word. They've learned how to take the Word and apply it to their lives. They put the Word in practice and it comes alive in them. It's working in them and they're growing in faith. They discover their spiritual gifts and find a place to serve. They're growing up and they're pressing on.

John next addresses those believers who are spiritually mature in the faith. "I write to you, fathers, because you have known Him who is from the beginning" (vs. 13). He says the same thing in vs.14. These are the spiritual adults, believers who have grown up out of childhood. Maturity comes from knowing God, by having true fellowship with Him, and by walking in the light with Him. 2 Peter 3:18 (NIV) says, "But grow in grace and knowledge of our Lord and Savior Jesus Christ." Their knowledge of God and their faithfulness to Him grows and grows and keeps on growing. Spiritual fathers have learned to apply their knowledge of God to life's experiences. 2 Tim. 3:17 (MSG) says, "Through the Word we are put together and shaped up for the tasks God has for us." They've fought the daily battles of life and have matured to the point that they trust God to get them through the hard times. They've lived through the up's and down's of life, the heartaches and the health problems and financial issues. They've trusted God and have come out the other side victorious.

The word "father" is a title of honor and refers to one deserving of respect and responsibility. They're the ones who have continuously demonstrated their love and relationship to God through their child-like faith and obedience. Such spiritual growth and faithful maturity doesn't happen automatically. It's not an afterthought. It must be your number one priority and the consuming passion of your life. A spiritual father is not a new convert or one that has been in the faith a short time. They are the ones who have been given by God the responsibility of leading others to the same path they're on. Ps. 92:14,15 says, "They shall still bear fruit in old age; They shall be fresh and flourishing, to declare that the Lord is upright." Fathers are called upon to take care of and look after those around them who are still growing in the faith. Joseph was made a father to Pharaoh (Gen. 45:8) and Job was a father to the poor and needy (Job 29:16). A spiritual father uses what he's learned to benefit others. They use what God teaches them through life's experiences to encourage others going through the same hardships.

2 Cor. 1:4 (NLT) says, "He comforts us in all our troubles so that we can comfort others. When they are troubled, we will

be able to give them the same comfort God has given us." Fathers speak the truth in love because they want others to avoid mistakes and benefit from the lessons they've learned. Fathers have grown in the wisdom of the Lord. Wisdom is applied knowledge. It is gained by applying their knowledge of God to daily life. They then seek to pass this wisdom on to others so they also can draw closer to God and grow up spiritually. 1 Cor. 4:15 (MSG) says, "There are a lot of people around who can't wait to tell you what you've done wrong, but there aren't many fathers willing to take the time and effort to help you grow up." Paul then said, "Therefore I urge you, imitate me" (vs. 16). Fathers always lead by example. Paul again said in 1 Cor. 11:1 (NIV), "Follow my example, as I follow the example of Christ." This is what spiritual maturity is all about. Hopefully one day you can say what Paul said in Phil. 3:17 (NLT), "Dear brothers and sisters, pattern your lives after mine, and learn from those who follow our example."

-29-

"AS JESUS WALKED"

As a child of God, you need to live in such a way that allows Jesus to one day say to you, "Well done, good and faithful servant" (Matt. 25:33). Make becoming a spiritual father your aim in life so you can faithfully take what you've learned and pass it on to others. Paul wrote in 2 Tim. 2:1,2, "You therefore, my son, be strong in the grace that is in Christ Jesus. And the things that you have heard from me among many witnesses, commit these to faithful men who will be able to teach others also." The Message Bible says to "throw yourself into this work for Christ" (vs. 1). You've been taught the Word of God, you've applied it to your life, you've been victorious in your war with the devil. Now throw yourself into helping others do the same. Col. 1:28 (NLT) says, "So we tell others about Christ, warning everyone and teaching everyone with all the wisdom God has given us. We want to present them to God, perfect in their relationship to Christ." With that in mind, Paul gives three illustrations of how to live as a father who passes on to others the truths of God's Word.

2 Tim. 2:3 says, "You therefore must endure hardship as a good soldier of Jesus Christ." Paul saw in the life of a soldier a picture of the life of a Christian who has grown up spiritually. A good soldier is conditioned to obedience. He is trained to obey every command given to him without

question or hesitation. He doesn't need to know the reason he's being told to do a certain command. It's not his duty to know the reason why. He just does what he's told. Period. The primary duty of the born again believer is to obey the voice of God along with the acceptance of that which he does not understand. A good soldier is loyal and is always ready to faithfully obey his commander without grumbling or complaining. If sacrifices have to be made, then so be it. The supreme virtue of a good soldier is that he is faithful even unto death. He is conditioned to hardship and sacrifice. It's who he is, it's what he does. The spiritual fathers in the world are forever ready to sacrifice themselves for God and their fellow man. It's the divine quality that makes them who they are.

To be a good soldier of Jesus Christ there must be a passion for victory, an unwillingness to back down. In his heart is the unquenchable desire for setting up the throne of God in the hearts of men. For that to happen, a soldier must live a life of total surrender. A lot of believers don't do this because surrender is demanding, it requires something of you. To surrender to the lordship of Jesus you've got to give your entire self to Him, all that you are and all that you have. You need to surrender your time, your talents, and your treasure to the will of God. You die to yourself as you yield everything to Him. Jesus prayed in the Garden of Gethsemane, "Father, if it is Your will, remove this cup from Me; nevertheless, not My will, but Yours be done." (Luke 22:42). At the most crucial moment of His life, in the shadow of the cross, Jesus surrendered His will to the will of the Father. It's not easy to give up your right to decide what you want to do with your life. For this reason many people remain sinners, destined for an eternity separated from God forever.

As a good soldier, you've got to have the right priorities. This is why surrender is so important. When you got saved, you entered a spiritual battle against the forces of evil (Eph.

6:12). Life isn't always easy anymore because you've made the wise decision to swim upstream. The good news is that in Christ you can endure anything the enemy throws at you, as long as your priorities are right. Paul says in vs. 4, "No one engaged in warfare entangles himself with the affairs of this life, that he may please him who enlisted him as a soldier." A good soldier is not preoccupied with the things of this world so he can concentrate on his role as a soldier. Jesus is your Captain and your top priority is not the affairs of this life but to please Him. A soldier "doesn't get caught up making deals at the marketplace. He concentrates on carrying out orders" (MSG). A soldier is a soldier and nothing else. Yes, as a believer you still must live in this world and make an honest living. What Paul is saying is that you must use whatever task you are engaged in to demonstrate your Christianity.

Don't be conformed to this world but do the will of God (Rom. 12:1,2). Live in such a way that your top priority is to serve God whenever He calls upon you. Be willing to go wherever He tells you to go and do whatever He tells you to do. Be like Isaiah who said, "Here am I! Send me" (Is. 6:8). It will take discipline and self-denial to say this. For this reason Paul writes in 2 Tim. 2:5, "And also if anyone competes in athletics, he is not crowned unless he competes according to the rules." Soldiers have the right priorities and athletes have the right lifestyle. 1 Cor. 9:25 (NLT) says, "All athletes are disciplined in their training." Only those who are self-disciplined have the spiritual determination to achieve their God-given goals. They put their hand to the plow and don't look back. They always run to win. Heb. 12:1 says, "Let us run with endurance the race that is set before us." What should you do? 1 Tim. 4:7 (NLT) says, "Train yourself to be godly." Vs. 8 (MSG) says, "Workouts in the gymnasium are useful, but a disciplined life in God is far more so, making you fit both today and forever."

In the race of life, you can't make up your own rules and do whatever you want to do. You must compete according to the rules of God's Word. If you don't follow His rules, you're disqualified and thrown out of the race. Paul is giving the church a very serious warning. He is saying you can't take a short cut when the race becomes difficult to run. Taking the easy way out disqualifies you from winning the prize. Samson did not have self-discipline. He lived to please himself and the consequences were tragic. He was led by his flesh and not by God who said in Ps. 32:8 (NLT), "I will guide you along the best pathway for your life. I will advise you and watch over you." You have a personal promise from God that He will teach you everything you need to know to live a disciplined and productive life. 1 Cor. 9:26,27 (NLT) says, "So I run with purpose in every step. I am not just shadow-boxing. I discipline my body like an athlete, training it to do what it should." Yes, the easy road may seem more attractive but those who have discipline are the ones who win the prize.

2 Tim. 2:6 says, "The hard-working farmer must be first to partake of the crops." Hard work today produces fruitful reaping tomorrow. This is not a lazy farmer but one who works hard day and night. The Greek word used here is "kopiao" and means 'to exhibit great effort and exertion to the point of sweat and exhaustion; to physically become worn out, weary, or faint; to engage in hard work with the implication of difficulty and trouble." This is the farmer's way of life and it should be yours also. Paul said in 1 Cor. 15:10, "But by the grace of God I am what I am; and His grace toward me was not in vain; but I labored more abundantly than they all, yet not I, but the grace of God which was with me." A person's reward from God is proportionate to the excellence of his ministry and the effort he puts into it. Press on in His power for He has already won the victory. Though the battle may now seem intense, it is only for a short time compared to eternity. 2 Cor. 4:17 (NLT) says, "For our present troubles are small and won't last very long. Yet they produce for us a glory that vastly outweighs them and will last forever."

Eph. 4:1 says "to have a walk worthy of the calling with which you were called." You need clear direction from God, based on His Word, on how you're supposed to live your life. You need to know what pleases Him and what He specifically wants you to do with your life. Eph. 5:16,17 (MSG) says, "So watch your step. Use your head. Make the most of every chance you get. These are desperate times! Don't live carelessly, unthinkingly. Make sure you understand what the Master wants." It matters how you carry yourself in the presence of others, the witness you proclaim by the things you say and do. Watch your step. Col. 4:5 says, "Walk in wisdom toward those who are outside, redeeming the time." The Message Bible says, "Use your heads as you live and work among outsiders. Don't miss a trick. Make the most of every opportunity." You live an observable life and people are watching you. Your neighbors and co-workers see how you are in stressful moments and how you treat those around you. They see what you're really like when you're not in church on Sunday morning. In other words, they see the real you.

Eph. 2:10 says you were "created in Christ Jesus for good works." You were created to have a positive influence in the lives of others. Believers are called salt and light in this fallen world which means you're supposed to live in such a way that you touch lives for Jesus Christ. You can share the gospel message with people but if you don't live a righteous lifestyle, the people won't listen to you. Examine yourself and the way you're living. Pay close attention to what you say and what you do. People are watching you and everyone who knows you has an opinion of you. Their thoughts toward you are all based on the way you've impacted their life. Think about that. God has given you the privilege of impacting another person's life, the opportunity to help them be better off than before they met you. You can do that if you're wise enough to listen to what God is telling you to do. One thing is certain, you are influencing other people's lives whether you want to or not. It's based on what you say or don't say, on what you do or don't do. This is why Col. 3:17 says, "And whatever you do in word or deed, do all in the name of the Lord Jesus."

Jesus said in Matt. 5:13, "You are the salt of the earth." In Biblical times, salt was more important than it is today. It was a valuable commodity and people were sometimes paid for their labor with salt. In times past, because of the lack of refrigeration, salt was used to preserve food, especially meat, which would spoil quickly in the desert environment. In the midst of a decaying world, you are called to show the world that there is life in Christ Jesus. Believers in Christ are preservatives to the world, preserving it from this evil society of ungodly people whose unredeemed nature is corrupted by sin. Think what this world would be like if there were no Christians to stand up for what is right. Salt is also used as a flavor enhancer. In the same way that salt enhances the flavor of the food it seasons, the followers of Christ stand out as those who enhance the flavor of life in this world. Where there is strife, they are peacemakers. Where there is sorrow, they bind up the wounds of the brokenhearted. Where there is hatred, they show the love of God in Christ.

Salt also produces thirst. You are being called upon to live in such a way that it produces in others a thirst for Jesus Christ. Christians are supposed to be the happiest people in all the world, even in the midst of trials and hardship. Show the world a different and better way to live. Many rich and famous people get depressed and commit suicide because there's something missing in their life. They're missing the sweet-tasting flavor of a relationship with God. It's your responsibility to show the world what such a life is like. It truly is a wonderful life, a life of love, joy, peace, and kindness. You are to show them a way of life that they'll never see from anyone else. Conduct yourself in a manner where people will want what you have. If you don't do that, Jesus said, "If the salt loses its flavor, how shall it be seasoned? It is then good for nothing but to be thrown out and trampled under foot by men" (vs. 13). Jesus is talking about believers who aren't doing what they're supposed to do. They're worthless to the kingdom of God and get thrown out and "walked on by people when the walkways are wet and slippery" (AMP).

You are the salt of the earth and you are also the light of the world (Matt. 5:14). The smallest light can be seen in a dark room. It breaks the darkness. A lighthouse shows the way and you're supposed to do the same thing. This whole world is in darkness and they need people to show them a way out. Phil. 2:15 (NLT) says, "Live clean, innocent lives as children of God, shining like bright lights in a world full of crooked and perverse people." The Message Bible says, "Go out into the world uncorrupted, a breath of fresh air in this squalid and polluted society. Provide people with a glimpse of good living and of the living God. Carry the light-giving Message into the night." Jesus told Paul his calling was "to open their eyes and to turn them from darkness to light, from the power of Satan to God" (Acts 2:18). A city on a hill cannot be hidden. People have got to be able to see you and what you stand for. You don't light a lamp and put it under a basket (Matt. 5:15). You put a lamp on a lampstand so it gives light to all who are in the house. Is your light dim or bright, or has it gone out altogether?

Matt. 5:16 says, "Let your light so shine before men, that they may see your good works and glorify your Father in heaven." This isn't a suggestion, it's a command. You are commanded by God to break the darkness and show the way. 1 John 2:3 says, "Now by this we know that we know Him, if we keep His commandments." It is only when you obey God's Word that you can be sure that you really know Him. Obedience doesn't cause you to know Him, it's the evidence that you already know Him. The word "keep" is a military term. It stresses the idea of being observant and watchful, of knowing the role you're to perform, to know who you are and Who you belong to. In Greek the word means 'to keep an eye on, to keep something in view, to hold firmly, to attend carefully, to watch over.' To keep His commandments takes diligence and effort. It means to be alert because the enemy is attempting to invade and dominate your life. 1 John 2:4 says, "He who says, 'I know Him,' and does not keep His commandments, is a liar, and the truth is not in Him."

The mature believer wants to obey God. 1 John 2:5 says, "But whoever keeps His Word, truly the love of God is perfected in him. By this we know that we are in Him." Maturity always expresses itself in actions, by doing good works, by keeping His commandments. Jesus said in John 15:14, "You are My friends if you do whatever I command you." Jesus told you to let your light shine before men. Don't hide the fact that you are a Christian. Yes, persecution will come and some people may not like you any longer. So what? Let your light shine anyway. Don't be like those people Paul referred to in Titus 1:16, "They profess to know God, but in works they deny Him, being abominable, disobedient, and disqualified for every good work." The Message Bible says, "They say they know God, but their actions speak louder than their words. They're real creeps, disobedient good-for-nothings." If you struggle with obedience, you need to be honest with yourself and see who or what you are most devoted to. Know this, you will obey what you love the most. Matt. 6:21 (MSG) says, "The place where your treasure is, is the place you will most want to be, and end up being."

The more grown up you are, the less difficult it is to do what God wants. Maturity will change you to the point where it's not drudging to obey. Pattern your life after Jesus who said in John 6:38, "For I have come down from heaven, not to do My own will, but the will of Him who sent Me." You're an ambassador of Christ (2 Cor. 5:20), a reflection of the living God. Do people see Him in the way you talk and act, in the way you dress and in the way you drive your car? They will if you've grown up spiritually. If you haven't grown up, if sin is running rampant in your life, then you're sending a false message to the world about who God is. Don't be that way. Don't give God a bad name. You're a child of the living God so act like it and talk like it. Let your light shine and be a reflection of who He is. You are under divine obligation to walk as Jesus walked, to do the things He did and say the things He said. You exist to express the life of Jesus in your words and actions. It's not your life you're living, it's His life. Him living in you is what makes a difference to those around you. Let your light shine. Be the person God called you to be.

Walking as Jesus walked is the result of spiritual maturity. 1 John 2:6 says, "He who says he abides in Him ought himself also to walk just as He walked." Anyone who claims to be intimate with God ought to live the same kind of life Jesus lived. If you say you're living in Christ and abiding in Him, then your walk should match your profession. The Amplified Bible says, "Whoever says he abides in Him ought, as a personal debt, to walk and conduct himself in the same way in which He walked and conducted Himself." The word "abides" means 'to remain in the same place or position over a period of time.' To abide in Jesus implies fellowship, communion, dependence, harmony, and friendship. Abiding in Christ is a living relationship. You live in Him and He lives in you (Gal. 2:20). As Jesus lives out His life through you (Col. 3:4), you are able to follow His example and walk as He walked. Rom. 8:29 (MSG) says, "We see the original and intended shape of our live there in Him." Live as a person who belongs to Jesus Christ. Choose to be different. Be the zebra among the horses. Live for the glory of God and be sound in the faith (Titus 1:13).

Martin Luther once said, "It is not Christ's walking on the sea, but His ordinary walk, that we are called to imitate." Walking as Jesus walked is not optional if you are a born again believer. The Greek word for "ought" is "opheilo" and means 'to owe something to someone' and conveys the sense of necessity, duty, or being under obligation. John is saying that the person who says they abide in Jesus is bound by duty, moral obligation, and necessity to walk as Jesus walked. It implies the closest conformity to Him in character and conduct. 1 John 4:17 says, "As He is, so are we in this world." If you talk the talk, then you must walk the walk. The obligation to conduct oneself the way Jesus did is placed upon all true believers. Change happens when you give your life to Jesus. Eph. 5:8 says, "For you were once darkness, but now you are light in the Lord. Walk as children of light." The Message Bible says, "The bright light of Christ makes your way plain. So no more stumbling around. Get on with it!" Vs. 10 (MSG) says, "Figure out what will please Christ, and then do it." Paul is saying to walk as Jesus walked.

Start living like you are alive. Eph. 5:14 says, "Awake, you who sleep, arise from the dead, and Christ will give you light." Paul is saying you have to be different in a fallen world. You are to live outwardly who you are on the inside. At one time you were dead in your sins but now you are alive in Christ. The old life has passed away and the new life has come. Your priorities have supernaturally been altered and what's important to God becomes important to you. You wake up one morning and find yourself loving a person you didn't love the day before. You then realize you're loving people you don't even know. You now have a sense of what's right and what's wrong. The commandments of God have meaning to you and you see the value of putting Him first in everything you say and do. You walk as Jesus walked so others can see Jesus in you. That's the purpose of spiritual maturity. It allows you to live in such a way that your life brings glory and honor to God. Is. 60:1 says, "Arise, shine; For your light has come." Vs. 3 then says, "The Gentiles shall come to your light, and kings to the brightness of your rising."

To walk as Jesus walked, you must do the things Jesus did. Acts 10:38 (NLT) says, "And you know that God anointed Jesus of Nazareth with the Holy Spirit and with power. Then

Jesus went around doing good and healing all who were oppressed by the devil, for God was with Him." As a follower of Christ, you must forever be doing good works just like Jesus did. Titus 2:14 (NLT) says, "He gave His life to free us from every kind of sin, to cleanse us, and to make us His very own people, totally committed to doing good deeds." You've got to see yourself as belonging to God and not yourself. 1 Cor. 6:20 says you were bought at a high price. That means you don't belong to you anymore. You belong to God so glorify Him by walking as Jesus walked. Titus 3:1 says "to be ready for every good work" and Paul then said in vs. 14, "And let our people also learn to maintain good works, to meet urgent needs, that they may not be unfruitful." The Message Bible says, "Our people have to learn to be diligent in their work so that all necessities are met (especially among the needy) and they don't end up with nothing to show for their lives."

Why were you born? What were you made for? You were created for the good of other people. 1 Cor. 12:7 (NLT) says, "A spiritual gift is given to each of us so we can help each other." The church was not made to meet your needs, you were made to meet the needs of the church. Most believers don't understand this so if the church doesn't give them what they think they need, they leave and go find another church that will. Because of this wandering from church to church, they never get rooted in a specific place and never do anything useful for the kingdom of God. People wrongly believe that the church was made for them when in reality they were made for the church. 1 Peter 4:10 (NLT) says, "God has given each of us a gift from His great variety of spiritual gifts. Use them well to serve one another." You were made by God to be a critical organ that the church can't live without. You need to seek God and find out what He wants you to do. The good news is that it's in the journey of finding and fulfilling your role that you come to know God in a deeper way. It's in the journey that you'll experience God and this is where spiritual growth happens.

There are some guidelines that will help you find and fulfill your role in the Body of Christ. First of all, go to God in prayer and tell Him you want to be used by Him. Rom. 12:1 says to "present your bodies a living sacrifice, holy, acceptable to God, which is your reasonable service." To be used by God you've got to walk in the light and stop walking in darkness. Vs. 2 (NLT) says, "Don't copy the behavior and customs of this world, but let God transform you into a new person by changing the way you think. Then you will learn to know God's will for you, which is good and pleasing and perfect." You must also walk in humility because pride kills your ability to serve God. Vs. 3 (NLT) says, "Don't think you are better than you really are. Be honest in your evaluation of yourselves, measuring yourselves by the faith God has given us." Seeking God and His will for your life allows the Holy Spirit to transform your life and tear down the barriers of pride and fleshly living. Vs. 6 then says, "Having then gifts differing according to the grace that is given us, let us use them." Use your gift for the good of the church and the world. Fulfill the role you've been made to fulfill. Allow God to transform you into a living sacrifice.

There are four things you must cling to in order to fulfill your role in the Body of Christ. First, be faithful where you're currently at. Jesus said in Luke 16:10, "He who is faithful in what is least is faithful also in much." God is not as interested in what you're doing as He is in how you're doing it. Second, be filled with the Holy Spirit (Acts 6:3). You cannot serve God in your own strength. This leads only to conflict, confusion, and burnout. Third, be flexible. In Acts 8, Philip had great success in the city of Samaria when an angel of the Lord appeared and told him to leave and go to a city where the enemies of God lived. How did Philip respond? Vs. 27 says, "So he arose and went." You also need to be flexible and go where God tells you to go even if it means you have to get out of your comfort zone. Keep pressing on for you are in the process of being transformed into what God has created you to become. Be flexible. Let God call all the shots. Fourth, be focused (Phil. 3:12). Your ultimate focus must be on the eternal purpose for which Jesus has laid hold of you. If you focus on anything else, it will be only a matter of time until you get taken out of the ministry. If you walk as Jesus walked, that won't happen.

Randall J. Brewer

-30-

"SAVED FOR TODAY"

James 4:14 (AMP) asks the question, "What is the nature of your life?" What does your life consist of? What is your life all about? An aching void will fill your heart if these questions are not answered. What you need to understand is that these are not questions you should be asking yourself, these questions should be asked of God. With a willing mind and an open heart go to Him and say, "Lord, what is the nature of my life? Why am I here? For what purpose was I born?" One of the first things He will tell you to do is stop allowing the world to shape and dictate the way you think. Prov. 16:25 says, "There is a way that seems right to a man, but its end is the way of death." The Hebrew word for "death" means 'to die prematurely because you did not heed wise counsel or have wise conduct." Listening to the wrong people causes you to go down the wrong path. 1 John 2:17 (AMP) says, "The world is passing away, and with it its lusts (the shameful pursuits and ungodly longings); but the one who does the will of God and carries out His purposes lives forever."

Don't go after things that seem right and never allow the world to shape your idea of success. Worldly success may bring you fortune and fame but inside there will always be a sense of emptiness because you didn't fulfill your eternal purpose. There is nothing worldly about eternal success because it is spiritual in nature, pleasing God. Surrender yourself to the plan of God and you'll discover what true success really is. You can do that when you understand that you were bought with a price (1 Cor. 6:20) and that you are not your own. You are His workmanship created in Christ Jesus (Eph. 2:10) and you must allow Him to do with you that which pleases Him most. Allow His will to be done in your life and not your own. This is how you fulfill your destiny and it all begins when you come to realize that you are His. He paid for you by shedding His blood on the cross. He died so that you may live. Gal. 2:20 says, "I have been crucified with Christ; it is no longer I who live, but Christ lives in me; and the life which I now live in the flesh I live by faith in the Son of God, who loved me and gave Himself for me."

Do you want to fulfill your purpose in life? Then put God first in everything you do. Love Him "with all your heart, with all your soul, and with all your mind" (Matt. 22:37). If you love Him, you'll obey Him. You'll do what He tells you to do, you'll say what He tells you to say, you'll go where He tells you to go. Don't be like Jonah who ran away from the call on his life. God told him to go to Nineveh but Jonah rebelled and took off in the opposite direction (Jonah 1:3). He soon learned that you can run from God but you can't hide. God got his attention in the belly of a whale and eventually Jonah did what he was called to do. He learned the hard way the importance of fulfilling your heavenly call. Don't let this happen to you. Don't wait until your head in entangled in seaweed and your body is engulfed in strong stomach acids before you submit to God and His will for your life. The people in Nineveh needed to hear the message Jonah was sent to proclaim. Likewise, there are people in your world who are on the heart of God, people to whom you've been called to minister to in word and deed.

The world is reached when ordinary people respond to their heavenly call for this is what allows God to step in and do extraordinary things in them and through them. Inside of you is something supernatural that other people need and their salvation is dependent on you showing them the true nature of God and what He is like. The end is near and you don't want to miss out on what God is doing on the earth today. 1 Cor. 3:9 says, "For we are God's fellow workers." It is indeed a great privilege to be regarded as laborers together with God. It should motivate you to be found laboring with God when Jesus returns, to be working with Him toward fulfilling His divine purpose. Other people are counting on you so daily pray for God to have you be at the right place, at the right time. This is what you're here for. People need you whether you realize it or not. The people of Nineveh needed Jonah and there are people who are counting on you to be the person God called and created you to be. There are people in your life who need what you have so don't sit on the pew at church waiting for and expecting someone else to do what you've been called to do.

The call that is upon your life was given to you before the world began. 2 Tim. 1:9 says He "has saved us and called us with a holy calling, not according to our works, but according to His own purpose and grace which was given to us in Christ Jesus before time began." Before the heavens and the earth were created, before Adam and Eve walked in the garden, God had a call and a plan for your life. It's a call according to His purpose (Rom. 8:28). This means you don't decide what your assignment is, you discover what it is. Remember, if Jesus is Lord of your life, you're no longer in charge. He is! He knew you before you were born and He placed you on this earth to do something that will advance His kingdom on earth. There is something inside of you of great significance that God can use if you'll submit your will to His will. Rom. 8:28 (MSG) says, "Every detail in our lives of love for God is worked into something good." Give all that you have to God and He will use you to do great things on the earth. Give Him your time, your talents, and your treasure and you'll be able to do things you never dreamed of in your former life.

Placing a call on your life is God's part, answering the call is your part. In Gen. 12:1 God called Abram to leave his country and go to a land He would show him. Vs. 4 says, "So Abram departed as the Lord had spoken to him." He answered the call and became the father of many nations. God would later tell him to do many things and each time Abraham did what God told him to do. You also must dedicate yourself to that which God wants you to do. Daily you must keep yourself in the will of God for this is what determines the direction your life will take. Rom. 1:1 says, "Paul, a servant of Jesus Christ, called to be an apostle." He answered the call and became a servant of God. He said in Gal. 1:15 that God "separated me from my mother's womb and called me through His grace." Before he was born, God had a call on his life. Paul dedicated himself to his heavenly call and wrote in Phil. 3:8,9 "Yes, everything else is worthless when compared with the infinite value of knowing Christ Jesus my Lord. For His sake I have discarded everything else, counting it all as garbage, so that I may gain Christ and become one with Him."

The Message Bible says, "I've dumped it all in the trash so that I could embrace Christ and be embraced by Him." Dedication is about obedience. It's telling God you'll do whatever He tells you to do. It's saying, "Here I am! Send me." Whatever you dedicate your life to is the direction your life will go. Prov. 23:7 says, "For as he thinks in his heart, so is he." All actions begin with a thought. If you'll think and meditate on what God wants you to do, you will see the fulfillment of your destiny. What was the key to Paul's success? Phil. 3:13,14 says, "But one thing I do, forgetting those things which are behind and reaching forward to those things which are ahead, I press toward the goal for the prize of the upward call of God in Christ Jesus." Paul was successful because he pressed toward the fulfillment of God's call on his life. In his final letter before his death, he wrote in 2 Tim. 4:7, "I have fought the good fight, I have finished the race, I have kept the faith." In other words, he fulfilled his destiny. On that day when you stand before Christ, hopefully you'll be able to say the same thing.

If you are born again, if today you are saved, then understand that you are saved for today. Yes, salvation is for eternity but you must realize that today is part of that same eternity. In the eyes of God, you are in His eternity right now. What that means is today you have the chance and the ability to do something eternal. The things you do for God lasts forever while everything else is fleeting and passing away. What you do today matters because so often in life you are transformed by the things you do. Don't ever forget that you were created to serve the Lord. Eph. 2:10 (MSG) says, "He creates each of us by Christ Jesus to join Him in the work He does, the good work He has gotten ready for us to do, work we had better be doing." God created you to do good works. You are His workmanship, His work of art, and the most exciting and fulfilling life you could ever have is to do what God created you to do and to be who God created you to be. Nothing this sinful world offers compares to that. God is building a kingdom in your midst and He wants you to be a part of it.

You were not saved so God could help with what you're building, you're saved to help God with what He's building. That's the purpose for your life as a Christian. 1 Peter 2:5 (NLT) says, "And you are living stones that God is building into His spiritual temple. What's more, you are His holy priests." This verse is written to every born again believer, and that includes you. The Message Bible says, "Present yourselves as building stones for the construction of a sanctuary vibrant with life, in which you'll serve as holy priests offering Christ-approved lives up to God." You are saved for today and you are a holy priest in God's kingdom. It is a high and holy calling to make your life a sweet-smelling offering to the God of the universe. You must have the same attitude Jesus had who "made Himself of no reputation, taking the form of a servant" (Phil. 2:7). Jesus served His disciples when He washed their feet. He served the hungry when He fed them. He served the sick when He healed them. He served the lonely and the outcasts when He interacted with and loved them. And He served you by dying on the cross for your sins.

Jesus was born to serve. If He did it, you can do it also. Eph. 5:1,2 (NLT) says, "Imitate God, therefore, in everything you do, because you are His dear children. Live a life filled with love, following the example of Christ. He loved us and offered Himself as a sacrifice for us, a pleasing aroma to God." The Message Bible says, "He didn't love in order to get something from us but to give everything of Himself to us. Love like that." If you'll do that, you'll be the beautiful masterpiece God created you to be. When God formed you in your mother's womb (Ps. 139:13), He made you just the way you are because He needed you right where He was going to put you. You're a living stone in the kingdom He is building. 1 Peter 4:10 (NLT) says, "God has given each of you a gift from His great variety of spiritual gifts. Use them well to serve one another." Don't squander what God has given you. Be a functioning part of the Body of Christ by using your gift. Do what God has called you to do with the strength and energy He supplies. This is how you bring glory to God through Jesus Christ. That is your highest calling.

People get desperate when they have a thirst that is not quenched. How desperate are you for the power of God to be manifested in your life? God's desire is to pour Himself into your life to the point where you'll act like Him and talk like Him. This is why you're here, the reason you were born in the first place. You're here to be an imitation of Him in this sinful world. God wants to use you to be a divine influence to those who cross your path each and every day. That's your assignment from on high. That's the reason God wants you to grow up spiritually. God changed your life and He now wants to use you to help other people get their lives changed. The word "influence" is 'the capacity to have an effect on the character, development, or behavior of someone or something.' What would it take to get you to serve God? Are you willing to put your comforts aside in order to do what God is calling you to do? When you serve God, you're following the example of Jesus. You're walking as He walked. He said in Matt. 20:28, "Just as the Son of Man did not come to be served, but to serve, and to give His life a ransom for many."

God has a plan for your life. You've been set apart to influence the world around you. God told Jeremiah, "Before I formed you in the womb I knew you; Before you were born I sanctified you; And I ordained you a prophet to the nations" (Jer. 1:5). God's plan for Jeremiah was preordained before the prophet was born and so also was God's plan for you. It matters not your age, gender, or nationality, God has a plan for your life. There is something God wants you to do today, tomorrow, and the rest of your life. Will you do what God wants you to do? You should because serving God is proof that you believe in Him, that you're one of His children. 2 Cor. 9:13 (NLT) says, "As a result of your ministry they will give glory to God. For your generosity to them and to all believers will prove that you are obedient to the Good News of Christ." As a born again believer, nothing should be as important to you as fulfilling the call of God on your life. It's what you were born to do. Like Jeremiah, you've been sanctified and ordained to serve God. The Message Bible says, "Before you saw the light of day, I had holy plans for you."

Every day you need to have the desire to live at your full potential. Give God an open door into your life "for in Him we live and move and have our being" (Acts 17:28). It's being in His presence that makes the difference, the assurance that your destiny will be fulfilled. It's what causes you to expect good things to happen. Joel 2:21 (KJB) says, "Fear not, O land; be glad and rejoice for the Lord will do great things." Take your life and point it in the direction God wants you to go. Pray for His will to be done in your life and not your own. Hunger and thirst for righteousness for God said in Is. 44:3,4, "For I will pour water on him who is thirsty, and floods on the dry ground; I will pour My Spirit on your descendants, and My blessing on your offspring; They will spring up among the grass like willows by the watercourses." Live a deeper life. Be strong in the Lord and in the power of His might (Eph. 6:10). Rise up and be the person God created you to be. Be different and act different. Don't be like those religious folks whose head is filled with the knowledge of God but their hearts are void of His power. 1 Cor. 8:1 says, "Knowledge puffs up, but love edifies."

You were made for greatness because you were created to do great things. 1 Peter 2:9,10 (MSG) says, "But you are the ones chosen by God, chosen for the high calling of priestly work, chosen to be a holy people, God's instruments to do His work and speak out for Him, to tell others of the night-and-day difference He made for you - from nothing to something, from rejected to accepted." You were chosen for a purpose. You were chosen to show the world what God is like by the things you say and the things you do. You've been set apart to shine bright in a dark world, to influence those around you. There is something divine inside of you that needs to be released into this world. The more you pursue God and His will, the more He will manifest Himself to you and through you. Prov. 3:6 says, "In all your ways acknowledge Him, and He shall direct your paths." Acknowledging God doesn't mean just turning to Him in times of trouble or publicly during worship at church. It's about living a life that reflects the fact that God is directing it. The level of your pursuit of God is the level that He will manifest Himself in your life.

Do you want to do great things for God? Ps. 92:13 tells you how, "Those who are planted in the house of the Lord shall flourish in the courts of our God." The word "flourish" means 'to strive, to increase, to enlarge, to grow, to be prosperous, to abound, to spread out and expand, to make steady progress, and to be at a high point in one's life.' The Christian life is a progressive life, a life where God takes you from glory to glory (2 Cor. 3:18) and faith to faith (Rom. 1:17). Paul wrote in 2 Cor. 4:6 (NLT), "For God, who said, 'Let there be light in the darkness,' has made this light shine in our hearts so we could know the glory of God that is seen in the face of Jesus Christ." To do great things for God, you must be planted in His kingdom and the way He does things. You need to be planted in the place where God dwells for the closer you are to Him, the more you'll be transformed into His image. He does great things and you'll do great things as well. Jer. 20:11 says, "But the Lord is with me as a mighty, awesome one." When the Lord is with you, there is no limit to the things you can do in and for His kingdom.

Being planted in the house of the Lord is about fulfilling God's plan for your life. It's about walking on the path He preordained you to walk on. At the burning bush God told Moses to take his shoes off for he was standing on holy ground (Ex. 3:5). What this means is God wants you the way He created you. He wants you to no longer walk the way you did before. Old things have passed away, behold, all things become new. At the burning bush God changed the direction of the life of Moses and it was then that his life began to flourish. In Greek the word "flourish" means 'to break forth and bud; to blossom.' God will change you on the inside so you can break forth and help change the world on the outside. Jer. 20:9 says, "But His word was in my heart like a burning fire shut up in my bones; I was weary of holding it back, and I could not." When God touches your life, you can't hold back telling others about the goodness of God and all that He has done. You've grown up spiritually and been empowered from on high. The Message Bible says, "I'm worn out trying to hold it in. I can't do it any longer."

Many people go to church but they're not planted in the things of God. If they were, they'd go out and turn the world upside down (Acts 17:6). It's being planted that brings you to the place where you'll fulfill what God has called you to do. Col. 2:7 (NLT) says, "Let your roots grow down into Him, and let your lives be built on Him." You will fulfill your destiny if you'll plant your roots deeply in God. Jer. 12:2 says, "You have planted them, yes, they have taken root; They grow, yes, they bear fruit." God wants you to flourish and to help those around you to flourish also. Don't limit what God can do in your life. Trust Him to help you fulfill your destiny. Jer. 17:7,8 says, "Blessed is the man who trusts in the Lord, and whose hope is the Lord. For He shall be like a tree planted by the waters, which spreads out its roots by the river, and will not fear when heat comes; But her leaf will be green, and will not be anxious in the year of drought, nor will cease from yielding fruit." The Message Bible says you'll be "bearing fresh fruit every season."

When you're planted in God, you'll break forth and blossom into the person He wants you to be. You're no longer driven to fulfill your own wants and desires but instead are desirous for the will of God to be manifested in your life. What He wants is what you want. You no longer live for yourself but now you live for Him. Jesus said in John 12:24,25 (MSG), "Unless a grain of wheat is buried in the ground, dead to the world, it is never any more than a grain of wheat. But if it is buried, it sprouts and reproduces itself many times over. In the same way, anyone who holds on to life just as it is destroys that life. But if you let it go, reckless in your love, you'll have it forever, real and eternal." It's when you die to yourself that you really begin to live. It's being planted that causes you to fulfill your destiny, to do many great and extraordinary things for the kingdom of God. Jesus died for you, now you die to yourself for Him. Vs. 26 says, "If anyone serves Me, let him follow Me; and where I am, there My servant will be also. If anyone serves Me, him My Father will honor."

Never see yourself as being insignificant. No, God has a special plan for your life. He wants you to flourish like a palm tree (Ps. 32:12). A palm tree is stately and beautiful. It has deep roots and can flourish even in the desert, growing tall and living long. It is perhaps the most useful of all trees. Not only does it produce dates, but also sugar, wine, honey, oil, resin, rope, thread, tannin, and dye. Its seeds are fed to cattle and its leaves are used for roofs, fences, mats, and baskets. It was palm branches that was laid on the road as Jesus made His triumphant entry into Jerusalem (John 12:13). In heaven a great multitude of people will stand before the throne of God "clothed with white robes, and palm branches in their hands" (Rev. 7:9). One of the best qualities of the palm tree is that its fruit gets sweeter as the tree grows older. This is why Ps. 32:14 says, "They shall still bear fruit in old age; They shall be fresh and flourishing." Every seed that is planted has an assignment to fulfill. When you are planted in the house of the Lord, your assignment is to be a light that influences the world around you.

Get excited about the future God has planned for you. Don't get in a rut thinking hard times is all you'll ever have. Stir up the passion inside of you knowing that you were created for such a time as this. Trust God knowing He'll set you free from your current hardship and give you direction for your future. Oh, what a glorious future it will be when you're planted in the house of the Lord. Jesus said, "But for this purpose I came to this hour" (John 12:27). The same can be said about you. You were not born by accident. For a specific purpose you were born at the right time and the right place. Lay hold of the fact that God has a plan and a purpose for your life. You were saved for today so submit your will to His will. He's the potter, you're the clay. God said in Jer. 18:6, "Look, as the clay is in the potter's hand, so are you in My hand, O house of Israel!" Allow God to mold you so you can do good works for Him. The word "good" means 'beneficial, useful, excellent, distinguished.' These words represent who God is. You're made in His image and this means you're to be the same way.

God is thinking about you right now. Jer. 29:11 says, "For I know the thoughts that I think toward you, says the Lord, thoughts of peace and not of evil, to give you a future and a hope." It is an amazing thing to know that the Creator of all the universe is thinking about you at this very moment. The Hebrew word for "thoughts" is where the word "machine" comes from. A machine is designed to accomplish a specific task based on a predetermined purpose. God knows intimately who you are and the purpose for which you were created. These are the things He is thinking about. You fulfilling your destiny is forever on His mind. Shouldn't this be on your mind also? Raise the level of your thinking knowing that like a well-oiled machine you were designed by God to do something great. He is looking for a people who will fulfill His will on the earth. How sad it must have made Him when He said in Ezek. 22:30, "So I sought for a man among them who would make a wall, and stand in the gap before Me on behalf of the land, that I should not destroy it; but I found no one." Rise up and tell God to look no further. Say to Him, "Here I am! Send me."

Its Time To Grow Up

Randall J. Brewer

Its Time To Grow Up

Randall J. Brewer

Its Time To Grow Up

Randall J. Brewer

Its Time To Grow Up

Randall J. Brewer

www.ingramcontent.com/pod-product-compliance
Lightning Source LLC
Chambersburg PA
CBHW071259110526
44591CB00010B/715